AF491182

STRONGER
THAN
TYRANNY
Political
Prisoner
in Cuba
ERNESTO DIAZ-RODRIGUEZ

Primix Publishing
East Brunswick Office Evolution
1 Tower Center Boulevard, Ste 1510
East Brunswick, NJ 08816
www.primixpublishing.com
Phone: 1-800-538-5788



Published by Primix Publishing: 06/29/2026

ISBN: 979-8-89194-634-7(sc)
ISBN: 979-8-89194-644-6(hc)
ISBN: 979-8-89194-635-4(e)

Library of Congress Control Number: 2026904859

# CONTENTS

# DEDICATION

To the heroic women fighters who, despite the agonies viciously imposed on them, wrote with courage, dignity and love the most beautiful pages of glory during their long years in the febrile shadows of the Cuban political prison.

To all the valiant men who suffered so many long years in prison too for defending the values of freedom, human beings and peace for all Cubans.

# ACKNOWLEDGEMENTS

To my son David, who painted the image of my youth which appears as part of the cover of this book.

To Scott Roberts, for his generous contribution in designing the front and rear cover of Stronger Than Tyranny, as well as the final editing of this translation.

To my friend, Angel De Fana, who contributed his experience publishing this literary work.

To my wife, Alicia Perez, for her invaluable support for the publication of each of my books.

# In The Voice Of Ernesto Díaz Rodríguez To Be Heard In Cuba

Political prison is a university: a mere mortal man enters it and leaves as a giant. In war, in revolution, in tyranny –the very begetters of prisons– one choice alone remains for the defenseless captive: say either yes or no, resist or give in. The oppressive State creates a penitentiary with the sinister purpose we know all too well: to break human beings, to strip them of their human dignity, and to push them with the tip of a bayonet into a pit of despair, where they are to lose their humanity. But it never works on everyone. Reduced to the level of animal subsistence –a jug of dirty water, rotten parboiled meat, a single light bulb blazing day and night– the political prisoner still looks at his jailer saying: *"I am stronger than you! I am more powerful than you! Because I possess my own free will and you have given up yours."* Each blow, each humiliation to which he or she is subjected, echoes in the hollow of that solitude. But who is calling? The spirit of moral resistance is calling, not allowing the prisoner to fall into a lethargy, making the prisoner know that he is not alone, that he is part of a beleaguered army kept sealed away from sunlight, but maintaining its luminous soul. To remind the prisoner that he has not surrendered his dignity, or surrendered anything in fact.

Today, our Cuban political prisons are crueler, longer lasting, and more numerous than anything ever before seen in the Americas, or in the world —except for Hitler's fields of extermination. But with a difference: the world wept, still shouts out, and will continue screaming until the end of time against the anti-human barbarity of Auschwitz and Treblinka, but remains strangely silent before the sealed-off horrors of our own prisons, Combinado del Este and Boniato. A wall of silence and complicity, has surrounded —since their very inception— Castro's crimes. All manner of atrocities are practiced there. All desecration of those more intimate human values is being perpetrated in the endless prisons that have become a sinister pox invading the green body of the island. But nobody notices, nobody stands up in protest. What true "revolution" continues to execute people with firing squads decades after its proclaimed victory? What Latin American tyranny —Trujillo's or Pérez Jiménez— has shot youngster just for stealing a boat? What country would take so many of its women —teens, students, respectable grandmothers, artists, and professionals— to lock them up with prostitutes, the mentally ill, and pathologically criminal? Did Duvalier ever sink a tugboat carrying dozens of his country's own children and drown them? Where else in the Americas have we ever seen slave labor camps, without trial or sentence, thousands of young people have been locked away for sporting long hair, liking rock music, practicing an unapproved religion, or engaging in sexual conduct unauthorized by the macho State? Nowhere, of course. In no other system of governance in the Americas has this pathological insanity been accepted. The question is: should this even upset anyone? Should anyone's moral conscience be offended by this return to barbarism? Where are those voices that shouted out protesting against the apartheid system of South Africa? Where is the support for the missing Cuban mothers, the mothers of May, June, and all the months of history? Nowhere, of course. Nobody knows anything, no one wants to know anything, and nobody has heard anything. The vileness and amorality justifying Castro's crimes can only occur because the discredited word of "revolution" burns shut the lips of those fools —among them the whitewashed tombstones of religion.

This book is being written to rip away that shameful veil. Who is the author? He is not one, but many, because in this book he speaks for an entire people. It has been written and bears the signature of a son of that people, Ernesto Díaz Rodríguez, poet and narrator. Thus, he is embedded in the very viscera of his homeland, rising up from its depths, having suffered a very long season in hell, giving this testimony its unique voice.

Yes, Ernesto Díaz Rodríguez, fisherman and son of fishermen of Cojímar (that small seaport immortalized by Hemingway), knows of what he speaks. Barely out of adolescence he was already facing Castro's tyranny. Why had they stripped everything away from him and his loved ones? Was it because he was a reactionary, a supporter of the old, just vanished Cuba? No. Rather, because he was one of thousands, millions really, of young Cubans who felt cheated out of their civic trust. Ernesto Díaz Rodríguez had believed in the revolution, had fought for it, joining ranks with that rebellious generation who had left behind such outstanding martyrs as José Antonio Echeverría and Frank País. Some of that generation, with hope of a greater, more transparent Cuba ruled by law and decency, found themselves tragically seduced by the verbal juggling and promises of national greatness emanating from the hypocrite-in-chief. It was a disastrous disconnection not of their own choosing, imposed upon them by a romantic con artist.

In 1961, Ernesto Díaz Rodríguez left Cuba clandestinely in a small boat. Why? To continue, from the outside, a fight that from the inside he found impossible to conduct. In Miami, he joined Alpha 66, which argued that against violence, violence is the only possible defense. Soon, in other boats as small as the one in which he had escaped, he secretly returned to the island several times to launch attacks against the oppressors who held the country hostage. On one of those raids he was given a special mission: to bring Commander Eloy Gutiérrez Menoyo and his guerrilla group into Cuba. After Gutiérrez Menoyo's capture, he took over as Alpha's chief of military operations. And after having carried out successful clandestine infiltration missions he was ultimately captured by Castro's henchmen and condemned to 15 years in prison. That's when the maturation of Ernesto Díaz Rodríguez begins. From jail, while he studies and writes, he organizes clandestine cells of Alpha 66, for which the dictatorship imposes 25 more years in prison. He is moved to the appalling, walled-off cells of Boniato, completely isolated, excluded from any process of appeal, along with a group of other *plantados,* stalwart unmovables called "rooted ones," moral titans like himself. Finally, on March 23, 1991, thanks to an intense international campaign, he is freed and sent into exile. During 22 years in prison, he had written several books, among them *Bell of the Dawn*, the finest, most beautiful book of children's poetry written in Spanish since José Martí's *Ismaelillo.*

The beardless youngster that crossed the threshold of his cell came out a fully mature human being. Political prison was his school; literary, political, and humanitarian. There he came to know Cuba, delving more deeply into its history and learning how to appreciate even more its best sons and daughters. He also saw the moral abyss which had swallowed up so many of those children. That is the secret and suffering of Cuba that appears in this book. That is the story of how a happy, carefree island where the tap, instead of giving water, gave forth music —a land blessed by God with natural warmth, where the bitter and the bad always seemed to apply to other parts of the world —became a nation divided between Cains and Abels. A territory of evil experimentation, a Mephystophelic lab creating incessantly poisonous swinish doctrines to for the youth to drink.

Books are to be read, not described. And that's what you are going to do right now with this one. Upstanding men are not to be quoted, but honored. And that is just what we Cubans do when hearing the name Ernesto Díaz Rodríguez. Fisherman from Cojímar. Poet and writer. Political prisoner and revolutionary. As intransigent today regarding any settlement with despotism as the day he went to jail. Ernesto Díaz Rodríguez, exalted example of a genre that will never die: Cubans who when forced to choose between surrender or death, will always choose death.

Agustín Tamargo,
Miami, Florida, June 20, 1995

It was May 1983 when I started writing this book using prison notes that I had been assembling clandestinely over the years, this very literary work which constitutes an important facet of my life. I won't talk of the high price paid in sacrifice to accumulate the experiences that today I share with you, because greater than all the torments of prison is the satisfaction of having served with love and decorum the sacred cause of freedom in Cuba.

It was not easy to fulfill the will of my spirit to testify to the compelling and exemplary history of the ideals of the Cuban political prison, written together with my brethren, many with their own blood. But sometimes fate gives us a flash of light in the darkest night and reveals such wonderful realities, reminding us that any just cause, sooner or later, has its just reward.

It was almost the end of November 1984, amid a repression so fierce that it exceeded all limits of vileness and ignominy from the jailers in Castro's employ, when I finally finished writing these memories of the experiences that had most impacted me during my forced and prolonged journey from prison to prison, from one end of the island to the other. Since then, much has changed, including the collapse of the Communist bloc in Eastern Europe, as well as the fall of the Soviet Empire, which, for a long time, gave the false impression of being a very firmly established dictatorial system, with absolute control over the population and with a machinery of terror and blackmail practically capable of paralyzing the human will. It also produced the release, in accelerated form, of all *plantados,* unbreakable political prisoners, a process that culminated in July 1991 with the freeing of Mario Chanes de Armas after having completed, to the last day, the 30-year sentence that in 1961 had been arbitrarily imposed by the military court, accusing him of crimes that Chanes had not committed and which would make him, according to known records, the longest-serving prisoner of conscience in the world.

I had the honorable privilege of sharing my last days of captivity with my esteemed fellow prisoners –Mario Chanes de Armas, Alfredo Mustelier Nuevo, and Alberto Grau Sierra– as the four of us, designated as being especially rebellious, had been excluded from the program of pardons which the Cuban government had established as a release mechanism at the end of the 1980s. The measure of our exclusion and confinement was such that our cell was built in a special area, one which absolutely off limits to all military not part of the group of officers assigned to our special custody by the "High Command." Our response, to those who had decided our fate, was a series of interviews recorded in secret, revealing and condemning before the world the serious violations of human rights being committed by the regime of Fidel Castro in Cuba's prisons. What must have enraged the arrogant officials of the political police, no doubt, was the joke on the government of keeping us confined in such total isolation, yet our showing of absolute contempt for their repressive machinery, in that our recordings were transmitted to Cuba in a special program of Radio Martí at the very moment when the UN Human Rights Commission team was carrying out an investigation of prisons on the island.

Perhaps someone might think that when writing down these memories I overlooked the political prison of Cuban women. Nothing is further from the truth. If there is an absence of reports about such courageous sisters in my telling, it is only because of the communication barriers to which we were subjected within the confines of the walled cells of Boniato when I started writing this book. Because of my respect for the dignity, stoicism, and courage that the hard rock of Cuban political prisons aroused in those self-sacrificing women, I dared not allow myself to conjure up inaccurate stories, even though our sisters were present in my thoughts and were always part of my daily inspiration.

My release, occurring on March 23, 1991, left me with the personal experience of the need to live with hope and with the certainty of a better future.

Ernesto Díaz Rodríguez, Ridgefield, CT, June 3, 1995

# PROLOGUE

My prison experience actually had begun back on December 4, 1968, when I was captured while fighting against Castro's forces. Little did I know then that I would remain a political prisoner for more than 22 years until my release in 1991. Only part of my prison experience is recorded here. But it is enough to give you an idea of all that we had to endure during those 22 long years. I was fortunate to have clandestine access to pen and paper and to have preserved the writing on pages buried inside cell walls until they could be secretly spirited out of prison. Within these pages, some photocopies of the original manuscripts are included.

Being able to write was part of what kept me sane in prison, as I felt that I was being productive in my own way by revealing what was actually happening to us there, so far away from the blinded eyes of the world. I fully expected what I had written would eventually see the light of day. I also firmly believe that for the integrity of historical archives it is important to be as accurate as possible. I must thank God, who often seemed to have scorned me, for ensuring that this book and some of my poetry actually survived my imprisonment.

***Stronger Than Tyranny*** is a beacon lighting the way to freedom, a triumph of the human spirit when it forcefully rebels against injustice and the adversities of fate, thus becoming invincible.

# CHAPTER 1

# "Plantado" Political Prisoners

The history of Cuba's political prisons is written in blood. Describing so much horror, so much human tragedy, is a painful task. Many times, I've thought it would be best to forget, to close my eyes and erase in one fell swoop all those bitter memories, all such harrowing experiences in the prisons of that enslaved island. But, how could I keep silent when an entire people has been subjected to such an absurd and prolonged suffering? When some of the world is still, perhaps, unaware of this grim and painful reality?

We, its victims, are well acquainted with the unsavory machinations of those who rule in Cuba. That is why to denounce the truth about this Caribbean "Gulag" is an obligation, and for me, an urgent one. To close my eyes heedlessly would be a betrayal of our dead, a betrayal of justice, of democratic principles, of the right to life, freedom, and happiness.

It would be hard to list all of Cuba's prisons, all the concentration camps, spread out all across the length and breadth of the island. Without a doubt, this has been the most significant achievement of economic, social, and political experimentation, carried out by a man without any scruples. Free expression, the freedom of press, and ideological pluralism were all deemed monstrous bourgeois defects. They had to be eradicated at all costs –he would repeatedly shout out– as the outdated schemes of capitalism. And that prodigious task required an iron hand and many prisons.

It is impossible to change imbedded structures rooted in an entire nation, abolish democratic institutions by firing squad, and implant by force the most abject tyranny without facing outrage and rebellion from a people not resigned to becoming slaves. And shortly after his assault, this warlord of the Americas filled up both the cemeteries and the prisons. Then, perhaps during an evening out on a binge or under a radiant moonlit night, came the idea of concentration camps, while Fidel Castro, the "liberator," lovingly caressed the tender head of an innocent child. This passionate disciple of Joseph Stalin knew perfectly well the extraordinary properties of barbed wire fences and immediately ordered construction to be started in all the provinces.

Of all of Cuba's prisons, Boniato is, without a doubt, one of the most brutal and repressive. On first impression, surrounded by mountains, one feels as if chained down at the bottom of an abyss. Then every new experience will show that it goes deeper still, and that you will have a chance to sink down even more and more, unless you should seek to float above it at all costs, risking your life for the sake of dignity every day.

To survive the physical fall, you need only a little bit of luck... or maybe a lot. Surviving the mental fall, the moral plunge, necessitates, among other assets, a firm and defined ideology, a strength of spirit, an awareness of historical responsibility, love of the homeland and of the cause of the struggle, self-denial, and, as a basic element, a smidgen —at least— of courage. It is necessary, finally, to be a *plantado* political prisoner, that is, one absolutely "planted" in his beliefs, with roots so deep and strong that as a plant, they are unmovable.

Beginning in 1971, the government began to extend the sentences of *plantado* prisoners while they were still serving their time. Any excuse took them before a military tribunal, improvised in some prison office. The process began when the prisoner was read the act of prosecution. The most serious crimes with which he was charged were of having participated during his incarceration in hunger strikes and of showing a recalcitrant attitude. Then came the prosecutor's interrogations, unvarying, almost mechanical in nature. Usually, the trial would be held one or two weeks before the date in which the prisoner was due for release, although sometimes even several months later.

"The revolution is strong and generous and wants to give you an opportunity."—the prosecutor would arrogantly intone— "Are you willing to accept the reeducation plan? The plan of collective work on a state farm?"

A simple "Yes" would mean an order for release. In most cases, acceptance of a work plan did not go beyond mere tokenism, a symbolic compliance with an arbitrary and repressive decision. A resounding "No!" meant that the prisoner was condemned to further time, renewed whenever the end of his designated term approached. Every one or two years, according to the new ruling, this farcical "trial" was repeated. With very rare exceptions, *plantado* political prisoners endured with admirable dignity that tempting test. For some, so-called "reeducation" meant compliance with a capricious will, humiliation, and the rending of their spirit. For others, it meant even more. The very officials of the regime recognized the arbitrariness of that measure. Those higher up on the hierarchy were ashamed, doing it only with a mixture of arrogance and irony. It was one of the many ways of demonstrating that they represented a government of force. As Comrade Lenin had said: "The end justifies the means." And the goal of the ruling caste is to stay in power against all odds.

As a genuine representative of partisan shamelessness, we could quote Interior Vice-Minister Brigadier General Enio Leyva. Opportunistic and of large girth, vulgar by nature, his rude vocabulary revealed his innermost personality. "Re-condemning those who have already done their time is a queer caprice of the courts," you heard expressed by him on that occasion in the dining room of Combinado de Este prison, words spoken in front of a hundred political prisoners. The general was heading up a delegation of high-ranking officials carrying out an inspection visit to our floor at the time. Members of his numerous entourages all smiled in unison. Then the vice-minister added a string of stupidities, and made several promises that were never kept. Without a doubt, he had imbibed more than a few drinks. His gait was awkward and his conversation incoherent. Our companions closest to General Enio Leyva assured me that the stench of alcohol exuded from his pores.

The first stage of re-condemnations lasted for about seven years. As a result, many colleagues who had an original punishment of nine or ten years confronted fourteen, fifteen, and up to seventeen years of imprisonment. Very little word spread around the world about this terrible injustice. The Western press, official radio stations, some as important as the Voice of the United States of America, were inexplicably silent, which allowed the regime to curb liberties indefinitely. This allowed an increase in abuses in the prisons of Guanajay and La Cabaña, in unseen firing squads in the concentration camp of Manacas, in prison massacres inside the wall-enclosed inner citadel of Boniato.

In a 1977 interview, American ABC journalist Barbara Walters, with marked concern, asked Fidel Castro why, in Cuba, children were taught to hate. The day before, during a tour of the island's capital, Walters, had heard a group of primary school students chanting: "Yankee, go home! Yankee, go home!" Castro, apparently surprised, could not come up with a convincing answer. (There *is* no possible answer that justifies such diabolical teaching of children.) And then, in a fantasy improvisation, he responded that children learned what they'd heard daily, simply old slogans. The people had felt a great deal of contempt from the Yankees... He failed to mention that such disinformation was instilled beginning in day care and was basic to the systematic hate promulgated in all the nation's schools.

In Cuba, work begins at the root to create the "new man": a mechanical human machine capable of murder and of hate whose only pleasure derives from following orders. But the savvy journalist was not only worried about the shameful education of children. Barbara Walters unearthed from international press files the dusty memory of Cuban political prisoners. Thanks largely to her fortuitous intervention, a few months later, Cuba's communist government would revoke the order to re-condemn the *plantados* and, soon thereafter, decreed a massive pardon which, although it failed to include the whole imprisoned population, benefited some 3,600 political prisoners.

The program of pardons has a history both complex and dark. It was a way without defined paths, full of falsehoods and traps. And from a government of force, fair actions cannot be expected. For such a government, the law is a weapon. Reason, justice, will always be relative truths, although truth, as we know, is only one –unique and indivisible. In Vietnam, according to Communist theory, the United States practiced genocide. The Soviet invasion of Afghanistan, in contrast, purportedly obeyed humanitarian principles, including the use of chemical and germ warfare, fully justified by the dialectic of proletarian internationalism. This was the same dialectic used by Castro during his program of pardons to orchestrate the fantastic myth that certain people and ideas were supporting terrorist groups.

It is well known that in totalitarian regimes, a priority is suppression of freedom of movement. A man lives like a bird with cut wings, looking up nostalgically at the unattainable sky. Or like a worm, always dragging along on the ground. Following that invariable tradition, the Havana regime maintains millions of Cubans with their wings clipped. They are, in fact, hostages of the state. You would need to ask: who are the real terrorists in our country? Whose side are they on? What interests do they defend and what moral compass allows them to so unscrupulously judge those who have come into their prisons only through the love of homeland and freedom?

Not that Fidel Castro has had enough honesty to recognize when his appetite for revenge had not been satisfied to satiety.

In Cuba, everything goes awry, including in the mind of the tyrant. This opens doors to a myriad of questions. It could have been any reason; any, except that used to justify our exclusion from the program of pardons. It's not easy to negotiate with a sword pressed against your chest. Those who came in from exile to dialogue with the tyrant arrived in Havana with their hands tied. Never mind what noble intentions motivated some of them, or how many hopes they represented. That didn't matter. "With dialogue or without dialogue, the result would always be the same. The government of Cuba [read Fidel Castro] had decided beforehand how many political prisoners would be released and this would happen regardless of the results of the negotiations." That would be the later comment of the colonel of Cuban counterintelligence, Manuel Blanco Fernández. Among other things was the approaching Sixth Summit of the Movement of Non-aligned Nations to be held in Havana where Castro would assume the presidency for a period of three years, so he was pressured to repair his tattered image as much as possible. Also at its peak was the campaign by American President Jimmy Carter to defend human rights, and Cuba was not invulnerable to international pressure.

The deplorable economic situation, housing shortage, and growing popular discontent were other reasons forcing the Cuban government to decree the massive pardon. The freedom of some 3,600, however, would come with the condition that several tens of thousands of former political prisoners and their families also be expelled from the country. Authorized as well was the return to the island, as tourists, of Cuban exiles, as announced by the official media. That was how, overnight, so-called "worms" came to be hypocritically considered by the Communist clique to have become "members of the Cuban community abroad." Some joked that Castro acknowledged, with tears in his eyes, his error at having them called "worms" for twenty years.

At first, although the prices established for a brief visit to Cuba were exorbitant, exiles enjoyed certain liberties. They were allowed to take their relatives clothes and shoes, appliances, and certain consumer products. This brought on a collective euphoria, awakening among youth an awareness that, on the other side of the Florida Straits, there existed much more than violent police officers with nightsticks, taser guns, and attack dogs who suppress an endless queue of unemployed, a deplorable dunghill of "worms." Then urgent measures were taken to curb what was considered "a waste of opulence." Astronomical duties were imposed and, finally, everything was banned that was not regular luggage. However, nothing could suppress the clamor of the young. The dragon had bitten its tail in the attempt to collect a few million dollars for the ailing economy. In the spring of 1980, the more than 10,000 exiles in the Peruvian Embassy in Havana were more than convincing evidence. There had been an explosion, and fire was threatening to break out everywhere. Castro lifted the restrictions to rid himself of the protestors, allowing people to leave from the port of Mariel, which was no surprise to anyone. It was a long-awaited and necessary measure, what might be called an escape valve.

# CHAPTER 2

# Tony Cuesta: Heroism and Selflessness

The case of Antonio Cuesta Valle is, without a doubt, among the most touching in the long history of Cuba's political prisons, one of the greatest acts of cruelty committed by Castro and his jailers, who systematically refused to free him for more than 12 years, despite his pitiful physical condition, which prevented him from withstanding harsh prison conditions.

As chief of Commandos L, an infiltrating organization composed of Cuban exiles, Tony had directed numerous attacks against military objectives on Cuba's coasts. One night in 1966, while trying to make a landing in the area known as Monte Barreto, west of Havana Bay, the group was surprised by a reconnaissance patrol. The landing had coincided with a mobilization of Castro's troops (a state of alert had been decreed), devolving into an intense gunfight in which the valiant anti-Castro revolutionary Erminio Díaz and other colleagues were killed after having landed there. It was a bloody battle with the men under Erminio's command bravely attacking members of the more numerous and better-equipped enemy who had swarmed into the conflict area to wipe them out. The action at Monte Barreto is, and will remain, an example of heroism in the long history of the struggle against Communism which, for decades, Cuban patriots have been carrying out with selflessness and stoicism.

Facing the impossibility of picking up Erminio Díaz and the rest of the command, Tony Cuesta had decided to move away from the coast with the men already aboard his boat. He experienced some delay in trying to rescue one of his frogmen who was still in the water, forcing an intense exchange of gunfire resulting in the speedboat's presence being detected very close to the coast. Finally, his companion grabbed onto a rope and was towed slowly away from the area of fire. Once out of shooting range, the rescue was completed and they continued north, full speed ahead into the deep waters of the Florida Straits.

After about fifteen minutes of navigation, the sea became calm and everything seemed to indicate they would not face greater difficulties. But soon enough, about 200 meters off the bow, perhaps a little more, they detected a Castro torpedo boat, then another on their port, and one more that approached directly, trying to cut off their escape. All three boats began closing in and a ferocious gun battle ensued. Cuesta had no choice but to return fire to prevent them from coming aboard. In vain, he tried to open up a gap. As would be expected, despite the tenacious resistance of the anti-Castro commandos, the overwhelming superiority in firepower and disproportionate advantage of the Communist patrol decided the battle's outcome. When a large-gauge shot into one their engines, the exiles' boat exploded in flames. With the exception of young Eugenio Zaldívar, who had been hit by a projectile in a leg and another in his chest, and Tony Cuesta himself, all of their companions, including a nephew of Celia Sánchez Manduley (Sierra Maestra veteran and Fidel Castro's "secretary"), had died in the combat. It was then that Antonio Cuesta, facing immediate capture, exploded a grenade, as he himself told me, intending to commit suicide. Shrapnel pierced his stomach, severed his left hand at the wrist, and seriously injured both his eyes. Nonetheless, both Eugenio Zaldívar and Cuesta miraculously survived, one of those inexplicable twists of fate.

Sentenced to 30 years by a military court and deprived, on Castro's orders, of adequate medical assistance, Eugenio Zaldívar was left lame in his wounded leg and the chief of Commandos L permanently lost his eyesight. Since then, numerous governments and humanitarian institutions from around the world tried to obtain their release, or to have them subjected to less rigorous treatment given their delicate physical condition. But, again and again, Cuba's leader ignored such pleas, clinging as a beast to the politics of hate, the policy of intransigence, and the systematic denial of any humanitarian gesture.

It has been known for some years, according to testimony of the very doctors who attended him on several occasions, that Antonio Cuesta would have been able to recover at least 70% of his eyesight through timely surgical intervention. But that privilege, under various pretexts and arguments, was denied him. Castro preferred that he remain blind forever.

After a dozen years of cruel imprisonment, twelve long years in the dungeons of torture, of misery and humiliation, of wanton cruelty, "humanist" Fidel Castro, as a goodwill gesture, would include Antonio Cuesta Valle among the first 46 prisoners pardoned.

# CHAPTER 3

# Combinado Del Este Prison

Combinado del Este Prison was initially envisioned as a fabulous project. Twenty million pesos were allocated by the Cuban government for its construction. Its multiple buildings, four stories high, would have capacity for about 20,000 prisoners. However, like everything else that happens in an anarchic and archaic administrative system, the 20 million pesos authorized were wasted indiscriminately, and the Interior Ministry's repressive machinery would have to make do with a prison only able to house, even with overcrowding, only four to five thousand prisoners. Since three-fourths of the original project had to be sacked because the budget had been prematurely exhausted, the labor force ended up being comprised mostly of thousands of common prisoners. Viewed at a distance from the other side of the barbed wire, from the other side of the multiple watchtowers with guards and machine guns surrounding the penal area, from beyond the reflectors and sharp fangs of police dogs roaming freely night and day along prison hallways, Combinado del Este looks rather like a modern hotel complex with a recreation area for middle-class tourists. The four buildings glow in attractive colors. No less attractive is the showcase hospital, located between buildings 2 and 3, right next to the new athletics track and baseball field. Of course, these sports facilities will never be available to the prisoners unless a specific event for propaganda purposes requires the timely presence of a certain number of victims.

The transfer of political prisoners to Combinado was carried out via an unprecedented military operation. We were in La Cabaña Prison when a large group of officers appeared outside the bars of Gallery 8. It must have been about 5 a.m. Someone, among the prisoners, cried out: "Search!" And, immediately, a frantic hustle ensued, with all of us trying to hide things we wanted to keep out of the jailers' reach. But it didn't take us long to realize why that surprise mobilization had actually occurred. A stubby official, a genuine classic henchman with twenty years of experience in looting and opportunism, grabbed the loudspeaker, shouting "Attention!" "Attention!" Then he began reading off nine names: Remberto Zamora Chirino, Luis Zúñiga King, Jesús Silva Pontigo, Servando Infante Jiménez, Segundo Elejarde Capero, Argelio Aparicio, Heriberto Bacallao Espinosa, Gustavo Areces Álvarez, and, my own, Ernesto Díaz Rodríguez.

Without further delay, we were instructed to pick up "all belongings." Soon came the inevitable dispute, because, as always, the guards pressured us in the vain hope of forcing us to hurry us according to their whims. Since none of us complied, this irritated them. In Cuba, the only ones daring to openly disobey the capricious orders of the authorities are political prisoners. And they don't do so because they are braver than others; it's simply that they already have nothing left to lose. Out on the street, any disobedience means jail. Under a police regime such as Havana's, the citizen has become a machine managed by the military, an instrument of perfect passivity. Not even the supposedly free man can afford the luxury of looking a uniformed monster demanding respect straight in the eyes, convinced that it's not worth living in chains, instead deciding meekly to protect his precious skin.

We ended up picking up our possessions as they continued calling out names in different groups. All prisoners were given the same instructions, convincing us that it was a general transfer, even though there was speculation about whether we were actually going to the new prison, Combinado del Este, where we had heard that some buildings were still under construction. Among the prisoners there were always some super-optimists, like the beggar who enters a casino hoping to become a millionaire, always a few who speculated with boundless joy that the time had come for their long-desired freedom.

After gathering up our few possessions, the first nine of us were taken to the visitors' room. There we were delighted to find ourselves suddenly reunited with our compatriots Húber Matos, José Pujals Mederos, and Antonio (Tony) Lamas de la Torre, who, along with Eloy Gutiérrez Menoyo and Reinaldo Figueroa Gálvez, Lauro Blanco, and the poet Jorge Valls Arango, had been kept incommunicado from the rest of the prison population over the past seven years, first in Castillo del Príncipe, and, later on, in an underground cell in the same prison of La Cabaña... now, finally their brutal isolation had ceased. They could now breathe somewhat lighter air, even feel a little freer within the stark limitations to which we would always be subjected as the beasts that we were considered to be, at least according our treatment by the prison authorities.

We warmly embraced each other as brothers meeting again after a long journey. A moment of intense joy! In the visiting room, also with us was a platoon of officers and guards who immediately began searching thoroughly through all our belongings. Despite an unusual courtesy that at first surprised us, we found ourselves victims once again of the most indiscriminate looting. Many of our possessions were piled up in a corner. Once more, we would have to endure capricious dispossession without any right to the most minimal claim, because in such cases the jailers' response is always the same: "We follow orders." And "we only follow orders" is dutifully repeated by each and every one and, finally, by the prison director. "We just follow orders" is also the refrain of the director of jails and prisons, and of the interior minister, if someone should insist on wasting his time with a protest, a claim. Because in Cuba everyone follows orders with the exception of the Maximum Leader himself, with the exception of his Majesty Fidel Castro Ruz.

Loaded up with whatever we could salvage we were marched toward the prison headquarters, escorted by half a hundred gendarmes. On both sides of the alleyway several dozen guards lined up wielding AK47 Soviet rifles with fixed bayonets. During the whole journey of some 50 meters we were photographed over and over again. In front of the prison's headquarters we saw many high-ranking officers: generals, colonels, lieutenant-colonels, a range of magnificent examples, all well fed and trained to unconditionally serve Commander-in-Chief Fidel Castro, without any need for reflection, or even thinking. And there was also a mobile cart (called a "cage" by our jailers, nicknamed "pigsty" by us prisoners) into which we were pushed, one by one, until all twelve of us were squeezed into that small space with barely room to move. We were soon locked inside with a padlock and chains for good measure. Then four guards with AK47s assumed their positions. The outer door of our transport vehicle was slammed shut, plunging us into complete darkness. We began to sweat profusely and a sticky sweat was soon burning our skin. The heat was stifling, so suffocating that we could scarcely breathe. Moments later we heard the purr of the engine as the truck lurched forward.

Half an hour later, in the midst of a cumbersome military deployment, we entered the Combinado del Este visiting room where we were searched again to take away many of the few belongings that we thought we'd saved at La Cabaña. As might be expected, new and even more violent disputes took place between prisoners and guards. That resulted in pretexts to take away items that we really needed. They began by taking away some unimportant stuff and, if the prisoner did not resist, they continued taking items away until he was left with nothing. As you might guess, among the military, there were both left-wing extremists and more tolerant officers. The former did all possible damage, while the latter, less mischievous, did their job less rigorously. The former are full of hatred and resentments, heartless Communist; their greatest pleasure would be to stab out your eyes and display them out on the street on the tip of a bayonet. The latter are there to earn a paycheck, and may not understand the ignoble cause they are defending. They recognize the boundary between human and beast, perhaps a small difference, as a barrier that they should not cross and they do not do so unless circumstances require it. After all, they have not had a chance to learn any other trade and need to honestly earn their daily bread. Who knows if they have a wives and a couple of children, and maybe even mothers who they need to feed?

As long as the pat down continued, the Interior Ministry kept filming us from different angles. Photographers too, apparently, considered us a magnificent distraction, fantastic entertainment. Later we found out, as was announced in the magazine *Moncada* (the official and exclusive organ of information for members of the Interior Ministry), about the deactivation of La Cabaña for conversion into a prison museum. Previously, a long report had appeared in that magazine, and in several state publications along the same lines, when we political prisoners had been transferred from La Cabaña to the prisons of Guanajay and Castillo del Príncipe shortly before the spring of 1970. However, in September of 1972, we were unexpectedly returned to La Cabaña.

The idea of the museum had been put on hold a long time ago, when the government, having exhausted the capacity of all its concentration camps and jails, had to resort again to using the old fortress to hold some 3,500 soldiers, sanctioned mostly for repudiation of the Communist regime and breach of orders, and in part also for ordinary criminal offenders. A very few had even arrived there at age twenty-one. It is well known that the treatment these mostly adolescents received was brutal. Some were actually murdered with bayonets or by bestial beatings, or shot at close range. And these weren't just rare flukes, as they tried again and again to convince the victims' doubting relatives.

I heard about a mother who committed suicide shortly after being told that her only son, age seventeen, had been killed "accidentally" when an officer's Soviet-made rifle went off during a search. The boy's father had fallen in battle in Angola, a former rebel army officer called back to duty in November 1975 to advance the noble cause of proletarian internationalism. The young man, then serving his compulsory military service, went AWOL when he learned of his father's death, which led to his arrest. I was told by a comrade of the murdered young man, years later, when he came to Combinado del Este because of an illegal attempt to leave the country, that the boy had become an irreconcilable enemy of the Communists and in La Cabaña maintained an attitude of constant rebellion, despite the many beatings he endured. Most of the time, he told me, the boy was kept in punishment cells, and once cried out while jailers were beating him that one day he would kill Fidel Castro to avenge his father's death.

Once our search was over, we were taken by bus to the building designated for political prisoners. This, like the other buildings for the prison population, was divided into two sections, each four stories high: a north wing and a south wing. In the center, between the two areas, was a control board for the cell doors using an electronic system operated by a soldier, and three small office rooms. Across the way were a bathroom and a lounge available only to the chief floor officer and the jailers. Also, situated between the north and south wings were the main staircase (with an aide assigned to the far end of each section), a freight elevator, and the dining room with barred doors to be used alternately by inmates of both wings. Sometimes, in specific situations, occupants of each cell were only allowed access one by one. When this happened, prisoners intentionally dawdled as long as possible, to such an extent that at suppertime, from 4:30 to 5:00 p.m., the last ones still had not finished lunch. Thanks to this collective stalling, what was at first a very common practice came to be applied only at very critical moments, when it was sensed that the prisoners were at a critical juncture.

The twelve men in our first group, when we arrived at the Combinado del Este prison, were placed in cell #1404 at the end of the north wing of the fourth floor, building #1. Half an hour later came the second group, twelve more, who occupied cell #1403. Then others came and others still, until the building was filled up by some one thousand political prisoners in all.

The first floor held a section of small enclosed cells with steel doors in the north wing that, during the first six months, were used as punishment cells. There I personally met for the first time with the poet Ángel Cuadra. Previously, I had known him through his literary work, but during the pilgrimage from prison to prison, we had never before coincided. When he was at La Cabaña during the 1960s, I was in the provincial jail of Pinar del Río, known as 5 ½. Subsequently, his block was transferred to Guanajay prison, shortly before they did the same with me to La Cabaña. From Guanajay, Ángel went to a concentration camp and a few years later he was released. But his days out on the street were brief. One of his more vigorous poems was published abroad, so, immediately, in retaliation, the government revoked his freedom and the poet, after receiving a rash of threats at the headquarters of the political police (State Security), was sent to atone for his horrendous literary crime in the Combinado del Este prison's punishment lock-up.

From the very first moment we became good friends, and that friendship grew over time to become a true brotherhood. Many of us shared great joy when on April 6, 1982, the poet Ángel Cuadra Landrove, after completing the very last second of his fifteen years of deprivation of liberty, left Boniato Prison to reunite with his family in the peace of his own home.

Only two galleries of the first-floor section of the north wing of building #1 —each accommodating up to 36 men— plus the whole south wing, with the exception of two other similar galleries— were reserved for new inmates, that is, for those still pending trial.

The north wing of the second floor was also comprised mostly of small cells. Some *plantado* prisoners, wearing blue uniforms, were housed there. The south wing was entirely occupied by more than one hundred young men belonging to the so-called "re-education plan." The rest were assigned to both sections of the third floor. I feel it appropriate to highlight that while the vast majority of these young men were sent to prison for confronting the regime, a good number of them, as well as others caught trying to leave the country illegally, were not allowed to choose freely between the so-called re-education plan and the path of the *plantados*. I was one of those young men. In order for the government to recognize my status within the rebellion *(plantado),* I had to impose my will and display my firm determination and stoicism against a regime of frightening cruelty. Confined for many months to one of the special narrow cells for those sentenced to death, I met and endured the most humiliating harassment, most degrading and miserable perversity that can possibly be imagined, merciless torture in all its forms and nuances.

The whole fourth floor was designated for *plantado* political prisoners, about 250 to 300. We were put on the top floor to isolate us as much as possible from the rest of the prison population so as to keep us from fostering rebellion among the young people coming in.

Buildings 2 and 3 in a just few days became crowded with common prisoners. In all the Cuban prisons where these unfortunates had to live, if you can even call it living, conditions were truly inhumane. The modern Combinado del Este prison was no exception. If we political prisoners were being treated as beasts, the treatment that common prisoners received begs description. I happened to witness at Castillo del Príncipe the terrible overcrowding that those condemned by so-called "popular tribunals" were being subjected to. I spoke with many of them, so very young, almost still children. Their sentences generally were short, between one and six months, but excessive in that their so-called offenses mostly merited no more than a simple reprimand. Dozens and dozens of those teens came in every day. They usually were given only one set of used clothing for changing into and sometimes a rusty tin to hold their meager food ration. When there were not enough cans to go around, the corn meal slop or badly boiled spaghetti was served on pieces of cardboard. They had no spoons. Everyone ate with whatever they could improvise. Many used their hands. They slept on the frigid and grimy floor between rats and bedbugs, on top of each other, using shoes for pillows. Never actually absent were the nightsticks and bayonets. "They have to be treated roughly so as not to relapse," I heard various officials say on more than one occasion.

# CHAPTER 4

# Inaugurating The New Prison

Many of the facilities were still half finished, including the hospital, punishment pavilions, and the laundry room, when we were transferred to the new prison. The official opening of Combinado del Este did not take place until June 6, 1977, a national day of annual celebration by the Interior Ministry (MININT). On this occasion, the High Command organized celebrations that included mass participation by common prisoners. They had to perform dances and rhythmic gymnastics in the small athletic field located between buildings 1 and 2 and the visitors' hall. Around a hundred female prisoners from different women's centers were brought in daily from about mid-May until the designated date. They weren't able to learn much in just two or three weeks. I don't believe that they were particularly interested either. What mattered most to those girls was to be distracted from the grey monotony of their cells, or of the rustic barracks of the concentration camps where they were being held. We observed them from the fourth floor at meal times, appearing almost playful, like butterflies escaping from the cocoon. Some were so young that they looked like schoolgirls, children really. It caused a lump in my throat to think that fate had allowed them to be born in a corrupted world under such a cruel police system, often leading them to be jailed for the slightest infractions without anything ever being done to remedy the ills behind their alleged crimes. Now, those unhappy souls had appeared quite close to us, reminding us that much still remained to be done in our beleaguered homeland. They were silent reflections of a tragedy for all of us to remedy. Maybe it was the only time they smiled since they had become ensnared in that spider's web of prison bars and thorns, trapped so that the monster of the Caribbean could suck out their blood and dash their dreams. Occasionally, one would lift her hand to greet us, but discreetly, as from the outset, they had been forbidden to do so.

On one side of the visiting room, the political commission of the Board of Directors had placed a huge photo of Vladimir Illich Lenin, about 10 meters high, and, beside it, but considerably smaller, one of José Martí. That sad spectacle was depressing. Not only was the Bolshevik leader's image –a despicable, abominable symbol of slavery– placed next to that of the Apostle of Cuba, representing love and justice, but the arrangement tried, unscrupulously, through the symbolic difference of height and representation, to show what they, the pawns of Moscow, saw in Lenin and Martí. Anyone curious enough to carefully examine any Cuban newspaper or magazine will not fail to notice the invariability of that complicit practice. The ideologues of the Communist International have always occupied a privileged place. Next, according to those in charge here, comes the figure of the Commander-in-Chief, followed by Che and Camilo. Finally, the heroes of our independence, Martí, Gómez, and Maceo. Of course, if there is something that Fidel Castro does not like, it's the "cult of personality." And, as he assures us… he *never* lies. However, from one end to the other of the island, he has been unjustly viewed as the Kim Il Sun of the Americas.

A week before the designated date of the prison inauguration, we heard that the interior minister would be giving the closing speech. Right away, a group of *plantado* prisoners decided on a coordinated action to show our discontent with this new act of provocation before thousands of victims of the repressive prison system.

From the outset, we considered several proposals and counter-proposals. All agreed on the need to do *something*, but we couldn't agree on what. So, we tried to reach a consensus regarding just a simple protest. If majority approval was reached by the date of the inauguration, we would simply refuse prison food throughout the day. But, inexplicably, we could not reach agreement even on that, so we stopped trying. Would we simply observe, with arms crossed, the bitter spectacle mutely from our bunks, with our liver quivering within us? It was impossible to resign ourselves to doing nothing at all, I mused bitterly. And, my colleagues agreed. No, it was not possible to simply resign ourselves, as I repeated to myself, so, in one way or another, it was necessary to strike a blow. And we would see how when the opportunity arose.

Since our jailers were well aware of the machinations of the *plantado* prisoners, they felt pressured to take proactive security measures. To intimidate us, they always fell back on repression, the only deterrence Communists use to silence their opponents, especially if these are political prisoners. They did so despite the reality that time and time again, their results fail, as political prisoners usually respond to repressive measures with rebellion.

# CHAPTER 5

# Captain Raúl Álvarez Visits Cell 1404

On the afternoon of June 3, the chief of the political prisoners' building, Captain Raúl Álvarez, entered our cell apparently intending to browse around, something that he did quite often. He had no idea of the earful he would receive from Commander Húber Matos about his ill-timed visit. It happened that a few days before, in the newspaper *Granma,* official organ of the Cuban Communist Party, there had appeared a lengthy article miserably maligning Commander Matos. Not only did it unscrupulously twist actual history, but it tried, with marked cynicism, to make him appear before public opinion as a coward of the worst stripe, forced to climb up to the Sierra Maestra at gunpoint to fulfill a mission entrusted to him by the leadership of the 26 of July movement in Manzanillo. Nothing more villainous and ridiculous could be leveled against a man of such personal integrity, someone who was often tested in the insurrectional struggle against the dictatorship of Fulgencio Batista and, then again, during 20 years of imprisonment under Castro.

Defamation is a weapon which Communists often fall back on to confront their ideological and political foes. Becoming a good Marxist-Leninist requires something more than simple mud-slinging, something more than being full of hatred and envy or acting a bit ridiculous, or as an apprentice to becoming a fool and a knave; you need also, among other virtues, to erase all shame and sensitivity.

Captain Raúl Álvarez was a perfect Marxist-Leninist. Never before had I seen Commander Húber Matos more furious or more eloquent than on that occasion. He began by recounting all the intrigues leveled by Mr. Fidel Castro against his person, some so early that they went back to his very first days after joining the guerrillas in the Sierra Maestra. Matos had arrived in the area of operations leading an expedition of Cuban exiles on a clandestine flight from Costa Rica on the afternoon of March 30, 1958. In an undeniable example of heroism, the pilot, Pedro Luis Díaz Lanz, had made a rare landing on an inhospitable field, not far from enemy advances. After unloading the valuable war cargo of weapons and ammunition, and facing the impossibility of taking off again due to the terrible condition of the terrain, the expeditionary forces proceeded to burn the aircraft that had brought them to the island. A few days later, after his men had been incorporated into the rebel ranks, Matos would confront his first difficulties with Castro, strongly rejecting a despotic reprimand from the commander-in-chief. Now Matos pointed out to Captain Álvarez similar incidents throughout the long trajectory from his arrival in the mountains up until the day of his resignation letter to Prime Minister Fidel Castro, resulting in his arrest and arbitrary 20-year sentence, a sanction that he would have to fulfill up to the very last day. Using very energetic and precise language, Commander Matos openly accused Castro, in front of the building's chief, of being a traitor and a coward. He called him a murderer, a blockhead, and even more still, words so violent I dare not repeat them here, though I much enjoyed them at the time.

"Don't pay attention to all that crap written by folks at *Granma*," was all that Captain Raúl Álvarez had to say, and added, with a disgusting dismissal, "You know, Húber, that's politics. And you know, history is written by the winners. You lost."

"Look, Raúl, it's best to not talk any about more about this," Matos cut in. And, then, with the precision of an arrow, emphasizing each word with a gesture of open contempt, he added, "You are all the same, completely shameless."

Captain Raúl Álvarez's own story had begun like that of many reporters at *Granma*, including the writer who had signed the article published on January 1, 1959, when Batista had fled after the overthrow of his regime. He did not react to the whiplash given him by Húber, not at all demoralized. He merely shrugged, smiling (a cynical smile) without saying a word. Then he left, displaying the tranquility of a devoted Communist, wrapped in the aromatic smoke of his exquisite cigar.

It was June 4, late at night, when all the buildings were enveloped in a peaceful silence. For much of the time, most of the guys had already gone to sleep. Perhaps at that moment, some dreamed of their elderly mothers, their estranged wives and children, or of the wife and child they hoped to have in the future because quite a few of those unfortunates had entered the regime's dungeons in their early teens, without time for any lover except the homeland. And who knows if they dreamed of their village's streets and parks and the vast blue sea, and of all those ineffable chimeras about which each man, happy or unhappy, tends to dream about?

Soon enough, the chilling squeal of tires against pavement made us jump up startled. Almost immediately, we heard another car, and then another and another. We recognized it as a clear signal of the arrival of several political police patrols. Soon the vehicles stopped, discharging our handcuffed companions Silvino Rodríguez Barrientos, Eleno Oviedo Álvarez, Víctor Miguel Cantón Gómez, Antonio López Muñoz, and Remberto Zamora Chirino, who were all led to State Security Department G2, then held hostage there to prevent them from arousing any disorder during the inauguration of the new terror and torture chamber.

The next morning came the news that the police on that same night had also occupied the prison hospital, where they had taken our fellow Orlando Molina Contreras, despite his being seriously ill. "When we arrived, we feared them from the very first," I would be told later by Eusebio Peñalver Mazorra. They had come in like angry beasts, their voices amplified throughout by the loudspeakers.

"Molina was rudely ordered to get out of bed. The nurse was angry about that, asking for an explanation. But they said that they were in charge and, without further hesitation, threw her out of the room. She left crying, I don't know if from rage, fear, or helplessness. We never saw her again. Molina was then led out barefoot and handcuffed. As soon as they had left the room, fearing their prompt return, I slid into the bathroom. I immediately took out items that Pepe Pujals had given me to deliver personally to César Páez, letters with accounts critical of the government, and threw them into the toilet. I could not breathe easy until I saw them disappear in the swirl of water. Imagine that close call, as Pepe had warned me that those papers must not fall under any circumstances into military hands. Had they found these, Pepe would suffer their retaliation. Already that same evening, word had been sent to César to collect them in room B, but this happened in the first hours of the following morning. I was mortified, but César was understanding, even pleased to a certain extent, that I had destroyed them."

After a brief pause, he continued. "'You did well,' he told me. And then repeated the same warning given me by José Pujals; that the only thing that could not have happened was that those papers to have fallen into hands of the Communists."

Then Peñalver continued on with his story, "When I came out of the bathroom, I went and peeked out through the blinds and saw the three alfitas (Alfa Romeo cars, used by the Cuban political police) leaving Post #1. That night we stayed awake until very late, as there was much uncertainty and tension, so no one could fall asleep."

# CHAPTER 6

# Conceiving A New Type of Protest

Almost without realizing it, the eve of Combinado del Este's inauguration was upon us. Since we weren't able to reach agreement about mounting some type of protest, many felt disappointed, thinking we might do nothing at all on such a significant date. However, that same evening, pondering what to do to save the situation, it suddenly occurred to me that although there was no chance to run it by my eleven prison mates (Segundo had been released after having had his sentence commuted days before), we might actually have the solution at hand. I first shared my idea with Servando Infante. I was sorry not to have come up with it sooner to be able to consult with our other companions in both sections. I was sure that they would prefer this new variant, something much more appropriate than not eating, which already almost everyone had rejected as it had usually been ineffective in recent months. But now there was no time to lose.

"Hey, Servando, what do you think about tomorrow?" I asked him, not caring much about his response, just a way to get the conversation going.

"What do you mean?" he answered me with another question, sounding a little surprised.

I realized that his mind was somewhere else, perhaps traveling among the asteroids, because at that moment, he was engrossed in reading *The Little Prince,* that extraordinary literary work by Antoine de Saint-Exupéry. (At times, our relatives were allowed to bring us books —non-political ones, of course, to family visits. These books, some in English, were cherished and passed hand-to-hand. During other long periods of time books were forbidden.)

"Tomorrow is June 6," I reminded him, "MININT Day, the opening of the...

"Damn it, sure, Yes, fuck!" he interrupted sharply, slapping himself on the forehead. And slowly, stretching out the syllables, he said, "The inauguration of Combinado del Este."

Servando closed the book and sat up on his bunk. His was on the top tier, with Jesús Silva in the middle and Húber Matos at the bottom.

"Move over," I told him, gesturing left, then adding, with my foot already on Silva's bed, "I think that for me, the spark has been lit. Move over a little bit more."

I climbed up onto the bed and sat beside him. There was a brief silence; then:

"Put this into your noggin, Servo, I just had an idea. What do you think if tomorrow we hang a Russian flag outside the dining room and light it up on all four corners?

"Shit!" he exclaimed enthusiastically.

That was Servando's personal expression of approval. Apparently, it had been a mechanical response, because suddenly, a little astonished, he hastened to ask me: *"A Russian flag? From where in hell are we going to get it?"* And, after a short pause, "You're pulling my leg, right?"

"How would I be kidding? Not at all. I'm talking seriously, very seriously. A Russian flag and a big one, so that they can see it all wrapped up in flames, the minister and all those bastards who will be applauding him."

Servando was becoming more and more intrigued. Not that he doubted that we would solve it somehow, but he wanted to know from what magic hat we were going to pull out that flag.

"Stop beating around the bush," he insisted, pressing me, "Where are we going to get it?"

"It's not question of where. We are going to make it ourselves. Yes, we're going to make it. Wait and see."

"How?"

"Well, very simply, with a sheet... and with blood."

"Shut up! You expect me to buy that!" he exclaimed, slapping his forehead again with both hands.

Servando had raised his voice, causing everyone to turn to stare at us.

Matos, stretched out on his bunk ready to go to sleep, turned over smiling and, in a jocular tone, asked Luis Zúñiga, "And at what party will we pick up those two little fish?"

"You really don't want to know," Zúñiga replied, "Looks like they've already discovered how water gets into the coconut." This reference to how water gets inside a coconut was a Cuban phrase used to describe mysteries and curiosities.

In fact, with the exception of Remberto Zamora, who at that moment was locked up in a dark State Security dungeon, and Tony Lamas and Heriberto Bacallao, admitted to the prison's hospital – Bacallao for more than two weeks, recovering from a terrible ulcer attack– all cellmates suddenly had become engaged in our conversation. First of all, because it was really difficult, not to say impossible, to stay out of the conversation in the close quarters assigned to us by our jailers. Second, because in our own tiny universe, we got along so well and had so much spiritual affinity –regardless of everyone's individual philosophy and daily habits, personal character, culture, and emotional state —that we had come to consider ourselves true brothers, giving us a certain liberty, a liberty that in a less intimate setting might be interpreted as indiscretion. But certainly, there were logical and reasonable limits that everyone understood without anybody having to say so.

I still enjoy looking back on those days in cell 1404. We actually spent some entertaining hours there and even, at times, had fun playing practical jokes.

The cell's two most serious men, not only because of their gray hair, but also in terms of character, were Pujals and Matos. Pepe was usually reserved and rarely joked around, although he enjoyed my idea of a flag in his own way while feigning disinterest. Húber liked engaging in entertaining talk and telling us about his experiences fighting in the mountains against Batista's army, something important historically. To be fair, Luis Zúñiga, though much younger, should have been considered an equally serious member of cell 1404. A fourth-year engineering student, he was expelled from the university for standing up against Marxism and had been obsessed with learning English, which he had acquired almost to perfection, spending no less than 10 hours a day immersed in books. Argelio Aparicio was, without a doubt, the most introverted.

Tony Lamas, one of the most noble and battle-hardened, was obsessed and meticulous about organizing his things. He alone had more possessions than all the rest of us put together. So many, that on two or three occasions, when he had to go into the prison hospital, he felt it necessary to send us a curious outline indicating the location of each and every object, because otherwise, it might have taken us days to locate something as simple as a pair of socks, a handkerchief, soap, or a toothbrush. And this, even though, just six months earlier, he had lost a similar number of items in the search before our transfer.

I could have a lot to say about the daily disputes between Bacallaito and Chuchú Silva. They engaged in constant battle without drawing blood. While they exchanged horrors in jest, neither was ever actually bothered by what the other had to say. The only thing that really got Chuchú's goat was being awakened by a blow to the head while asleep. Of course, it was only a momentary anger. Bacallaito, as we called Heriberto, suffered from delicate health, spending most of his time in the Combinado hospital. He fell in love with any sort of skirt, even if it hung on a broom stick. And there in the hospital, he saw many female nurses, some very beautiful and affectionate. Chuchú took advantage of this to tease him mercilessly.

"Hey, buddy," he told him, "stop all this play acting, because even your corns don't hurt. You are just crazy about the nurses, which arouses your ulcer. Look in the mirror and don't be so glum; you couldn't attract even a monkey with that sour puss."

His friend, of course, retorted, "And you, you old goat, who are you going get with that bald head? You're dying of envy because that round dome of yours wouldn't interest even a witch."

And they wouldn't stop.

# CHAPTER 7

# A Russian Flag

As soon I'd finished telling Servando about my idea of burning the Russian flag, and he had agreed, I took the idea to Zúñiga, who, as always, got excited. Despite our dire circumstances, he always managed to maintain his boundless optimism. It's not surprising, then, that every year, he would bet me a barrel of beer and a roast suckling pig that by the next Christmas, we'd all be back out on the street.

"Forget that, pal. Plant your feet firmly on the ground and don't get delusions," I joked, more to challenge him than anything else. After all, our banter was a way to break our daily monotony.

Immediately, he'd repeat his bet, always the same: the suckling pig and drinks all around. After a few years, when he owed me I don't know how many piglets and barrels of beer, I turned the tables, arguing that perhaps a change of course would bring us better luck. Since the chances that Fidel Castro would decide to free us were so slim, that gave him the opportunity to amortize his symbolic debt, symbolic because neither of us would have charged the loser. The real point was that, someday, we would celebrate the planned family dinner.

Shortly after midnight, before going to bed, we outlined our entire enterprise in structured detail, planning to implement it the next morning. That night, I dreamed that I was with my brother and my kids, out walking together on the streets of New York. On our walk, we arrived at lower Manhattan, where we boarded a sailboat that took us out to the Statue of Liberty. We climbed up to the crown via a narrow spiral staircase, stopping there to gaze out, entranced at the beautiful city. At that instant, a huge fire broke out inside the statue. Flames flared up, preventing us from being rescued from the inferno. Suddenly, a deafening explosion was heard, and then I found myself floating under a huge multi colored parachute along with my brother and children, falling gently down onto the park in the town of my birth. I spent the rest of that hot, humid night wide awake nursing a severe headache.

Morning dawned. Just as we were opening up for breakfast, I sprinted to the small nursing corner of our section to ask the nurse for two or three of the largest syringes he had and ten or twelve needles number 19 or 20.

"Whatever are you up to?" he asked with undisguised curiosity and surprise.

The nurse was Arcelio Ramos Lechuga, a political prisoner in the rehabilitation plan, a former Batista military officer, sentenced to 30 years. He was often short-tempered, but got along well with me.

"Don't worry, it's not to make an atom bomb," I parried, trying to downplay the matter, "Are they sterilized?"

"Not the syringes. Why sterilize them if those big ones are never used? Furthermore…" he paused, glancing at his watch, "it's only 6:10 am."

"Let me have them just as they are," I said, having no other choice.

At that moment, I recalled that prisoners are like mummies; there is no microbe that can destroy us.

"There's something fishy here somewhere," he murmured, not giving up, adding in a more jocular tone, *You bastard! I'd dare bet my neck that you're up to something.*

"Never mind! I'll tell you later. Hurry up before everyone starts leaving the dining room and the guard comes in to shut the door."

Lechuga wrapped up everything in a green cloth, which he handed me without further ado. Instantly, I tucked it under my shirt. Our cell was just two steps away from the nursing station.

When the others arrived, I showed them from under my pillow how we were going to draw blood.

"Go ask Lechuga for a little alcohol and cotton," I told Luis Zúñiga, as, in my unbridled haste, I'd forgotten that detail.

Zúñiga grimaced in disgust.

"Okay, if you want, I'll do it myself," I retorted, "but he's cranky. Don't you think that it's better that you go? You never get on his bad side."

"If you insist, then I'll go. But by God, watch out for Areces (a fellow prisoner), as he might climb up onto your bed to get to his top bunk and accidentally plant his foot right onto your pillow and spoil everything."

I went out myself, because already the guard had begun closing up the cells of our section.

I returned in less than a minute, along with the tourniquet, which I'd also forgotten previously.

The guard had closed the door of 1404 and had gone over to the other hall. Everything was now ready to put into action.

"How did everything go in the dining room?" I wanted to check with Servando and Zúñiga, although already Húber and Pujals had told me that everything went fine.

"Buddy, everything is hunky-dory, nothing special, as we already told you," I was assured.

"Lieutenant Mauricio was watching from his office door," Luis Zúñiga added, "maybe a little suspicious, but nothing more."

Lieutenant Mauricio is a devoted goon. It was he who had ordered the mutilation by machete of Eduardo Capote when we were in courtyard #1 of La Cabaña Prison. Now he was in charge of *plantado* prisoners in both wings, of the fourth floor, north and south. Those in the north area of the second floor, also *plantados,* had another floor officer.

Without delay, we began getting everything ready.

"Who's the first victim?" I asked, smiling.

"Are you drawing blood?" they all protested almost at once.

In our cell, Tony Lamas was the only one who knew something about injecting, but at that time, he was in the Combinado hospital.

Since someone had to do it, then that someone had to be me, based on my experience in having once injected vitamin B12 into an anemic cat at Castillo del Priíncipe.

Her delivery had turned out badly, perhaps because of the many prying eyes observing her during the birth of her very first kittens. We all had wanted to see how a cat would give birth, but she seemed to have decided, after having released the first creature, that was all she would display that afternoon, and made no further effort. Several hours later, fearing that the cat was having a serious setback, I picked her up and took her to Tony Cuesta's bedside. On several occasions, Cuesta had told me that in his youth, he had been a student of veterinary medicine.

"Here is María Luisa, who needs a thorough checkup," I hastily explained, giving details of what had happened.

After a thorough examination and feeling her abdomen due to his poor eyesight, Cuesta intoned authoritatively: "Don't keep on waiting. She's completely empty, having given birth to all she had."

I took the cat and gently deposited her into the drawer where the newborn was waiting. We then forgot all about mother and baby. After about an hour, it occurred to me have another look. To my surprise, I found a whole litter of kittens, all nursing beautifully. A few days later, our "veterinarian" Cuesta prescribed six injections of B12 for the new mother. (I think he wanted to make up to the cat for having so badly misdiagnosed her.) But the first time I stuck her, she landed a tremendous bite on my thumb, enough to make me give up the vitamin treatment. This time, I hoped that none of my colleagues would do the same.

Servando, resignedly, was the first to extend his arm. As soon as I had wrapped the tie around his arm and before he could change his mind, I plunged in the syringe. The needle smoothly pierced the vein and the blood began flowing slowly. But it proved harder than I had expected, with the plunger offering me more and more resistance.

Finally, the syringe was filled and I took it out to install another needle firmly, to make sure it would stay in the vein. We tried several times.

It was not until after finishing with Servando that we discovered why the syringe had offered so much resistance: Nobody had remembered about removing the tourniquet around the arm. When I untied it, almost instantly, a bruise appeared and by the next day covered his entire forearm.

To Luis Zúñiga, I had to give several punctures. It was not his lucky day. Areces was not so hard, and two or three was enough. The rest, more or less, had their ups and downs.

Things got complicated when my turn came, as no one volunteered. Well, to tell the truth, though some offered, none inspired me with confidence. As often happens in such circumstances, the choices could not have been worse. Zúñiga gave me I don't know how many sticks, some so deep they almost went through my elbow. I started to break into a sweat, as if in a Turkish bath or locked in a punishment cell. He stamped his feet and, at each failed attempt, lamented his bad luck. But he didn't stop. That needle entering and leaving my arm reminded me of a woodpecker, although for me, certainly, my arm was my arm and not a tree trunk.

"ENOUGH!" I managed to scream, "No more needle-pricks!"

"Don't give up now, the vein is right there and I have it pegged; it's mathematical. Give me another chance," he almost begged.

"Not one, not even a half!" I protested vehemently, jumping up to show that I meant business and would not allow even one more stab.

"Okay, then let someone else try," he sighed in resignation.

"No more, it's over!" I interrupted dryly. "I'm going to draw the blood myself."

Everyone looked astonished.

I thought that by working slowly, I could hit it, but wasn't sure if I had the courage to drive the needle into my own arm so cold-bloodedly.

Before deciding, I contemplated on the sheet stretched out on the floor, already half filled in. The strong smell of blood churned my stomach. However, our effort was looking magnificent. Then I went to the door, trying to breathe in some fresh air through the bars. I spent a few minutes there, thinking about the surprise that within a few hours we had in store for the Interior Ministry's High Command. Maybe that was enough to give me the boost I needed.

With a sigh of resignation, I came back to the bench that we had set up for our effort. I don't know what would have happened if I hadn't hit the vein on that first try. This time I didn't forget to loosen the tie in time. While I held the syringe in place, Zúñiga pulled slowly on the plunger, so that blood began filling it up, centimeter by centimeter. Those minutes felt like an eternity. Collapsing with fatigue, I threw myself onto the mattress where they gave me a cotton swab moistened with alcohol to revive me. Soon, I was once again soaking a brush in my own blood and smearing it with satisfaction on the sheet, now nearly transformed into a flag.

It was necessary to resort to several donations from the folks in cell 1406, communicating our thanks via a snippet of fabric hoisted by a rope improvised with bootlaces. Cell 1406 cell was in Hall B, but its bottom met the bottom of ours, separated by a narrow corridor about two meters wide. The upper part of both walls ended in columns of steel and concrete, with a connected vertical opening approximately three inches wide, open to the air (and the rain) that allowed us to exchange secret communications. Thanks to this opportune opening, we got the rest of the blood we needed to finish dyeing the sheet. The hammer and sickle was the first thing we depicted, before the door opened for breakfast, using a jar of yellow synthetic paint that only days earlier, one of the building's painters, in a lucky twist of fate, had given me. Just in case a guard happened to glance into our cell, we hung the finished flag inside the bathroom. However, the strong smell of blood persisted. As we didn't have much time, we took turns waving air at it with a towel.

Throughout the morning, we were figuring out the best way to take action to catch them all by surprise and not give them time to react before the flag was enveloped in flames. To avoid allowing the fire to burn the mooring ropes, causing the flag to fall abruptly, we hung it up with wires. The bed and frame that Segundo de la O. Elejarde had left empty after being released days earlier provided us with everything we needed, something not more than two yards long. The facade of the dining room, as well as 80% of the exterior building walls, were constructed of panels of pre-cast concrete, with columns of vertical openings of the same type as the backs of cells 1404 and 1406, and all the others, with the only difference being that the outward openings stretched from the floor up to half a meter from the ceiling.

Zúñiga and Servando would take care of tying up the flag. I would set it on fire. Anticipating that the blood might not have dried properly by the time we went to lunch, we had a small bottle of gasoline that someone had given me to clean the brushes. With that, it was guaranteed to flare up immediately.

At last, the time had come and they began to open up all the doors of the north wing simultaneously. That meant that we didn't have to take special safety precautions, because, otherwise, the exit to the dining room would have been cell by cell, with all the drawbacks and limitations that represented. So, the path was clear. Confident that we faced no major difficulties, we waited a few minutes to be sure that everyone would be quietly having lunch when we arrived.

Once a short time had elapsed, we put everything inside a gunny sack and dashed out to carry out our mission. Who knows if by pure coincidence, the moment we arrived at the dining room, we found Lieutenant Mauricio there. But, in fact, this unexpected finding did not present any sort of obstacle. Improvising, I sent out Gustavo Areces and Silva Pontigo to ask him some questions. And if we had to tie him up, we would have gladly done so. Once our decision was made, we were prepared to burn the flag in one way or another.

Zúñiga and Servando worked quickly, so that when Lieutenant Mauricio looked up, the Russian flag was already firmly clamped and hanging over the main entrance. Very surprised, and angry, he ran towards us, screaming with unbridled fury: *"No, no, no, you can't do that! You cannot do that!"*

I couldn't help smiling as I emptied the bottle of gasoline on the sheet stained with blood, which still had not finished drying completely. All the prisoners, more than one hundred, were astounded and immediately raised their voices in a crescendo of deafening cries of joy.

"Down with Communism!" cried one.

"Down with Lenin's flagship!" bellowed another. It was the voice of Teodoro González Alvarado.

"Down with tyrant Fidel Castro!" rang out with the power of a million speakers.

José Oscar Rodríguez Terrero and the poet Jorge Valls approached us right away, eager to do something, to lend a hand or to accompany us at least with their physical presence, just with their very breath. Others also came, wanting to participate in our modest act of rebellion.

"Get out of here! Get out before we burn you too along with this shit!" Zúñiga threatened, in a very energetic tone, Lieutenant Mauricio, who tried in vain to unleash one of the wires.

Mauricio didn't have time to utter even one syllable, because at that instant, a wonderful flare rose up to almost scorch his craggy face, and us also. Very frightened, he leapt backward and hurried away. When he was on the other side of the dining room door, he communicated with his office. He flipped down the metal grating over the dining room door and from there, he stood watching the show from the other side, his eyes wild and flashing, I don't know if from horror, rage, or shame.

"Quiet! Quiet!" a strong voice calling for silence was heard while the flag still burned. Then, it said, "The anthem, the national anthem, let's sing the anthem."

Immediately, the prisoners all stood up excitedly and, in unison, sang the Cuban National Anthem.

A little later, when we were back in our cells, Captain Raúl Álvarez arrived, accompanied by a platoon of guards, to remove the rest of what had been a Russian flag. We thought that we would be taken immediately to the punishment dungeons. But that did not happen, perhaps because the new punishment pavilion was still under construction and the walled first floor cells were not sufficiently rigorous according to Soviet technicians, experts in the art of repression. In any case, there was no rush. We would pay our dues when the time came…

I later learned that José Oscar Rodríguez Terrero (Napoleoncito) had first set fire to the flag before I had had time to do it, and I also met Rigoberto Pérez Roque (Telto) and other colleagues, after they had sent us their blood donations from cell 1406, and was informed of their own project of making a banner denouncing the crime against Pedro Luis Boitel, student leader and a prominent figure of the Cuban political prison, which was also hung up at lunchtime, not far from the place where we had burned the hammer and sickle flag.

We could never confirm whether the interior minister at the time, Dr. Sergio del Valle, who had ended up leaving in his wake, as the maximum representative of his repressive institution, a veritable rosary of maimed and dead, was in fact present or not at the official opening of Combinado del Este.

Four days later, six colleagues who had been taken out as hostages to State Security, returned.

# CHAPTER 8

# Devoured by Sharks

We could have a lot to say about the various methods that, over the years, prison authorities have used to assassinate political opponents. The classic, most common way was the firing squad— the execution wall. From 1959 to date, Cuba's Communist government has executed tens of thousands of its opponents this way. The effort started with the wholesale execution of Batista's ex-servicemen. Then came the dissident revolutionaries and, later, intoxicated or alienated by power and blood, the authorities continued executions in prisons all over the island on the flimsiest of pretexts.

In the summer of 1970, a prosecutor of the so-called "Revolutionary Court No. 1" in Havana, surnamed Camacho, told my comrade Emilio Nazario Pérez, Dr. Edmundo Pujol, and me that in the years 1967 and 1968, the government had been seriously considering applying the death penalty to all those accused of trying to leave the country illegally. "Imperialists did not stop encouraging young people to commit such crimes. Having those youths reach their coasts aboard a raft allowed them to exploit that sensational news for propaganda purposes. We had to stop them, to impede that effort in any way possible, and we thought an effective measure could be the firing squad," Señor Camacho had explained with a despotic shrug. And then, as someone trying to make believe that the universe is just a tiny kernel, he concluded: "We were sure that with such measures, the revolution would save many lives, because half of them have ended up drowning in the sea."

Not mentioned by Mr. Camacho was how the other half had died, machine-gunned down on the coast, or even in international waters when they were surprised by the regime's patrol boats, or that the Cuban government denied their legal right to travel freely, then forced them to live on bended knee in the most appalling misery.

A few months later, this same official would tell the accused, Alberto Lazo Pastrana, "I will do everything possible to have you shot."

I saw the prisoner Lazo Pastrana arrive at Castillo del Príncipe suffering from a severe crisis of nerves. He was assigned to live in Gallery #6, Zone 5, very close to me, almost at the same entrance door. There he found many of his old prison colleagues and told us, between tears and sobs, his heart-rending story.

After having served 10 years in prison, Alberto Lazo Pastrana was freed at the concentration camp called "Fajardo," located on the outskirts of San Cristóbal, Pinar del Río province. It was a welcome relief after his exhausting pilgrimage from prison to prison during a decade characterized by savage abuses, beatings, and torture. Doubtless that had been one of the bitterest stages of Cuba's political imprisonment. La Cabaña, the fields of forced labor on the Isle of Pines, the terrible punishment cells of 5 1/2, the blows, solitary detentions, despotism. None of this was escaped by the prisoner Alberto Lazo Pastrana. But now he felt fortunate, enjoying the peace of his home, sharing love, bread, and hope with his long-suffering wife and their four young children.

In 1971, Alberto Lazo Pastrana and his wife decided to leave the country, finding it impossible to continue living in Cuba in the face of the constant harassment and discrimination visited upon those daring to dissent against the dictatorial regime of Fidel Castro. They duly went to the immigration office to carry out the necessary and rigorous legal procedures. *"We'll let you know,"* they were told by Cuban authorities. Months later, they received an official communication notifying them that their request for permission to leave the country had been denied.

From that moment on, the former political prisoner and his family were subjected to new and greater retaliation. Cornered like a beast or a worthless animal, Alberto began mulling over the idea of escaping from the island by the only door remaining: a rustic raft.

"One way or another, I had to get out of this hell," my beleaguered friend would explain to me later at Castillo del Príncipe prison, "I had been left without work and was getting desperate. Sometimes I couldn't even afford to buy the four nonsense items allowed us by the ration book. I was sorry to have to borrow from friends without much hope of ever repaying them, at least until I could find some work. One day I said to myself: 'I can't take this anymore,' and decided on the raft. My idea was to go by myself and, once there, to find a way to bring my wife and kids. I thought that by going to the U.S., not only could I find work and send them whatever they needed, but perhaps any efforts to get them out legally would also be easier. What would they care about my wife and children? I knew I was the obstacle, that they would never give me permission. That was what I had decided at first. But then my wife told me:

"'No, Alberto, the day you came home, we swore never to be apart again, so let's not break that vow. For God's sake, I don't want to be separated from you. Take me with you. Don't leave us.'"

Alberto paused in his narrative to swallow hard. Then he continued, his voice quivering, as if his soul were choking on a painful internal sob. "'And what about the children?' I'd asked her, puzzled.

"'The children would also risk the same fate. We all live or die together. Anything is preferable to having to live without hope,' she'd said. And then, with tears in her eyes, she added: 'Already, we've been apart too long. Yes, we'll go with you. Let God's will be done.'"

Two weeks later, the Lazo family moved quietly to the Isle of Pines. There, with the help of his wife and children, all enduring a hellish plague of mosquitoes, in a hidden bower very close to the mouth of a stream, Alberto built a homemade raft to reach their dream of freedom.

On a starry night, they rowed out to sea, taking advantage of a gentle breeze that helped propel them off the coast. They were already in the gulf, approaching the intersection where ships sail west through the Yucatán Straits toward the Panama Canal. They had spent several days adrift, but felt blessed to have escaped the coast guard, the humiliation of the Defense Committees, the miseries, the slavery. Those unfortunate drifters could not have imagined that just at daybreak, when they least expected it, they would be detected by a Communist patrol boat, manned by a group of monsters.

First, the patrol boat circled the raft several times, lighting it up with its powerful searchlights. Then, the official craft rammed its steel bow against the fragile vessel over and over, crushing its fragile structure which bounced atop the water like a walnut shell. Nothing came of the mother's desperate cries, imploring them not commit to such an appalling crime; nothing came of the screams of the children with their terrified faces. Hatred proved stronger than reason. One by one the children began falling into the water, wounded, crushed. So, in this dreadful and monstrous way, Lazo's wife and four small children were killed in their desperate attempt to achieve freedom, thanks to the torturers in Castro's service.

The next morning, the unfortunate woman's body was extracted from the water after sharks, already attracted by the blood, had devoured her breasts and both arms. None of the children's small bodies could be found, gone forever; who knows if they were also eaten by sharks? By the irony of fate, Alberto was the sole survivor of this dreadful disaster. Apparently, death was too good for this humble and honorable man, forced to escape his country with those nearest and dearest to save them from frightening misery, hunger, and slavery. To his infinite pain, he had miraculously survived, perhaps to bear witness, so that someday, the civilized world would know about this horrendous crime.

Despite the insidious brutality of the prosecutor, the accused Alberto Lazo Pastrana escaped the firing squad. However, one or another way, Cuba's communist government had decided to stop that shadow of a human being who raised his accusing finger at every step. Though sentenced to 18 years in prison for his attempted illegal departure from the country, "President" Fidel Castro announced via radio and television on August 6, 1978, that Lazo Pastrana would be one of the 3,600 political prisoners pardoned. But, inexplicably, on September 1 of that same year, just 20 days after the pardon announcement had been made to the world, Alberto Lazo Pastrana died of a mysterious illness in a cell in the Combinado del Este prison hospital.

# CHAPTER 9

# Punishment Dungeons

Two weeks after the burning of the Russian flag, Servando Infante, Luis Zúñiga Rey, and I received a written notice informing us of the suspension of family visits for four months. The only break from our isolation had been monthly visitation with our family, and they now took even that away. The same punishment was imposed on Jorge Valls Arango and José Oscar Rodríguez Terrero. It was not the first time that we had been deprived of our family visits, and we knew it would not be the last.

The next few days continued with their usual monotony and scarcity. However, we didn't know if the latter was because in reality the prison was out of supplies (as we were assured by Lieutenant Mauricio, as well as Captain Raúl Álvarez, the head of supplies, and the prison director himself), or if it was a retaliatory measure applied collectively for our disorderly actions. Regardless, our food quality had fallen sharply to the lowest levels.

Tired of requesting that adequate food be served to us in an acceptable manner, and seeing the authorities not making even the slightest effort to comply, the leaders in each cell agreed to a protest the following noon, whereby each prisoner would throw his food onto the dining room floor. This was done, and consequently, twenty of us were notified of a two-month visit suspension in retaliation. Lieutenant Mauricio punished only those who angered him most. That was lucky for the others, which actually gratified us, because nothing is really resolved by punishing more than 100 prisoners for such a simple thing.

In early July, the new punishment pavilion was put into operation, one of the harshest dungeons I've ever encountered. The criminal directorate named it a "disciplinary" unit, so with all the irony in the world, we started calling it "human rights."

Each black hole cell was just 2.33 meters long, 1.40 meters wide, and 2.43 meters high, barely enough room to lie down, turns around or stand up. There was no light or water except when the jailers felt it opportune to grant these privileges, rarely more than for 15 minutes a day. The bed was a rough concrete slab that chafed the skin, making it impossible to sleep more than half an hour without having to change positions. Underpants were the only clothing allowed, requiring us to remain practically naked lying on top of that rustic cement. You were not allowed to have a pillow except for your own shoes, without their laces. In winter, the cold penetrated; in summer, the heat was stifling, as the only opening in that sealed tomb, enclosed by double metal planks, was in the small skylight in the ceiling, where barely enough oxygen penetrated to prevent suffocation. The usual stay there for an offense which the directors deemed "serious" was for 21 days.

The first of the *plantado* prisoners inaugurating those dreadful dungeons was Teodoro González Alvarado. That same evening, in protest, we threw on the dining room floor all our ration of foul-smelling boiled spaghetti and a spiny fish we had baptized with the nickname "lizard."

Then on July 15, Servando Infante Jiménez was sent to "human rights" after having thrown a plate of pasta at the dining room wall and shouted out some strong phrases against the dictator Fidel Castro and his gang in the presence of several guards. That same night, the political police came for him. Servando was taken to State Security, where after being subjected to harassment and abuse he was informed that a new accusation had been opened up against him. Several weeks later, appearing before a military court, Servando Infante Jiménez received an additional five years for having taken part in the burning of the Russian flag during the inauguration of the Combinado del

Este prison. In addition, he was accused of slander against "President" Fidel Castro and other leaders of the Revolution and to have placed on the prison's outer walls allegorical signs referring to the death, in a hungry strike, of Pedro Luis Boitel. This last sparked a serious dispute between the accused, Infante Jiménez, and the presiding judge, when the latter, referring to the murder of the student leader, called him a "counterrevolutionary."

"Pedro Luis Boitel was not a counterrevolutionary, Your Honor. He was a complete revolutionary," Servando replied in a firm and angry voice.

A low prolonged whisper rumbled through the judicial chambers, where only the military of MININT were allowed access.

"Boitel was a counterrevolutionary!" shouted the presiding judge, his face flushed with anger. He was not accustomed to being contradicted, especially in front of a uniformed audience.

"Revolutionary, Pedro Luis Boitel was a revolutionary! Revolutionary! Revolutionary! Revolutionary!" Servando repeated even louder. And without giving the judge time to reply, he continued shouting, "You are the counter-revolutionaries! And Fidel Castro is a counter-revolutionary who betrayed the Revolution and sold himself to the Russians as a disgusting mercenary. Yes, listen now all you soldiers present here, witnessing this farce, many of you just young boys confused by Communist propaganda, know that it is all a lie, a huge scam: The counterrevolutionary traitor is Fidel Castro; a counter-revolutionary killer, miserable and cowardly!"

"Expel him from the room for lack of respect!" roared the judge, standing up while banging on the table with his fist in a foolhardy attack of hysterics. "Get him out! Take him out of here immediately!" he ordered.

Instantly, four guards armed with AK47 rifles landed on top of him. After putting him in handcuffs, they forced him from the room at bayonet point.

Servando was sentenced to five additional years in prison.

He was sent back to Combinado del Este, where the director ordered that they imprison him again in "human rights" until he had served 21 days of punishment.

# CHAPTER 10

# Lieutenant Mauricio Retaliates

On the first of August, 1977, we returned to our cells after being allowed to take some sun out on the yard. On the way, I was intercepted by the watch officer, asking me to accompany him to the office of the captain in charge, located on the first floor. I immediately imagined that something was wrong, but had no idea what it might be. During our two hours outside, I couldn't recall the slightest incident that might have aroused any official attention. That day, I had spent most of the time conversing with Mario Chanes and some other prison colleagues, while we took turns walking around the courtyard next to the fence so as not to interfere with a game being played in the middle with a cloth ball.

I followed the officer, a little intrigued, but without much concern. After all, what could happen? Were we not already accustomed to the worst? Whatever the reason for that unexpected interview would soon become clear when we got to the office.

Many of my comrades had gathered around expectantly, curious and impatient, at seeing me depart with the guard.

"Go ahead," I told them, "Don't worry; there's no problem."

Lieutenant Mauricio greeted me at the door and invited me inside the room. I entered and he followed me inside. A dozen officials and guards were waiting there. The first thing that occurred to me was to look over some figures and data written on the blackboard hanging on one of the side walls. Realizing this, an officer hurriedly pulled a white curtain to completely hide whatever had been written. Nonetheless, I committed to memory some data and some very interesting numbers.

Lieutenant Mauricio was the first to speak. Without looking at me and with his usual verbal clumsiness, he told me: "I sent for you to let you know that you have to shave off that mustache right now."

"What mustache?" I asked surprised.

This was the biggest absurdity that could have occurred to anyone with eyes and with a brain. But Lieutenant Mauricio had neither. Paradoxically, among the guys who had been out to the courtyard, not few wore two-week beards and others even had respectable mustaches. I, on the other hand, had not shaved in 48 hours. In addition, there was no rule requiring us to shave with a certain frequency, and even if there was, we would have regarded it just as another unacceptable disciplinary measure.

We engaged in a fierce discussion. Finally, Lieutenant Mauricio threatened: "Well, you decide. You must shave right now or be sent to the punishment dungeons!"

"I'll shave when I feel like it! Who are you to tell me when to shave?" I replied emphatically to leave not the slightest doubt that I would not be intimidated.

We kept on arguing for a few more minutes. Aware that this was all a provocation orchestrated with premeditation and malice, I was not surprised in the least when Lieutenant Mauricio took from a bureau drawer a summons, already drawn up, where I was accused of showing a lack of respect and a few other stupidities. And then I was taken to solitary in the punishment pavilion.

That same afternoon, my fellow cellmates Luis Zúñiga Rey and Remberto Zamora Chirino were sent by the same official to "human rights," after protesting about my arbitrary punishment. Miguel Ángel Alvárez Cardentey also protested and so all three were sent there.

It was not until shortly after midnight that I became aware of that beautiful gesture of fraternal solidarity, when, taking advantage of the silence, each comrade informed me by shouting out the number of his dungeon and why he was there. Besides the four of us, also in the fourth-floor punishment unit were three others from our tight-knit fraternity, making us a total of seven: Teodoro González Alvarado, Servando Infante Jiménez, and Reinaldo López Lima.

A few days later, they brought in Sergio Bravo and, finally, an American citizen, Rafael del Pino. After our arrival at the punishment pavilion, the situation there became very tense. Without a doubt, the official aim was to completely crush us. If they could manage to do that, not only would we ourselves be demoralized, but our example would dampen the rebelliousness of other *plantados* (or so their thinking went).

The first thing being tested out was obligating us to appear before a disciplinary court where we would be officially judged and punished. One by one, without any prior notice, we were led into a spacious office in the same building as "human rights." I was taken there on the pretext that the section chief wanted to talk to me. Everyone would have been taken there using the same deception except that the first of us loudly shouted out the true intention to the others after we had returned.

In that office, a ridiculous display unfolded. Caught by surprise after putting one foot inside, I immediately turned around to leave, as I had suddenly found myself facing 20 fat-bellied, pasty-faced officers, all assembled there with so much ceremony just to condemn a prisoner to 21 days in jail!

As I was leaving, Lieutenant Saborit, head of the punishment pavilion, tried to stop me, "Let's discuss this."

When he ran out of patience, he called on a group of guards who forced me inside. They grabbed me by the arms and held me there for two or three minutes while the accusation and sentence were read aloud to me. In fact, although I struggled and acted angry, that improvised show rather amused me. After all, I was no longer appearing in court of my own volition, but by force, a purely symbolic force used to justify my punishment. Not only was I being sanctioned for growing a so-called mustache and speaking some strong words to Lieutenant Mauricio, but also for an incident three years before at La Cabaña prison, when, confined indefinitely to the torture dungeons, I had refused for several months, as a sign of protest and rebellion, to shave my beard and did not allow my hair to be cut.

The rest of my colleagues also attended the disciplinary court under similar circumstances. Luis Zúñiga sang the national anthem while a soldier was reading the act. The officials became furious, but responded with only a few grunts. On this occasion, nobody was beaten.

# We Awaken to Music in the Punishment Dungeons

To our great surprise, a few days after our appearance before the disciplinary court, we woke up to soft music entering through the upper reaches of our cells as if coming from the sky. The previous evening, we seemed to have felt footsteps above, but not for the world would I have imagined that those same guys who had tormented us would then engage in the noble task of installing speakers in each cell skylight to humanize the sting of our monstrous loneliness. Was it a dream or a simple hallucination? But no, there it was above us, exquisite music delighting us somehow.

"Yes, that's it!" exclaimed someone whom I couldn't identify by his voice.

I later learned that his name was Miguel. He was 32 years old and belonged to the rehabilitation plan. He had become mentally disturbed after being tortured by State Security, but he had some lucid moments. He told us that he didn't know why he had been sent to the punishment cells or how long he had been there. With incredible frequency, he asked us if we thought he was going to be executed. Apparently, that was what the political police had told him and, possibly, what triggered his madness.

"We're being exchanged!" cried another prisoner. This time the voice sounded familiar.

Shortly before dawn the next day, we woke up to a brand-new surprise. Unavoidably, our joy soon became a torment. The powerful loudspeakers were now blasting at maximum volume, with two different radio stations synchronized to emit noise at the same time.

All morning long, no military appeared, apparently so we would have no one to complain to.

Shortly before noon, suddenly the deafening noise was halted. Then two police officers appeared handing out our lunch. When we protested to them about the new and unusual torture to which we had been subjected since dawn, both acted surprised. They said they had just had relieved the previous shift and had found complete calm all over the pavilion. With extreme courtesy, they said that to bother us in this way was not only unfair, but was strictly forbidden by the Interior Ministry, as well as by the humanitarian principles of the Revolution. And without our asking them, they offered to inform their superiors so that such an unpleasant incident would not be repeated.

"Don't hesitate to let me know if you need anything," the shorter one told me with admirable courtesy as he was closing the interior iron door of my cell.

Lunch was awful: a tablespoon of cornmeal with worms, three or four strips of dried shark meat, and a piece of bread. The appearance of that food hardly enticed me to take a bite. I got rid of the cornmeal by dumping it in the toilet hole in the floor and resigned myself to chewing on the dried shark and eating the bread. Then I rushed to brush my teeth with my finger and, since it was stiflingly hot, although I had no soap, I decided to take a shower. But as soon the water began to drip onto my head, the valve was shut off. Anyway, it was better than nothing.

Almost immediately, the speakers were turned on again with the same frightening intensity as before. "Sons of bitches!" I thought. They are not only evil, but on top of that, they are making fun of us. I decided the next time they popped their heads into my cell, that I would cuss them out royally. They would have to hear me out…No, that would only please them. They would enjoy watching the outraged prisoner and never feel insulted because they have no principles or shame. We already know them only too well. Rather, although our eardrums and brains were bursting, it would be best not to mention anything about the amplifiers. Nothing. Not one single word.

And so, I said nothing at all when they returned, nearly at dusk, delivering our modest supper food ration. As had happened at noon, the speakers were turned off only for a few minutes before the two guards with the meal arrived. This time they served us rice with corn and a boiled egg. While I still felt a little dizzy, I ate everything with a voracious appetite. The rice was well cooked and tasty.

After 15 minutes, the damned amplifiers started blasting again. This third barrage lasted until midnight. From then on, that sinister plan increased the daily torture of the lonely dungeons. Even the brief lull at mealtimes ceased. Apparently, they considered that a respite of 15 or 20 minutes twice a day was too good for us.

Although my head ached almost constantly, I was gradually adapting to that infernal noise. Although I lacked a piece of cotton to put into my ears, I managed to chew up some paper to block some of the sound, an effect perhaps more psychological than real. In any case, I needed to resist with stoicism. My colleagues also resisted with admirable fortitude.

# CHAPTER 12

# From Passivity to Counter-Offensive

For one whole week, we had endured the racket patiently, really much longer than we had expected the torment to last. Then Remberto Zamora came up with an extraordinary idea to move us from passivity to counter-offensive. He let us know his idea shortly after midnight, as soon as the 18 uninterrupted hours at full volume had ceased.

It took us only five minutes to agree. We immediately began to give out shouts against Communism and started beating the locks against the steel of our interior door planks. From that moment on —so we had decided —the trajectory of noise and tensions would be extended to cover all 24 hours in a day: they, through their amplifiers, from dawn until the midnight; we, from the moment the speakers were disconnected until they returned between five and six o'clock in the morning.

We had spent more than an hour screaming and banging the locks when the top official of the guard corps, who at that moment was circling the prison's interior roads in a jeep, stopping at each building, appeared at the punishment pavilion and was very alarmed. As would be expected, our reaction was violent; we redoubled our blows and screams against all those scoundrels who had endeavored with so much cruelty and deliberate excess to drive us crazy. We blurted vulgar insults, something unusual among us, but our tempers were red hot, and under those conditions, the rants often became Olympian, emanating from prisoners crushed, tortured, and totally fed up after supporting so much humiliation and vileness.

"I've come to resolve the situation," the official announced hesitantly from the center of the hall. "We will talk like sensible people, talk like human beings who understand each other."

"But you aren't human beings. You are monsters," shouted Servando, still furious.

"Wait a moment, just a moment! We are not all equal here," protested the officer. "I already told you that I've come to resolve the situation. I imagine that when you are so upset, it's because something bad has happened. I just got here now. Let's see; please tell me what's happened."

The old story, as always: "I just got here." No one could doubt that a true cynic would hide behind that apparent kindness.

Several voices were heard at the same time.

"One by one, please. One by one. It's impossible to understand you all talking at the same time."

"Let Zamora explain, just Zamora," suggested López Lima.

Immediately, everyone fell silent.

"Officer, come over here! To cell number 53, please!"

By the tone of his voice, you could tell that Zamora was still very upset. After they had talked quietly inside his cell for about 10 minutes, the guard officer turned to all of us again to say that they would take measures so that we would no longer be bothered by the speakers.

"I will discuss the matter with the director," the officer promised us. "I'll go to look for him right now."

Accustomed to the usual taunts of the jailers, to systematic cheating, we received this news with some skepticism. However, we accepted a truce until the next morning. If the officer's promise was not fulfilled, we would restart our counter-offensive on the very next morning.

That night I slept well, sometimes up to two hours at a time. I don't know if it was because my body was already getting used to the rough concrete, or if my nerves had relaxed due to the ray of hope that a solution to such a horrible and prolonged torment was in sight.

The sun rose. With boundless joy, we heard for the first time in a week the sweet rustle of the sparrows who challenged and courted each other up on the rooftop.

"They're not like people," I thought of the sparrows. They simply fight and love each other instantly. They don't know hatred or rancor, a most beautiful way of life. Or one more balanced and reasonable, at least. But we are said to be the purest and most intelligent creatures on earth. We need to review such concepts. It would be worthwhile to know the criterion of birds, butterflies, and silkworms. What about bees? Don't be silly; they don't think, perhaps that would be the right answer. Maybe bees don't actually think, but do have their own particular intelligence, so they wouldn't attempt to make honey with mud. Or with grains of salt on beaches. Or from the tears of orphans. Test tube babies are so not far off. The human being is an insatiable machine, never satisfied with anything, even with nature.

Give a man a pinch of power and see him stand up against his own people, imposing a gag and a yoke. Teach him to master the atom, to discover the secrets of physics, and already you have a cluster of bombs above your head, your child's head, and the head of your future grandchild. Of course, not all humans do bad things. Eagles have talons and some genuine humans are doves. Perhaps a day of enlightenment will reveal our true mission as human beings and then we will demolish all borders and gather all languages into a single tongue that allows us to understand each other. What does white, black, Chinese, Indian, mestizo, or Eskimo mean? Is their blood any different? What about the color of their souls? Yes, we look forward to the happy day when we will find the lost portal, the path without kinks or obstacles that will guide us from a borehole to the summit of a fertile mountain. Such were my utopian musings there in my solitary cell.

"Breakfast! Breakfast! Breakfast time!"

"Ah, yes, yes, excuse me; my head was in the clouds."

It seemed impossible that the guard had entered my cell without my awareness, but there he was, standing right in front of me inside the two metal doors, holding a bucket of boiled milk by its handle.

"I don't understand why you are in the clouds, since today we have not turned on the music."

Music. Could there be any greater irony? I don't know how I let him get away with such nonsense. I had before me that same idiotic guard as on the first day of the loudspeakers, the same guard with the same stupid face. It was perfectly understandable that he would not comprehend that one might no longer be tortured by the speakers, yet might still have concerns and worries that required the deepest meditation. He didn't understand, just as he failed to understand that he was holding up a tyrant –and what a tyrant! –and so I wasn't going to waste my time trying to convince him pointlessly of his ignoble work, of the absurdity of his miserable abjection, whether due to either depravity or cowardice. The talented Aitmatov had already said it, "It's useless to try to prove to an ass that it's an ass."

The guard took one of the rusted cups strung on a wire hoop and awkwardly dipped it into the tub. The boiled milk splashed, burning his fingers. He winced, swearing aloud. Then the cup slipped from his hand, sinking to the bottom of the container. He took another cup from the wire hoop and repeated operation, this time with exaggerated care.

"Take it!" grumbled the guard without looking me in the face. "No bread today. I'll come back for your dish in ten minutes."

This is guy is not from Havana, I told myself, a Habanero would have said "cup." My observation made me feel like laughing, but I did not actually laugh aloud, just smiled inwardly. Anyway, I thought, what is important is not always expressed.

I passed a peaceful morning. Shortly after noon, Lieutenant Saborit began visiting us one by one to let us know that we would be allowed an hour outside.

"All together," he promised, "so you can talk and unwind a bit".

Later on, we would be granted that privilege once a week, on Wednesdays, he said. The issue of the speakers also had been definitively resolved by the prison directorate, he told us. For the first time, his face looked relaxed and he seemed communicative.

At about 3:00 p.m. we all went outside. The patio turned out to be much smaller than we had imagined. In fact, it seemed like a large cell, 15 feet long by 12 wide, with walls of concrete and roof bars above that allowed the sun's rays to penetrate.

Still, we were glad to be meeting all together again. We warmly embraced. Among political prisoners, our hugs sometimes seem fierce enough to deflate a lung. An absence of just 24 hours can evoke boundless joy when we meet again, requiring us to listen patiently to the same stories being repeated a thousand times over.

Already, these men had shared so much pain and such a terribly long prison experience, usually more than 20 years. For nearly a quarter of a century, they have lived together harmoniously in a cramped space, 24 hours a day. Many came into prison in their early teens, even as children. More than half of their life has been spent sharing friendship and affection with their comrades, perhaps now and then even a fleeting smile and always with their tears held back, because the prisoner is required to mourn in silence, despite flooding his lungs and struggling for breath.

It's not easy to go suddenly from complete darkness into bright light, especially the tropical sun's direct rays. We blink our eyes at first arriving outside, then avoid sunburn when a headache propels us toward the shade. Even before our designated hour is up, we call on the guard to take us back to our respective cells.

During the short time that we were together in that tiny sun room, we agreed on collective measures if the speakers should be reconnected. Similarly, what to do when our 21 days of solitary punishment were up, in case we were each taken out separately, one by one.

Since I might well be the first one going back again to the fourth floor, I proposed two conditions. First of all, as I had been sent to "human rights" on a whim of Lieutenant Mauricio, claiming that after only two days, I needed to shave off my so-called mustache, therefore I would not accept under any circumstances allowing myself to be shaved in the punishment pavilion. Second, if after 72 hours outside the black hole, all my comrades had not been released from there, then, one way or another, I would return to meet with them again in "human rights" and would declare a hunger strike.

"Okay," they all approved, "but be careful."

Everything seemed to indicate that Lieutenant Saborit wanted to be done with us. Our presence in the punishment dungeons was just too troublesome, risking spreading our rebellion among other prisoners, especially among the young, who are rebellious by nature. That is why, without anybody asking him, he had offered to let us go outside together. Perhaps his strange generosity was offered for a particular purpose: promoting a reasonable solution that we could accept without our jailers having to sacrifice their authority.

# CHAPTER 13

# The Death of Pedro Luis Boitel

Between 1970 to 1972, I tried to escape from the ironically named Castillo del Príncipe (Prince's Castle) prison four times–four different efforts. All four failed. My destiny was to continue living behind bars, perhaps a strange privilege, one allowing me to expand my horizon of accumulated extraordinary experiences. Paradoxically, despite the barbed wire and machine guns, the sentinels, despite the walls that hid the heavens above, and the boot against my throat, and the walled-up doors, and the thick bars against my chest, I was feeling tremendously happy because they had not been able to reduce my will or stop my thoughts. For me, the important thing is not where I am, nor my living conditions imposed by force, but that I am still able to reaffirm my existence. In Cuba, many regime collaborators consider themselves free because they roam the streets and repeat slogans. None of them has the slightest idea of what true freedom means. Indeed, some don't care if they are always sliding around in the mud; slime is their element. To collect enough crumbs, all they need is a viscous tongue, as if they'd been born from a serpent's egg.

A serpent's egg: that's the secret! If we had all been born from a serpent's egg, who would write the story of how the life was ripped out of Pedro Luis Boitel? A modest, simple story, a story that will fit into a child's hands or in a kiss from Clara, his tormented mother.

The sky was clear, the clouds seemed to barely breathe as if someone had nailed them onto an invisible plank. Neither did *he* seem to breathe, crushed in his bed by the weight of the famine that consumed him in spurts that day. It was May 24, 1972, the eve of his departure for the vastness of nothingness. His last day of life.

For fifty-two days, Pedro Luis Boitel had gone without eating when he fell into a coma. During that whole time, on no occasion was he heard complaining, nor did he allow anyone to interfere with his irrevocable determination to immolate himself for the sake of his homeland, for the sake of liberty and justice. He wanted his death to show the world a little more about the monstrosity of the Cuban prison system, to know a little more about the suffering of mothers, wives, children.

The sun was shining intensely a little off-center in the sky when the door of a special dungeon holding Pedro Luis was opened. Two sturdy guards went inside his cell and, with the greatest indifference, deposited that bunch of sharp bones onto a rustic stretcher. Sometime before, I had been conversing with Eloy Gutiérrez Menoyo and César Páez, who along with Húber Matos, Lauro Blanco, José Pujals Mederos, Tony Lamas, Osvaldo Figueroa Gálvez, Atilano Gámez, Silvino Rodríguez, and Jorge Valls, were all sharing the isolation and solitude of the small gallery located on the second floor of the central area of Castillo del Príncipe. On orders from Fidel Castro, ever since December 1970, they had remained incommunicado there, kept away from the rest of the prison population in the hands of a special guard corps directed by State Security.

The main topic of conversation when we were together now was, of course, the extreme gravity of our compatriot Pedro Luis Boitel's condition. From them, I learned that he had fallen into a coma. If that same morning, they had started giving him medical assistance, he would have had a good chance of survival. But the authorities, following the orders of the interior minister, so they argued, had resisted allowing any doctor to approach him while he remained on hunger strike. Only when they realized that their patience had rebounded beyond the limits of prudence, inevitably obligating them to deal with a serious conflict with the rest of the group, did they agree to transfer him to the prison hospital.

The door opened again, giving way to soldiers carrying the stretcher. Pedro Luis's arm dangled down, which, given the careless progress of the guards, swung like a slow pendulum, like the pendulum of a clock that has exhausted almost all its cord and is about to stop.

A lieutenant with a very protruding belly, who had been following along closely, with a sudden movement, lifted the bony limb back onto the bed of the dying one. Almost instantly, the arm rolled back in reply.

"Stop!" ordered the officer.

The soldier carrying the foot-end of the stretcher nodded to his partner. And then they immediately resumed the march. Throughout the tour, I followed them with my eyes to the door of the infirmary. What happened next was reported to us the next morning by political prisoners admitted to the same room as Boitel who were able to track the movements and hear some comments from the military.

They had taken him there shortly after 1 p.m. They sealed off the area around his deathbed, using several plywood panels, so that no one could observe what might be happening inside. Despite his extreme gravity, no doctor came to visit him for the rest of the day. Only the special military guard, the prison director, and one or another hierarch of the High Command had access to the interior of that makeshift cubicle. Around five in the afternoon, when food was being distributed to other patients, his food ration was taken to Pedro Luis.

'There you have it. Are you going to eat or not?" was what was heard by several of our colleagues occupying beds close to the barrier.

There was no response; there could not have been because Pedro Luis Boitel had been in a coma since morning.

"Leave it on the floor for him until his appetite returns," was heard said by one special guard to another. And then, after a whisper of complicity: "It's time he learned a lesson!"

Several high-ranking officers appeared very late at night. They went in to see the dying man. Some laughter was heard after an unintelligible comment. The visit was brief, just a few minutes. Finally, in the early morning, Interior Ministry Colonel Medardo Lemus, National Chief of Jails and Prisons at the time, appeared and gave instructions in a low voice. He was accompanied by the prison director and two other officers. The latter stopped next to the panels, carefully surveying the room where political prisoners were lying in their beds.

Then Medardo Lemus and his companions left.

A few minutes later, a member of the political police, who had been instructed by Lemus, hurried toward the door where he shouted out a single word: "Now!"

Immediately, the Chief of Jails and Prisons reappeared with his entourage and with a big smile on his face. The order of Interior Minister Dr. Sergio del Valle had been carried out. The student leader, Pedro Luis Boitel Abraham, had been physically eliminated. A new triumph of the revolution.

The sad news reached us with dawn's early rays. Despite herculean efforts to isolate us in Castillo del Príncipe's section 5, the prison directorate was never successful at doing that. Knowing the vital importance of timely information, ever since our arrival at Príncipe from La Cabaña on March 16, 1970, we had embarked on the urgent task of organizing a good communications network. In a futile attempt to keep the death of Pedro Luis Boitel secret, our jailers redoubled their special security efforts, but already, as previously indicated, some of the trustees secretly collaborated with political prisoners, even on such sensitive issues as providing military information. Also on other issues of great importance, for example, when the garrison was about to carry out an inspection, we used to receive an alert notice from them via a password. Two weeks before the death of Pedro Luis, I reported on the instructions issued by the interior minister banning all types of medical assistance. Boitel would not have accepted it anyway, of course, even when it did not involve any dereliction of his purpose, since he was irrevocably determined to die in that historic protest. The minister's order, as far as I know, specified letting him die. Pedro Luis knew about this miserable, cowardly measure thanks to our timely communications. They told me that he had received the news with a smile on his lips and had even expressed satisfaction.

Despite exceptional security measures, it was not difficult to pass on to our fellows being held in the "special ward" news of that sensitive and painful loss of our beloved student leader and prominent political prisoner. The bitter reality, although not a surprise, set hearts beating and aroused manly tears that do not reach the eyelid, but do flood the veins.

Rest in peace, Pedro Luis Boitel. Your brave example is our flag and weapon in our struggle for our homeland's freedom. The murderers of ideas chipped away at your body, pulverized your veins, crushed your dreams to pure dust, but your reason is reflected in all the mirrors and your name is made a beacon, germinating the future arising from the center of the dawn.

The life of this martyr of the Cuban political prison is full of beautiful pages, pages of true heroism. It is a long history so magnificent that you cannot summarize it in a mere drop of ocean spray. We will have to write someday more than just a review of his death, but also a living trajectory of his years of struggle so that the world may know the true size of this revolutionary giant. For now, I have proposed just highlighting his departure in an honest attempt to awaken the conscience of those who still believe in the siren songs of Mr. Fidel Castro, in his clumsy lies, in his vile hypocrisy.

Vile hypocrisy?" someone naïve might ask.

Let them draw their own conclusions.

Here is another crystal-clear example. Nine years after the death of Boitel, at the 1979 conference in Havana of the Inter-Parliamentary World Union, in defense of the patriots immolated in a hunger strike in Maze prison in Northern Ireland, with well-rehearsed drama, "President" Fidel Castro declared:

"Talking about international politics, it is not possible to be silent about what is happening in Northern Ireland. I feel a duty to refer to it. I believe that the Irish patriots are writing these days one of the most heroic pages of human history. They have won the respect and admiration of the world; they also deserve your support. There are now ten people who have died in the most dramatic gesture of sacrifice, personal disinterest, and courage imaginable. Humanity, seeing with its own eyes such a crime being committed, should feel ashamed. To cease their strike, these young fighters do not ask for independence, do not make impossible demands; they claim only something as simple as recognition of what they are, political prisoners. These are not Marxists-Leninists or Communists for whom we are seeking solidarity in this conference. They are militant Catholics. How is it possible that in the very heart of the West, this cold and dramatic holocaust can be tolerated?

"We cannot become accustomed to crime in Ireland, or in El Salvador, in Angola, in Namibia, or in South Africa, nor in Lebanon or anywhere else.

"The stubbornness and intransigence, cruelty, and insensitivity to the international community shown by the British government, in addressing the problem of the Irish patriots on hunger strike until death is reminiscent of Torquemada and the barbarity of the Inquisition in the middle ages.

"Legend has it that once early Rome was besieged. Two young Roman soldiers had fallen prisoner. In order to test them, when the besiegers threatened to burn them alive, as a sign of contempt, they spontaneously put their hands into the flames. It is said that the gesture so impressed their enemies that the siege of Rome was lifted.

"Tyrants tremble before men able to die for their ideas after 60 days on hunger strike! And next to this example, what were the three days of Christ on Calvary, which were a symbol for centuries of human sacrifice?

"It is time for the complaints and pressure of the world community to stop this disgusting atrocity."

The humanist Fidel Castro never mentioned the "disgusting atrocity" that his government had committed with Lidia Pérez López, kicked to death in Guanajay prison in 1961, when she was pregnant. Nor did he reveal to his visitors how Ernesto Díaz Madruga was killed with bayonets at the Isle of Pines prison, or how the life was ripped out of Julio Tang Texier, murdered in the same way in the Isle of Pines forced labor camp on September 3, 1966. Not to mention young prisoners Raúl Balmaceda, Mario Fernández Rico, and Rafael Peña Torres, executed at close range by firing squad in the Boniato prison on March 19, 1971. Neither did he bring up the deaths of Pedro Martínez Fernández in Camagüey prison in May 1962; Eddy Álvarez Molina at the forced labor camp of Isle of Pines on December 9, 1966; Diosdado Aquit Manrique, forced labor camp, Isle of Pines, on December 17, 1966; Danny Regino Crespo, forced labor camp, Isle of Pines, on December 24, 1966; Juan Sosa, concentration camp Minjial, Oriente, January 1967; Francisco Novales Méndez, forced labor, Isle of Pines, February 28, 1967; Caciano López Jorge, concentration camp Minjial, Oriente, May 1967; Luis Corrales, concentration camp Sandino, Pinar del Río, December 1968; Armando García Valdés, Boniato prison on September 2, 1969; José Oriol Acosta, concentration camp Manacas, August 5, 1970; José Pereda Reyes, concentration camp Agüica, April 1967; Gonzalo Echevarría Chacón, Melena concentration camp No. 2, 1971; Miguel Peña Verdecia, Melena concentration camp No. 2, September 12, 1974, all murdered by firing squad with impunity.

Why did this Cain of the Americas fail to tell the 1968 conference of the World Inter-Parliamentary Union about the Cuban patriots who died on hunger strike: Roberto López Chávez, Isla de Pinos on November 12, 1966; Luis Álvarez Ríos, Castillo del Príncipe on August 9, 1967; Carmelo Cuadra, Havana Military Hospital on April 21, 1969; Olegario Charlot Spileta, Boniato prison, March 15, 1973; Enrique Garcia Cuevas, Manacas concentration camp, June 23, 1973; Pedro Barrios Pedré, concentration camp of Manacas on August 22, 1977, and we could cite the names of even more, dozens and dozens of victims of the repressive system implemented in the Cuban prisons of "President" Fidel Castro and his "humanitarian" government.

And so that the world will have a more accurate idea of how Cuban political prisoners are harassed as beasts, tortured, and forced to die freakishly according to the insane whims of the tyrant, here in brief summary, is another case to contemplate.

A peasant of very humble origins, Reinaldo Cordero Izquierdo, was sentenced in 1962 to ten years of deprivation of liberty for opposing Castro's communist dictatorship. During his prolonged enclosure, he was forced to endure, along with his companions in misfortune, hunger, humiliation, isolation, and all imaginable and unimaginable miseries. Sent to the fields of forced labor on the Isle of Pines, Cordero suffered firsthand the worst psychological and moral torture that can afflict a human being. He suffered brutal beatings, bayonet stabs, and burns. However, despite such horrible torments, this courageous young man had enough dignity and courage not to kneel down. He lived standing up, with his forehead turned up toward the stars, as befits those living by ideals. His life was very short. The enemies of his people wanted it that way. He died of hunger and thirst in a dungeon in the provincial prison of Pinar del Río 5 1/2, according to the express will of the master of Cuba.

Although the dictator Fulgencio Batista had made Fidel Castro spend only 21 and a half months in prison —he and the rest of those sanctioned in 1953 for the assault on the Moncada barracks— now this sheep with wolf's claws considered that a decade of martyrdom in his own dungeons was not suffering enough. But, as we have said, Castro is forgetful. In addition, according to the Communist dialectic, 21 and a half months can be equivalent to more than ten years. Is not Cuba –despite its countless jails, firing squads, millions of exiles, and repressive system–"The First Free Territory of the Americas?"

In 1972, Reinaldo Cordero had completed his ten-year sentence, which, according to the nation's laws, entitled him to immediate release. But, showing once again an absolute contempt for the law, the Cuban government used force to keep him behind bars. The authorities put forth the fallacious argument of "future dangerousness."

Without the slightest proof justifying a new sanction, Reinaldo Cordero was arbitrarily sentenced by an improvised court to an additional year in prison without any right to a defense. Then the interior minister ordered him sent to the common prisoners' ward, claiming that after completing his first sentence, he had ceased to be a political prisoner. Reinaldo strongly resisted such a humiliating and treacherous measure.

Retaliation was swift. Stripped of all his belongings, he was locked up, completely naked, in a punishment black hole.

The unfortunate inmate was never again allowed a family visit, correspondence, nor any other right, not only as a political prisoner, but as a human being. He never saw sunlight again. His water was rationed to three glasses a day... wasn't that enough to quench his thirst? Who knows if he prayed in that special section which, as a further measure, had removed any acknowledgement of his status as human being in his new sentence. After all, everything might be fully justified by the Marxist-Leninist dialectic.

Under those terrible conditions, Reinaldo Cordero completed the newly imposed sanction. He thought that maybe now he would have the opportunity to embrace his mother, his loved ones, meet with them again, happy in the bosom of the humble home that he had so longed for during his long years of absence.

But, soon enough, he was forced to grasp the bitter reality of his destiny: Cuba's communist government would communicate through a jailer, verbally, that he should stay in prison one more year. In this second re-condemnation, they didn't even have the decency to present him in court. It was enough to issue the ministerial order, cold, rough, inviolable.

The same communication in identical form, that is, verbal, reached Cordero for the third time a year later. He found himself apparently condemned to life imprisonment. A few months later, we found out that he was still in the punishment dungeons.

The reports that reached us were very painful: "Cordero's skin is riddled with fungus. It's been eight months since he has been given soap. His testicles are so infected that they have become a bloody mass.

"Cordero is on hunger strike." It was December 1975 when Reinaldo Cordero, despite his fragile health, decided on that course.

Immediately, water was suspended to increase his agony. It was not the first time that the shameless regime took that repressive measure against political prisoners.

Twelve days later, he was in a coma. He was tied up so he wouldn't be able to resist if he regained consciousness. Once in a while, he was given an IV.

Completely naked, bound by hands and feet with cords that cut him to the bone, he was kept face up on the rustic concrete slab that served as his bed in that infernal cell.

That atrocious situation might have continued indefinitely except that they ordered a stop to the IV solution, which saved him from further days of suffering. As might have been expected, on May 21, 1976, Reinaldo Cordero Izquierdo stopped existing.

Yet, as we have seen, "President" Fidel Castro defended the right of the Maze prisoners to be recognized as "political prisoners," the same right that Cordero was expressing.

After learning of these measures of extreme cruelty, any honest person will arrive at their own conclusions about who Fidel Castro really is and how he acts. Cuba's dictator can tamp down his rhetoric, hide his assaults, cover up his crimes by putting on the mask of a saint (or a clown), but no honest person can believe in the purity of his tears.

# CHAPTER 14

# La Cabaña and the Model Prison at Isla De Pinos

In all of Cuba's prisons, inmates are invariably held in subhuman living conditions. Overcrowding, doubtless, is one of the most serious difficulties. In La Cabaña, there were times when every gallery housed an average of 280 prisoners, sometimes even more than 300, when 60 were enough to be considered crammed.

Water has been another very serious prison concern. Nobody is surprised to learn that on quite a few occasions, for several months running, each prisoner received less than a liter a day to meet all his needs. Depending on what you were able to save, a difficult goal, you might be able to bathe once a week.

But as difficulties are not always insurmountable, over time, the water situation became less critical. For example, in courtyard No. 2 of La Cabaña, several outdoor showers were installed. This had its small pitfalls. The benefits were to be staggered, since, after all —the island's authorities must have thought— this undeserved award was a real privilege. And so they established certain norms, or what they called "rules of the game," and rules are made to be observed. One of the conditions to exit out to the patio to rinse off in the showers (no time for more), was having to go back and forth completely naked. *Plantado* prisoners are by nature not only rebels, but also a bit stubborn. They resist any disciplinary measure, especially one of this type, whose only objective is to humiliate, so, every few days when the chance for bathing arose, they covered themselves with a towel. When this happened, they usually did not make it to the showers. Before they had time, they felt the bayonets stabbing into their backs, driven by the fierce fury of the jailers. At other times, they managed to soap up. Then, the exit would be locked and so, in addition to suffering blows, they had to go back to their cell with soap still clinging to their bodies. In fact, it was a tactic characterized by savagery and evil without limits.

Regarding this inhumane spectacle, perhaps the most shameful and depressing was the invariable presence of unscrupulous military women hysterically screaming and urging on the guards from the rooftop to increase their merciless beatings. What level of moral degradation had befallen those unhappy women, brainwashed by the fanaticism of an alienating materialist doctrine? There is not much difference between a woman who has lost all decency and sensitivity and a spring without water. It's always pitiful to see, so empty inside, those useless victims shouting frenetic blood-thirsty slogans. Fate had created them as women, but ignorance had turned them into rag dolls.

If ruthless beatings were authorized for bathing, prisoner counts exceeded the limits of cruelty. Two platoons of guards armed with bayonets, dowels, and sticks lined up in a double row outside the door of every section. At the shout of "count!" —emitted by the guard officer—two hundred or so prisoners trotted out in pairs, two by two, passing through the gauntlet of guards beating on them to force them to run faster. Without stopping, prisoners filled up the courtyard from one end to the other, until the latest arrivals spilled out into the hallway and into the bloodbath. Then the return order was given, and again, two by two, the prisoners were subjected to beatings. Twice a day, the ordeal was repeated.

Of the approximately 3,500 political prisoners in La Cabaña's prison population during the first half of the 1960's, a good number had short sentences (less than five years); the rest, with very rare exceptions, were sick, very sick or elderly men and therefore not sent to the Isle of Pines forced labor camp. Isla de Pinos' prisoners, on the other hand, mostly had been given long sentences of 20 to 30 years. They were what we might call the dynamic mass, the tip of the spear of the rebellion.

The model prison of Isla de Pinos, although its first circular building was inaugurated in 1928, was completed in 1931 during the dictatorship of Gerardo Machado. The main core of the buildings intended for holding prisoners was composed of four imposing circular units, with 465 cells of two bunks each (double folding bunks, which the prisoners baptized with the name of "aircraft"), symmetrically distributed on five floors of each building. The sixth floor lacked cells, but was divided by a series of panels or hanging cloths, each unit housing six to eight inmates, bringing the number of prisoners in each circular to 1,100, approximately. In the center, was a two-story round dining room.

In addition to four prison circulars and the dining room, there were two rectangular buildings called "Selection" and "Conduct," inhabited at first by inmates of the rehabilitation plan. At the beginning of the Camilo Cienfuegos' forced labor plan, in June 1964, buildings five and six were reserved for *plantados*. A little beyond, at the entrance, was the building's headquarters. At the opposite end of the circular units were the punishment dungeons and prison hospital.

The entire complex of facilities for the prisoners was enclosed by a double metal fence, with multiple outlook booths interspersed, occupied by guards armed with machine guns. A tower, very similar to a lighthouse arose from the courtyard in the center of each circular. At the top, a guard brandishing a gun guarded all internal movements of the 465 cells.

Every morning just before dawn, the convicted were called to formation in their respective blocks (work brigades) to then be recounted, awaiting their orders to mount the trucks carrying them to the forced labor camps. Thereafter, no one could be sure he would return alive that night at the end of an exhausting day. There were many blocks, each made up of around 100 prisoners divided usually into two groups. Despite the brutal beatings and murders, these men maintained an admirable rebelliousness. You might not be able to imagine how much brutality and vileness those henchmen of tyranny unleashed against their helpless charges if you have not experienced it firsthand or heard direct accounts from some of those victims.

Every day, streams of blood gushed forth. Everything, even the most insignificant action, merited a ruthless beating. It was enough for the "chief" or "overseer" of the block to indicate that someone deserved punishment for a given failure than for blows to rain down on the unlucky victim. Their extreme ferocity and their constant beatings of prisoners earned certain chiefs nicknames such as "mad dog," "golden arm," etc. A failure could involve something as simple as taking a break to dry the sweat off his brow, sneezing on a plant (or stepping away from it to do so), having green eyes, being bald, cross-eyed, too tall, too short, or any other nonsense excuse. Other more serious offenses included falling a few meters behind the row of fellows digging trenches or spreading fertilizer, or failing to pull up a blade of grass. Those merited even more severe punishment, ranging from a bayonet through the thigh or buttock to a bullet in the brain. The latter almost invariably occurred when a prisoner, consciously or unconsciously, made the slightest gesture of self-defense. However, despite the assassinations and blows, the usual prisoner strategy was to maintain constant passive resistance, which completely stifled production. This caused even more repression, while increased repression, in turn, fostered increased resistance. This caused the injured and the dead to multiply, and the injured and the dead further hardened prisoners' individual character and helped consolidate their awareness.

Already during the second half of 1966, it was rare that prisoner transport trucks did not return at dusk with dozens and dozens of wounded, many gravely so, and sometimes among them, some dead.

There were exceptional cases, examples of true heroism, of colleagues who, at the risk of their own lives, refused emphatically from the very first moment to accept forced labor. The journalist Alfredo Izaguirre Rivas was one of them. Another, also a journalist, lawyer, and polyglot, was Emilio Adolfo Rivero Caro. A few more arrived at the same decision weeks later. Some were beaten until they lost consciousness. Locked in punishment dungeons, they remained there subjected to the cruelest tortures, Rivero until May 1966 and Izaguirre until June 1964.

At the beginning of 1967, before the failure of the so-called "Plan Camilo Cienfuegos," intended to break the stubborn resistance of *plantado* prisoners through barbarism and terror, Cuba's Communist government chose to renounce its aspirations of enforcing submission, accepting the transfer of some 5,000 political prisoners. A good portion of them were assigned to the concentration camps of greatest rigor, Sandino No. 1, Sandino No. 2, Sandino No. 3, and Tacotaco in the westernmost region of the island, where the regime, perhaps having forgotten the rebelliousness of those men, tried to carry out a new plan of forced labor. This time, it was in Antonio Maceo, which ended shortly with a setback for Castro, similar to the Isle of Pines.

Others went to the prisons of Pinar del Río 5 1/2, Boniato, and the main center of La Cabaña. The rest were distributed among multiple prisons and concentration camps across the length and breadth of the island.

Soon after the return to Isla de Pinos, a few months later, one of the more sinister retaliations occurred to the arrogant mind of Fidel Castro: a change of clothes. The new provision dictated that political prisoners, including *plantados*, now dressed in yellow pants and shirt, would be forced to wear the same blue uniforms of common prisoners. As there was a wholesale refusal by enraged *plantados* (since re-education plan inmates always wore blue uniforms), the authorities tried to impose this measure by force. In every concentration camp or prison, *plantados* were called out one by one. By refusing outright to abide by this capricious requirement, first you were beaten, then knocked down on the floor, undressed (15 or 20 guards fell on top of you all at once), and then you were dressed in the blue uniform. Usually the immediate reaction of the prisoner was to tear the clothes right off again. Then he was kicked, he endured another huge beating, and was immediately dressed again by force and, this time, he was tied up so he could not undress. Tied up, they were all piled up together into a separate room. Those who accepted the humiliating measure and stayed dressed were moved aside to prevent them from helping their companions untie the ropes.

Since I, and some 850 other *plantados,* did not accept this imposition, and the government couldn't maintain them indefinitely tied up with ropes, the authorities chose to leave them without any clothes. From that moment on, they were deprived of all their rights: visits, correspondence, and medical assistance. All their belongings were confiscated, and food, already meager, was reduced to just the necessary minimum to prevent death from starvation. Thus, arose the so-called "naked" or "underpants" prisoners. Later, many of those who had accepted the blue uniforms were stripped of them. This was most frequent in the concentration camps in the western region of the island (Sandino), while repression in that area surpassed all limits of savagery. Those transferred there were usually sent to the punishment dungeons in the provincial prison of Pinar del Río, which prisoners renamed "the Naked City."

On August 4, 1968, the interior minister ordered restoration of the *plantados'* yellow uniforms, as well as their rights to a family visit of two hours once a month and some other benefits that, in practice, never became more than purely symbolic.

Then, something happened that the government had not anticipated: 238 *plantados* refused, in protest of the abuses and sustained harassment they had endured, among other reasons, to accept the yellow uniform this time.

A new wave of repression, fiercer than ever, fell on those unfortunates who had decided to remain naked. Months later, on February 8, 1970, a transfer of 194 of them was initiated to Boniato prison, where they were soon locked inside small dark cells with sealed windows and thick plates of metal over the doors. That was the beginning of the infamous walled Boniato prison.

One of the first measures adopted by the *plantados* returning from Isla de Pinos to La Cabaña in the spring of 1967 was deciding not to run to make the count, in order to end that depressing spectacle. As some of the elders considered so drastic a determination nothing short of collective suicide, it was agreed that those who would prefer to continue running could do so, provided they leave first in a separate group. The rest would follow them without rushing, stoically enduring the sticks and the bayonets.

So that's what happened.

Dozens of heads were split each day. Broken arms. Fractured ribs. A real massacre convinced *plantado* prisoners to postpone that experiment. Nonetheless, again the executioners of the Interior Ministry took a step back according to the will of those men of steel. Several weeks later, aware of that the decision not to run was taken up by the *plantados* arriving from the Isle of Pines and would remain unchanged whatever the price to pay, the prison director gave the order that two counts per day would be held without the double row of guards inflicting blows. An important battle had been won.

# CHAPTER 15

# An Achievement of the Revolution

On January 10, 1977, we left La Cabaña to be transferred to the modern prison of Combinado del Este, where, although still subjected to unjustified overcrowding, we soon found ourselves living in cells that were much cleaner and more acceptable. They were freshly painted with joyful, pleasant, and soft colors, easy on the eyes. The granite floors were shiny. The lighting was not bad, and although at the beginning, the jailers took over control of the lighting system from the outside, they gradually began allowing us to turn lights on and off at our own convenience. The bathrooms were comfortable and hygienic. In cells designed for 12 people, such as 1401, 1402, 1403, and 1404 of the north wing, we had a urinal, a double sink, a superb shower, and a toilet! Drinking water was available 24 hours a day, so abundant and with such pressure that it could restore our energy.

But, as often happens in all Communist regimes, when the building was fully occupied, the capacity of the water storage tanks was insufficient to service a thousand people on an ongoing basis, not even to supply them in an acceptable manner. The solution the jailers came up with, obviously, was not to increase reserve capacities by building an additional tank, but to ration water to half an hour before breakfast, one hour before lunch, and an hour before dinner, causing serious conflicts. No prisoner easily gives up improvements already obtained. Also, when through experience, it becomes obvious that many of these deteriorations in living conditions do not always stem from real difficulties, but are simply destabilizing maneuvers, the moment arrives when behind each inconvenience, each obstacle, each deprivation–justified or not—a perverse, a premeditated, evil is discerned. The immediate reaction, therefore, is indignation, angry rejection, and even aggression. Finally, the enemy achieves the objective of destabilizing the prisoner unless the latter proves to be especially calm and cold-blooded.

If we recognize that during that period at La Cabaña, each prisoner was given only three glasses of water per day (three glasses for all their needs!), we will also understand that with 2 and a half hours of good flow daily, that would be sufficient. And indeed, it was. But no, not at first, simply because all the containers we had brought with us from Combinado del Este prison were seized during the transfer inspection, including plastic buckets, something making no sense, as in any prison, at the very least, a plastic bucket has multiple important uses. Of course, knowing how the jailers tended to interpret orders, it could not be expected that in the search of our possessions, it might have occurred them to analyze, much less to understand, that between an old can and a plastic container there is a considerable difference, just as between a rat and a rabbit, or between a cucumber and a banana.

For a time, they were apparently imagining that with water kept in our pocket, we could, like magicians, be able to meet our daily needs. In truth, they made not even a minimal effort to remedy the new crisis while weeks went by. We decided, therefore, to apply the "rattle" formula, consisting of hitting the cell bars and metal plates covering the electronic door system with anything capable of making noise: aluminum plates, steel spoons, pieces of pipe, and metal rods picked up when we went outside to the patio. Although each instrument alone wouldn't have done it, put all together, they created a concert big enough to shake the whole building.

Only a few hours of uninterrupted racket were sufficient for us to be given some containers, some of them the very same plastic pails confiscated in the inspection. They also promised to supply a 55-gallon tank for each cell. Now that would be a solution, a really practical solution, and therefore quite acceptable. We were glad to hear it.

Indeed, a week later, Captain Raúl Álvarez appeared at our building with 16 metal tanks, all freshly painted black, gleaming. But only two or three appeared to be new. The rest showed dents, some discrete — like a grumpy mule had given them a couple of kicks–others, as if that same mule had been kicking them all morning.

So, for a fair distribution, the same captain proceeded with a drawing. And what happened next was what was meant to be: we in cell 1404 were given the number 16. I doubt that even Victor Hugo would have been able to embark on an effort as grueling as that of describing the 444 profiles of that tank. A truly poetic effort, where each dent became a metaphor.

"Take that shit away!" was the first reaction of almost everyone in our cell.

"No, no, don't take anything away," I immediately protested. "How are we going to ask that it be taken away if such a treasure has fallen right into our hands? This is the best of the 16 tanks that has been delivered today!"

My cell mates looked on in amazement. "Has he gone crazy?" they surely must have thought.

To install the tanks, since the space inside each cell was so small, Captain Raúl Álvarez had authorized that they be placed opposite each door, outside in the corridor. Perhaps he did not anticipate that meant that from then on, high officials visiting the fourth floor, when entering the hallway as usual, inevitably would be bumping into those darn things. Envisioning the reaction that such a display might cause, I brought that battered vessel into our cell on the pretext of marking it with the number 1404, and over the black enamel that had been used to try to "rejuvenate" it, I traced a beautiful label with yellow paint: TAKE GOOD CARE OF ME, I AM AN ACHIEVEMENT OF THE REVOLUTION! The next morning, seizing the moment when we opened up for breakfast, we took that twisted piece of junk and strategically placed it outside our cell door, making sure the sign was clearly visible. We then immediately proceeded to fill the tank with water, but, since the bottom was all mangled, we had to slip wood chips underneath to keep it from swaying like a drunken sailor. Quite rightly, it has been said that prisons are where news travels fastest. You let out a scream from a nightmare, you vomit and your dentures fall into the toilet, you put your underwear on backwards, and, in no time, everyone knows about it. Such moments of entertainment are so rare! After all, prisoners have the right to have fun too, don't they?

In light of this, it's no wonder that minutes later, a parade of curious onlookers enjoyed viewing the "achievement of the revolution," a true mirror of what Cuba had to offer the people after almost 20 years of our brand-new form of Communism.

Although Captain Raúl Álvarez and Lieutenant Mauricio must have been aware very early on that morning, after being informed by the hall guard (he had been contemplating the "achievement," smiling naively, unable to discern its true intention), it not was until noon that the officers arrived there. The captain read the sign with an ironic smile. Admittedly, he was kind of phlegmatic, able to withstand the worst insults with the same frozen, empty smile. In contrast, Lieutenant Mauricio's ears were burning. His character was so sour that even the great Charlie Chaplin would have been unable to relieve even for a moment, for one single moment, the bitterness reflected in his grim face.

Several weeks went by and everything went on as usual. That piece of junk remained outside the door of 1404, working wonderfully well. We were already becoming rather fond of it. One afternoon, unexpectedly, we heard about the arrival in the building of an entourage from the Interior Ministry. After they came up to the fourth floor, we noticed them stopping by our cell, contemplating that mass of iron storing our water. Among those imposing personages were General Enio Leyva, Deputy Minister of the Interior; Colonel Medardo Lemus, the National Chief of Jails and Prisons; Colonel Manuel Blanco Fernández, of counter-intelligence; and Colonel O'Farril, Director of Combinado del Este prison, as well as Captain Raúl Álvarez, Lieutenant Mauricio, Sergeant Cervantes, and a numerous retinue of other officials.

"Take good care of me, I am an achievement of the revolution!" General Leyva read aloud, and added: "That's rich."

Then he turned to the warden, arms crossed, asking, "Who brought this tank up here?"

"Well, General. You know..." (The warden had grown pale and tongue-tied). "We had a problem with the water several months ago."

"Yes, yes, all that is very well, but who brought that tank up here? That's what I want to know," insisted the general.

"I ordered Raúl to resolve the issue, to get some containers... and this is what we could find."

"Resolve, right?" Leyva interrupted the director. "Doesn't Raúl know these people yet? You'd have to be an idiot to bring them that beat-up old tank, that crap. I don't understand it, I just can't explain it," the general repeated these last words as if speaking to himself, passing his hand over his shiny bald dome in a gesture much like of a human petting a dog.

Colonel Medardo Lemus and two others dressed in civilian clothes peered in through our prison bars. We feigned complete indifference. We tended to receive them coldly to avoid arguments. None of us in the cell spoke with them, no one asked anything, but, usually, they either briefly entered 1404 or stayed only a few minutes at the door. Only when they called out to Húber, or addressed any of us directly, did we grant them the basic courtesy of responding, always ensuring that the dialogue stuck to essentials, and remained as brief as possible.

Enio Leyva also looked through the bars.

"How are you all doing in here?' he asked those closest to the doorway.

Two or three voices answered him at once: "Fine." The same "fine" would have been uttered though they were crushing our bones.

"Where is Húber?" he demanded.

Matos got up from his bunk and approached the bars.

"What's up? What brings you here?" he said.

"Wow, Húber, you're getting old," remarked the general in a jocular tone.

*"Not only I, you, too, even with all that good living. I thought that in this country, the generals would not grow old. Maybe you have too much on your mind?" Matos replied sarcastically.*

The general's face flushed, and veering away from that conversation, he chose someone else to talk with.

*"Mario, and what about you? Are you still here? I thought you got out."*

The question could not have been dumber, or perhaps more perverse. This time he was addressing Mario Gavilán Sánchez, who had come to spend a few months in cell 1404 cell after Segundo de la O. Elejarde Cepero was released after completing his sentence.

"Yes, Enio, I'm still here. But don't worry, I've only been trapped here for 17 years."

By Mario's response, I realized he was not particularly impressed by Leyva's hypocrisy, who, undeterred, continued with his teasing.

"How many years did we give you?"

"Twenty."

"Twenty years?' exclaimed the general in mock surprise, "Those damn judges. They keep giving out those absurd sentences, and the beauty is that none of them knows what happens then. They are barbarians. I think the best thing we could do would be to lynch them all."

And he continued on with his usual cynicism amid the hollow laughter of his guests. Mario Gavilán took the opportunity to bring up the case of Rigoberto Perera, "Rigo," who several years before had suffered a stroke that it left him semi-paralyzed. Despite his deplorable physical condition, he remained in cell 1406 without any chance of recovery because of lack of adequate medical care.

The general commanded an assistant to make a note of Mario's concern and conduct a further investigation. Frankly, I doubted that anything would come of it. However, several weeks later, Rigoberto was called to an interview. During the following days, he was submitted to a thorough medical examination, and a month later, to everyone's delight, the government decided to release him.

Perhaps the news was welcomed least by Rigoberto Perera himself. After all, he had spent 17 years of his 20- year sentence behind bars, the last 7 being very tough as a result of his physical limitations. Thanks to his iron will, he had managed to recover the minimum function necessary to barely fend for himself. His strong spirit would not allow him to remain inactive, and, little by little, he freed himself from dependency on his friends. We admired his dignity and his stoicism.

After he was officially informed of the release order, several officers came to his cell to implement his release, but Rigoberto flatly refused to leave the prison unless regime authorities promised to return him home to the humble dwelling built by his own hands, confiscated arbitrarily in political reprisal.

We worked hard to persuade him to forget his claim and to go live with his sister pending his eventual departure for the United States, where he had two daughters and the rest of his family. Luckily, after making many reasonable and objective arguments, Mario Gavilán, a brother to him his whole life, managed to convince him.

Still, before General Enio Leyva withdrew with his entourage, he glanced again at the "achievement of the revolution" and once more swept his hand over his bare noggin.

Seeing their chief peering again at the sign, everyone else followed suit, thereby observing the established motto to "imitate the top gestures." But they avoided copying his hand movement lest the general see that disciplined imitation as making fun of his shiny bald head.

The delegation's visit occurred on April 4, 1978, shortly before they had opened up the cells for supper. We thought that later that evening, we would lose the miserable tank that Captain Raúl had blessed us with. But they didn't take it out until the next morning. Sergeant Pedro appeared at about 10:00 a.m. to place a brand-new tank outside the entrance to 1404. He then borrowed a pail from Lechuga in the medical unit to remove the water from the old banger amid snickers from inmate onlookers, or so I was told. As luck would have it, I didn't have the opportunity to actually enjoy the final act of that great comedy. The day before, shortly before midnight, the political police had come for me, and, at the time, I was being held in a State Security black hole.

My return then to the dungeons of Villa Marista, as I was informed during interrogation, was due to the publication abroad of my book, the poetic epic *An Urgent Testimony*. For an entire month, I was threatened with an additional sentence of 20 years. Since I'd already been condemned to 40 years, the additional sanction made no sense, because my life expectancy would be unlikely to extend even one day beyond 40 years. Therefore, it was less a real concern than an amusing threat. Perhaps those in charge of the repressive machinery came to the same conclusion. There was no new sentence given after all for the publication of my first book of poems.

# CHAPTER 16

# Stiff Resistance Against New Repression

A few days after my return from State Security, Rigoberto Pérez Roque (Telto) invited me to attend a modest celebration of remembrance for our comrade Pedro Luis Boitel on the sixth anniversary of his death.

I accepted gladly.

On May 25, as scheduled, as soon we had opened up for lunch, instead of passing into the dining room, we gathered in a room used as a local barbershop. Telto himself uttered some brief, but very beautiful and emotional words.

Meanwhile, Sergeant Cervantes stood at the entrance, watching and listening to everything. Although at no time did he interfere, he looked nervous and angry. I did not imagine at the time that on the following day, some 8 or 10 of us who had been present during that meeting would receive a written communication from Lieutenant Mauricio, notifying us of the suspension of two months of family visits for being directly responsible for our commemoration of Boitel's death. Those sanctioned were Jorge Valls Arango, José Pujals Mederos, Eduardo Capote Rodríguez, Silvino Rodríguez Barriento, Luis M. Zúñiga Rey, Servando Infante Jiménez, Remberto Zamora Chirino, and myself. No one in this group had had any other role than simply to be there to honor the departed with our physical presence, along with some fifty other companions from the fourth floor. More significantly, not only we were once again being punished on a whim, but to clear up any doubt of the authorities' right to act in any way they wanted, not even included among those punished was Rigoberto Pérez Roque himself, even though he was the one actually speaking —as I've said— in the presence of Sergeant Cervantes, who was, no doubt, the only military man to have witnessed what happened.

This new repressive measure upset us all, but none more than Remberto Zamora, not just because of our visits' suspension alone, but because of the arbitrary way in which the punishment was imposed.

"If you want conflict, then conflict you will get. This is Cervantes' foolishness," Zamora indignantly protested.

Zúñiga and Servando complained as well.

"Forget it," I chimed in, "We're already used to having our visits suspended with the slightest pretext."

Zamora continued to get worked up. Not since the night when we had raised our voices on behalf of "human rights," nine months before, had I seen him so angry. Back then, he had agreed to serve as the head of our cell, to represent 1404 before the military in discussing certain rights and collective needs. To not be further bound by this responsibility, as he would tell us later, Zamora now immediately resigned his position as head of our cell. He did not tell anyone how he would respond to the new repressive measures, but at six in the afternoon, when the counting officer came to our cell, he found that the gate had been tied shut with a thick wire. Zamora also began knocking on the gate with a steel bar to warn the officer about not coming any closer.

"No prisoner count here today!" he cried out with bloodshot eyes.

The soldier, looking surprised, shrugged and continued on to the next cell. Immediately Servando and Zúñiga also found some iron rods, then, with one standing beside Zamora, the other, up on a wooden bench, they began banging against the metal cover of the electronic door system.

"The crazies have been let loose." said Mario Gavilán, who joined me in watching the spectacle.

"And now we are in the waning moon's last quarter," he added.

With all that loud banging, it was virtually impossible to talk. So, Mario and I gave up.

Night had already fallen when Lieutenant Mederos showed up to try to get the boys to stop.

"We need to do the prisoner count, like it or not," he began in a raspy tone, after our comrades had paused to listen.

"This isn't going right," I told myself. We weren't getting anywhere.

*"Forget it!" answered Zamora, almost shouting. "Don't bother us with the count! Don't try, Mederos. You're wasting your time. Go get the guards if you like. Today we're playing hardball."*

*"What's your problem?"* the officer inquired, realizing that tempers were red hot.

"Go ask Mauricio," Zúñiga interjected, "or Sergeant Cervantes. They can tell..."

"Just shut up," Servando interjected, starting to bang again.

Zúñiga and Zamora followed suit.

Lieutenant Mederos tried to say something else, getting very irritated. His words were drowned out by the noise, so he dragged himself away, limping slightly on his bad leg, nursing his wrath.

Years before, while traveling during a military mobilization and sitting on the back of a truck with his legs hanging over, another vehicle crushed them, leaving one leg practically shattered. At Lenín Hospital in Holguín, doctors were barely able to save that leg, but its mobility was reduced. He was such an obsessive Communist that, despite his physical limitations, he insisted on remaining on the repressive political police force and had stayed there for 15 more years. Extremely arrogant, I once saw him hit a prisoner full across the face. However, on occasion, he could also be polite, and even helpful. I never saw him steal, though most of the jailers did. In that respect, he seemed honest. It seems only fair to recognize that virtue.

Even though I had a splitting headache, I looked around for a piece of pipe and, just like my colleagues, I started banging. The guard watching the doors and our movements inside the cell stopped to look.

Already around midnight, two more soldiers were sent to reinforce the north wing post. We expected them at any moment to take drastic measures. One option would be to take us out by force back to the punishment black holes. Another would be that the captain in charge would come to try to convince us to stop the racket. But neither of these occurred. Instead, intending to surprise us into meeting on much less compromising ground for them, around one in the morning, Captain Raúl Álvarez sent up the guards to bring us down to the first floor, where he was waiting for us in his office.

"Why does that gentleman want us to go down there?" Zamora asked.

"I guess to chat with you," someone said.

"Tell the captain to come up here if he likes, but not to talk. Come upstairs with the garrison in combat gear and open the door, so he can see that he's going to have to kill us out in the hallway."

What Zamora tried to do was to make very clear that under no circumstance would we be swayed and, simultaneously, that if the captain came upstairs with the garrison, the struggle could not possibly avoid involving comrades situated beyond our cell. First of all, because any problems that any of us had with the enemy directly impacted the mood of everyone, not only because of our unwavering solidarity, but because the very same deprivations and suffering shared over so many years had created our true brotherhood. Secondly, because there were always confrontations with the guards, the jailers were prone to attacking here and there, indiscriminately. It happened frequently that a fellow, who might have had no more than minimal responsibility in a certain conflict, had suffered beatings, been gravely injured, or, on occasion, even been killed by guards. Because of these bitter experiences, it was not always possible to adopt an attitude of unlimited intransigence, unless required by reason of certain principles.

But this time Zamora had thrown down his foot, so despite all that might be lost, we had no choice but to confront with courage and dignity the worst situation that we might have to face. So, we kept on hitting metal on metal to reaffirm our determination.

Half an hour later, the guards came back. Facing our cell, they approached to tell us something. We couldn't hear them over the noise.

They went into the dining room while we never stopped our banging for even a single instant.

"They might have come up with an ultimatum," I thought. "We need to be prepared so they won't surprise us. Hopefully, they will take us out and the row with us will take place out in the hall."

Our uncertainty lasted for another half hour...and another...and another.

It was 3:30 in the morning by then, making us aware that the formula chosen by the head of the building to resolve that crisis would not be a showdown after all, so we decided to end our barrage and go straight to bed. And so, we did. Feeling completely exhausted, I still tossed and turned in my bunk. Excitement and a headache prevented me from falling asleep. Only after I took a dose of "Duralgina" (a liquid analgesic akin to ibuprofen), diluted in water to attenuate its intense bitterness, could I finally go to asleep.

The next morning, none of the four of us woke up when the doors opened for breakfast. I don't know why that also didn't happen to the others, because I don't see how anyone could have slept on through it all while we kept on pounding, yet Mario Gavilán, Chuchú Silva, and Aparicio assured me that they had slept by putting cotton in their ears.

As soon as I opened my eyes, Húber came over to suggest that I pay attention right then and there to the cell's collective affairs. "Zamorita needs a rest," he said "and since someone has to take over as head of the cell, I think that you are best suited for that job. We must not create a false sense of anarchy. We have to solve this matter now, early. Think about it and then let me know."

Being chief of a cell or gallery can be very simple or at times complicated. It's no easy task to bring together separate wills among a very heterogeneous group, though, paradoxically, in difficult situations, people cast aside trifles, close ranks, and become much more understanding. Luckily, in 1404, it was enough to have a little tact. In fact, we enjoyed a remarkable rapport, a very deep-rooted and sincere brotherhood. There were no group antagonisms because we all respected each other's personal judgment, and all agreed on the fundamental principle that Cuba needed a free system, a system of true democracy and social justice. At least, those were the concerns, among others, that we invariably brought up, something that made me feel good and encouraged me to think that in our country there still remained many honorable men who defended the values of civilization. Taking into account these positive aspects, one could come to a conclusion without running too many circles around the topic.

I accepted Húber's proposal and immediately submitted it to the consensus of the rest of our comrades through our usual method: the secret ballot.

To no one's surprise, I was approved unanimously. In our cell, all votes were unanimous, showing that we enjoyed truly exceptional mutual support.

Then Húber explained in more detail why he had urged me on: at breakfast, Lieutenant Mauricio had informed the dining room that Captain Raúl Alvarez had ordered a meeting at 10 a.m. of all cell or gallery chiefs with any urgent matters requiring attention. The meeting would take place in the first-floor office of the head of the building. Matos thought that the failure to attend by anyone representing our cell could lead to a misunderstanding. He didn't want the captain to remotely imagine – even mistakenly– because of the conflict of the night before, that we were avoiding facing him. His reasoning was very logical and sound; I understood it right away.

*"Today, don't let him put anything over on you," interjected José Pujals, referring to Captain Raúl, "Make certain that he gets it into his head that he doesn't impress anyone."*

"Don't worry, Joe, he's already well aware of that. And he knows also that the dice are loaded, more than ever before. If he comes out with a bunch of crap, I assure you that he will get an earful," was my response.

"That's right!" Pepe agreed. 'Without trying to offend him, put him in his place, so he won't get the wrong idea."

"Don't worry. I'll treat him with exquisite irony."

# CHAPTER 17

# American Tony Bryan

After first entering the patio on the right-hand side, you would find the cell of American Anthony G. Bryan, known to us affectionately as Tony.

Tony Bryan is one of those people whose nobility and sensibility have earned him the devotion of so many. My first encounter with him came about in a casual way. It was in the spring of 1970, when we both found ourselves in the Castillo del Príncipe. In those days, I had suffered immensely from a duodenal ulcer, so I was ordered to the prison infirmary. They carried me over there around five in the afternoon. Tony was the nurse on duty. At that moment, he was sitting down, eating his food ration. I recall seeing him with the plate in his hand, somewhat restless, looking me over. The doctor told him: "Tony, give him an IV, dextrose in a thousand at 5% with 2 anticonvulsants. Here's the prescription. Take care of that."

Tony stood up as if moved by a spring, leaving his dish on the floor.

"Lie down over there," he told me, pointing to one of four cots in the infirmary.

I was glad to see that it had a clean sheet, something unusual at Castillo del Príncipe.

"It's okay. But finish eating first, then take care of me," I said, sorry to have interrupted him.

"Never mind," he insisted, "The food can go to the devil. How can I make you wait, knowing that you're having an ulcer attack?"

There was a pause while he read the prescription, then he added:

"And from the face you're making, it seems this little old pain is one of the good ones, right?"

I appreciated his humanitarian gesture and his immediate willingness to help me, because I actually felt as if a crab was biting my stomach from the inside.

With the serum already in the vein, and right after the drip was regulated, Tony sat down beside my bed to talk with me, interested in details related to Cuba's tragedy under the Communist dictatorship. He was also interested in the overall situation of political prisoners.

"I'd like to know the truth as you see it, those who have suffered most, although I've already heard enough from folks passing through here."

His perfect Spanish surprised me, all the more when he told me that he had learned it in jail in just a few years.

"Are you feeling any better?" he asked me after a few minutes.

"Not much. But I will be. Don't worry."

"Then I'd better leave you alone to see if you can go to sleep. I thought that by talking with you, you might get distracted and that would help," he apologized. "I'm going to let you relax, okay...? If you need anything call me."

Tony stood up. He looked at his watch and began to again observe the serum drip. I kept quiet so as not to interrupt him.

"I'm going to speed it up and when you start to feel better, I'll return it to 30 drops per minute. Have you ever had an anticonvulsant in your IV before?" Tony asked.

"Yes, whenever I've had this pain for several days."

"And you've never had a reaction?"

"From the IV?"

"Yes, the IV solution with an anticonvulsant."

"No, it's never given me reaction, at least not that I can remember."

"That's good, no problem then," he said, as he patted my left leg as if to say goodbye. I enjoyed his company, and even more his conversation. Furthermore, when a person feels unwell, he prefers to have company.

"Tony, if you aren't busy, you can stay," I told him. "Let's forget about the ulcer and just keep chatting."

Tony Bryan shook his head smiling.

"You Cubans are always so thoughtful. Since I came to Cuba, I've noticed that. They get shot in the head and still joke around a little before dying."

I knew Tony was exaggerating, but also teasing.

"We owe that to the Spaniards, no doubt. That's the Spanish temperament and here in our veins we all carry a little of that blood... and also some African blood."

Without noticing, we had already resumed the conversation. Tony sat down again.

He told me that he was from San Francisco, California, recounting several street adventures from his childhood, all very funny and interesting. He was happy, in turn, to know that for several years, I had lived in New York City and also in Miami, where my parents, my only blood brother, and my three children still lived.

"I'm one of those big jerks who let myself get confused by Fidel Castro's misleading propaganda" he lamented. "So, when I heard him defending American blacks like me, I hijacked a plane and brought it to Cuba. And then what did they do? They slapped me in the face and sentenced me to 12 years in prison. That damn guy is an asshole, old buddy, a crazy demagogue ready to double-cross anyone. If the blacks of my country only knew what a cheat he is. But no, they're as dumb as I was and will go on hijacking planes and bringing them to Cuba for Fidel Castro to use as propaganda against the United States and then he puts us in jail to wash his hands."

Later on, Tony Bryan told me about the horrors of the common prison. He himself had been beaten several times to the point of losing consciousness. He knew in his own flesh the appalling cruelty of the torture dungeons, but none of that tormented him as much as the news coming in from prisoners' family from the other side of the bars. Bryan no longer doubted that the entire island was a huge concentration camp where 10 million victims were suffering. From that bitter reality, as he confided to me that afternoon, he began to experience a dizzying transformation, which he himself defined as *not only a timely decision of political and moral consciousness, but also the valuable discovery of the only road to be followed by every man who respects himself and loves true liberty.*

No doubt, Tony was well aware that there can be no justice under a tyrannical regime where only a single individual decides everything, from which semen inseminates a cow to the installation of nuclear missiles, converting an island of peaceful inhabitants into a virtual atomic aircraft carrier at the service of a foreign power directed by warmongering demons.

Upon entering the courtyard later on, I started heading right toward Anthony Bryan's cell. There, already talking with him, was Emilio Adolfo Rivero Caro, someone who greatly sympathized with Tony.

"That kid is a real treasure," he often told me. "His intelligence is tremendous and he has an exquisite sensitivity. Have you seen his poems? They are magnificent; most actually give me the chills."

Emilio Adolfo was not exaggerating; Tony was a poet with very deep roots, brilliant roots already germinating with his future promise.

"Look who's here," Tony alerted Rivero, as I approached.

Emilio Adolfo reached out his hand to help me climb up onto to a concrete ledge about four feet high, stretching from one end to the other of first floor cells. We then were both about two meters away from Tony's door.

"What's new?" I asked Tony. "What good tidings do you bring us today?"

*"Not much, pal, too hot."*

Bryan fanned himself with a piece of cardboard.

"Where'd you get that great fan? Did the embassy send it over?"

"The embassy" is what we called the U.S. Interests Section in Havana.

"How did you guess?" Tony gamely replied. And following up on the joke, he added, "The embassy did send it to me, but they bought it here in Cuba. It's a Russian fan."

Emilio Adolfo let out a huge belly laugh. I've never seen anyone laugh more vigorously. Then he bid goodbye to the American. "After I stretch my legs, I'll come back to chat with you again. I'd like to take a look at your recent poems. And listen friend, keep on writing. You're doing great."

Rivero Caro was a dynamic guy. He hated prison idleness, hours spent passing through life with nothing more to do than to tell old stories and contemplate cobwebs. Despite his considerable cultural heritage, he forced himself to study several hours a day and read one book after another incessantly. (During certain periods of our imprisonment, we were allowed to have books brought to us at family visits, books passed along hand-to-hand.) Among his favorite authors, Shakespeare and Dostoyevsky occupied a privileged place. He always gave good advice and was a warm friend. He was my tutor and a sincere critic of my poetry. I owe him a debt for encouraging me to demand more from myself than I used to do. That's why his release would be a great event and it would be even greater to meet him again in a land of liberty and embrace him as a father or a brother.

"Still no news from your family?" I asked the American, although I assumed that Tony remained as isolated as the previous week, the previous month, and all the prior years. If there had been any news on that front, surely he would have let me know instantly, letting out such a loud yell that I would have heard even in my cell.

"Nothing. They're getting tired of writing and those wretched Communists haven't delivered a single letter. I'm going to call them out for it, really. They're driving me crazy."

"Maybe there's some reason they aren't writing?"

"No, no. I thought so at first, until I asked another prisoner's wife to find out. She called and talked to my aunt."

"When was that?"

"Recently."

Tony stopped talking as if trying to recall the date.

"Maybe five or six months ago. Didn't I tell you?"

"Yes, you told me; I remember now," I confirmed. "Apparently, I'm getting more absent minded."

"Maybe your mind is getting rusty by being pressed up against the bars," Tony said.

"Not just my memory, but my bones are rusting."

"Do you think we'll ever get out of here?"

"For sure!" I retorted without hesitation.

"When?"

"That's harder to predict. But I always go to bed thinking that I'll be released the next morning."

"And do you really think that?" Tony asked, giving me a grin.

"No, actually I don't. But an optimist should imagine that nothing is impossible. I do it as a discipline. Defeatists never get anywhere."

"True," Tony agreed. "If Lincoln had been a defeatist, blacks in my country would still be slaves."

"But don't you think that Senator McGovern would have freed them by now?"

"Hey kiddo, forget that old fart! Don't you know about him sending his daughter to study here in Cuba?"

"That's not the worst of it... did you read his statements in Bohemia magazine? That old fox admires Castro's policies and embraces him."

"They'll throw him out of Congress when his term ends," Tony opined. "The American people are not so dumb. What kind of senator plays games with Communists? If they can't tell the difference between democracy and totalitarianism, between good and evil, let them give up politics and go raise chickens."

"Then McGovern as president... would not have abolished slavery?" I asked this time, just to continue hearing what Tony had to say.

"Shit! He would move the capitol to the Kremlin. And Americans would be sent to study in Moscow."

Since Bryan's temper was heating up, which was not my intention, I returned back to our original subject.

"Tony, why don't you try to have your family write to you directly through the Interests Section?" I suggested. "Doesn't an official from there visit you from time to time?"

Tony Bryan muttered something unintelligible, tightening his lips and smacking his forehead twice with the palm of his hand. Then he grumbled: "Folks from the embassy don't want complications, chico. They only dare to bring me what is authorized: cigars and one book or another. But anyway, I'm grateful to them."

That last sentence was quite sincere. On several occasions, Tony had expressed his gratitude for the friendly gestures of Interests Section officials.

Meanwhile, with a flick of his thumb, the American indicated the cell next door, where an Angolan (who we did not trust to maintain any secrecy from the guards) had come in three or four weeks before. I immediately understood that he was trying to alert me.

"Okay!" I said, with a nod indicating I understood.

A conspiratorial smile lit up Tony's face. Then he signaled that he would write me a letter to give me before we left the courtyard.

"Sorry to hear it," I said with a double meaning, as if referring to the impossibility of receiving letters through the Interests Section. I loved that game, and tried to prolong it to fill up his curious ears.

"It's unfortunate to be in the hands of those pigs," protested Tony.

With that attack, Tony sought to kill two birds with one stone: the jailers and the Angolan. I completely understood. However, just to hear him throw out another missive, I pretended not to understand.

"What pigs?"

The American's exclamation that was almost a shout: "What pigs am I talking about? The Communists!"

We were gradually diverting the conversation away from the Interests Section. The rest didn't matter. Our accursed neighbor could strain his ears as much as he liked and also let loose his forked tongue.

"It's because you are such a dangerous fellow," I reminded him. "Didn't you break Lieutenant Ferreiro's foot? You need to pay for that. Did you think that they wouldn't retaliate?"

"More reprisals? Didn't they have to hospitalize me because they beat me up so badly? That was six years ago and I still get headaches."

"They hit you with clubs, right?"

"And with chains too. A single blow split my head into three parts. But the one that hurt most was one I got on the shins."

"Now that we are on the subject, Tony, clear up something for me. Finally, how much time did you get?"

"Three years, chico!"

"Three years on top of the twelve you got for the aircraft?"

"Yes, three more years. They are something else, these knuckleheads."

"After they beat you up?"

"That's right. But they accused me because of Lieutenant Ferreiro."

"You bastard, Tony, I think you're pulling my leg."

The American put his hands over his mouth to stifle a burst of laughter.

"No, no, don't say that. I landed a few punches myself when they gave me the first blows. I had to defend myself, right? Then, they started running like rats, and that asshole got his foot caught on some wooden boxes and... CRASH! That's how he broke his leg and ended up rolling on the ground."

I remembered the event, but not the details. It had happened in 1972 at Castillo del Príncipe. Back then, they gave Tony such a brutal beating that for several days he was on the verge of death. Lieutenant Ferreiro, head of the garrison, had ended up with a broken leg. That officer harbored a terrible hatred of blacks and, even more, of a black American. *To put an end to crime in Cuba, we should start by beheading all blacks, not leaving even one alive. They're a real plague,*" I heard him roar once, while dragging a slim young Afro-Cuban guy across the floor, a boy looking young enough to be out sailing paper boats on a pond. The youth was leaving behind a trickle of blood. A very young jailer followed along closely making a horrified face, but not daring to do anything to prevent that crime. Common prisoners began shouting out from several windows.

"Ferreiro, murderer!"

"Ferreiro, murderer!"

"Arrest him!"

The officer dropped his hold on the kid's leg, kicked him in the ribs, and went over to thrust his bayonet through the nearest window bars.

My guts stirred with rage. "They're worse than Nazis," I thought. "The real plague is red and not black or white or any other color."

These sad memories flitted across my mind while Anthony Bryan paused to light a cigarette. It's incredible how quickly such images can spring up —a whole detailed human tragedy while a match is being lit.

"This is the life!" the American chortled in satisfaction, while the smoke cloud he'd just exhaled swirled whimsically one meter away from his lips.

"Life? I would say death," I opined. "It's also a fool's folly."

"Please, cut that out," the American protested. "In my country, almost everybody smokes," and, in a jocular tone, he added, "except children under five, unless parents send them to school early. I think that Superman began smoking at age three."

"In Cuba, smoking has also become fashionable. There's plenty of freedom to smoke, especially among prodigies" I said, playing on Tony's joke. "We have the case of a precocious Fidel Castro, who at six months old was already crawling around picking up cigarette butts."

"Certainly a phenomenon of nature, unique to this world," Tony exclaimed ironically. "No, you're wrong; he is not the only one. Previously, Germany had brought forth a genius with identical characteristics, a boy named Adolf, who also at six months of age smoked cigarette butts."

Tony again inclined his thumb toward the next cell

This time, I just shrugged my shoulders. Many years ago, I had arrived at the conclusion that while in jail, with the exception of honor and dignity, I had nothing left to lose.

As we had already chatted long enough, I waved goodbye.

"See you later," I promised the American. "I'm going to stroll around the courtyard to keep my legs from getting stiff."

"Don't forget to come by here before you go. Remember," Tony said, pointing to his temple.

"No worries. I'll be back by," I assured him, realizing that he wanted to give me the promised letter.

"That's right!" he said, and went over to sit down on his messy bunk.

# CHAPTER 18

# José Oscar: A Small Giant

The sun had retreated behind a dark cloud, which raised my spirits. On a morning of such intense heat, that was a blessing. Summer shade is a godsend to black sheep and to prisoners.

I began walking out toward the barbed wire fence rising up painfully from the ground; it seemed to extend to the very gates of hell. Out in the middle of the yard some fellow inmates were tossing a cloth ball; others were talking together, sitting on cement benches at the far end bumping up against the building. Among the latter, I noticed José Oscar Rodríguez Terrero, who because of his small stature –in contrast to his gigantic inner strength— we all called Napoleón. When he saw me, he jumped up and started striding along with me during my exercise walk. We had been waiting to talk and this seemed like the right opportunity.

Of peasant stock and with a very alert mind, José Oscar had an early awareness of the social injustices and ills bedeviling his homeland. Perhaps the most conclusive proof of his revolutionary orientation was that, when he was only thirteen, he went to the Sierra Maestra where he wielded a gun against the previous dictatorship of Fulgencio Batista. There he experienced all the hazards of war. One of the most difficult moments, as he confided in me that morning, was when he got news of the death of his older brother, José Spaulding, a courageous young man, only 18 years old, who like the youthful José Oscar, was part of the anti-Batista guerrilla contingent.

*"My father, three of my brothers, and I had joined a few months earlier."* They had sent José Spaulding down to the lowlands with special instructions. He had managed to easily infiltrate the city of Guantánamo. But once he had accomplished his mission, and was about to return to the sierra, he was betrayed and taken prisoner. (Oscarito pauses to take a breath here). They riddled him with bullets on a river bank on April 6, 1958, after he had been savagely tortured.

"My mother was greatly affected by my brother's death. But she had the fortitude to bear adversity with real stoicism." (At this part of his story, Oscarito's black eyes light up intensely with a mixture of sadness and pride). "Mom has always been very brave," he went on. "Batista's aircraft strafed her by mistake when she was traversing the mountains to find out news of her kids. Her pilgrimage was a tremendous odyssey. It happened that during the bombardment, she had lost her horse and was forced to continue on foot through the mountains, wandering on foot here and there."

José Oscar wiped the sweat from his brow before continuing with the story of his brother's death.

"It wasn't until 1959 that Mom and Pop were able to recover José Spaulding's remains. Then it was discovered that his skull had been shattered by rifle butts. We later found out about the monstrous way they had tortured him before machine-gunning him to death."

After the overthrow of the Batista regime, the Rodríguez Terrero family dedicated themselves with love and honesty to the great task of national reconstruction. However, very soon they would realize with infinite bitterness that Fidel Castro had betrayed them. When the stealthy Communists, who far from risking their own skin had been licking Batista's boots, began to assume power under the next tyrant in line, José Oscar and his family took up arms and again scaled the mountains in the struggle for freedom.

Captured by Castro's forces in unequal combat, José Oscar Rodríguez appeared before a military court that condemned him to 20 years in prison. Twelve years later, his sentence was commuted. He was only 16 when he was taken prisoner and already had participated in two wars for the emancipation of his people. As happens when shame and courage combine, his ruthless incarceration did not dampen his spirits, not even in December 1962, when the Communists pumped eight bullets into the chest of his brother, José Andrés, just a few hours after having sentenced him to death for defending the freedom and independence of his homeland.

"José Andrés was shot at the San Juan firing squad range at Santiago de Cuba on January 23, 1963, 36 days after having been captured and without trial. He still suffered fresh wounds from his last fight. As they had refused to provide medical care, the wounds had become infected and imbedded with worms, but he never complained. He died with great dignity and with much optimism. He died aware that someday Cuba will be free and for him that was most important," so José Oscar told me.

The dark clouds had dispersed and the sun had forced to seek shelter on the south side of the courtyard, under the shadow of the building. I had a keen interest in hearing Oscarito tell about his experiences at the Isle of Pines prison, where the "chief" of block 23 happened to discharge his gun in the forced labor fields, pointing toward José Oscar's testicles, after the latter valiantly pushed the sharp bayonet away from his buttocks. As the projectile crossed through both thighs, the teenager still made a defensive gesture before falling to the ground covered in his own blood. This time, the uniformed executioner aimed toward his head, but fifty angry voices thundered in unison, and fearing that the youth's death would provoke a riot, the chief holstered his revolver, uttering offensive threats against the prisoners and ordering them back to work. The cordon of security guards all pointed their guns toward the prisoners, but none dared to shoot.

Up to that point, I already knew the story, but wanted to clarify certain details about it, and who better than the victim to describe to me that cowardly and criminal act?

"Do you remember the name of the chief who shot you?" must have been the first question I asked.

"Adel Gutiérrez. No, I wouldn't forget him if I live a hundred years.

And just to show you the ironies of fate," added José Oscar, "during the earlier war, that same son of bitch was wearing an official army helmet, but then when Batista fell, he joined the rebel army to serve with Castro. He has the soul of a real sell-out. Adel Gutiérrez."

"Adel Gutiérrez... so that asshole was a Batista goon?" I was astonished by that unusual revelation.

"Yes, a Batista henchman, my friend. That's what galls me the most."

"As you said, a born lackey! Surely, he must be pleased these days. With this government, he has many chances to develop his vocation of murderer. He's probably a colonel by now."

"No doubt. Not just a colonel either. I wouldn't be surprised if he became a member of the Central Committee, like that bloodthirsty Julio Tarrau."

Julio Tarrau was the most despotic and criminal director ever at the "model" prison of Isla de Pinos (Isle of Pines), inaugurated in 1928. Because of his frightening cruelty and unbridled bloody attacks against political prisoners, because of those killed and mutilated in the forced labor camps of Isla de Pinos, because of all the orphans, because of the many tears shed by Cuban mothers, because of the mourning visited upon countless homes during the 1960's, Lieutenant Julio Tarrau was honored by Castro, who appointed him to the Central Committee of the Cuban Communist Party. His is an example of the relentless system of annihilation practiced by the regime in Havana, its real policy, not the policy of human rights that the unscrupulous Fidel Castro proclaimed deceptively in international forums, trying to confuse naïve leaders and world public opinion.

'I'd like another detail," I told my diminutive buddy. "Do you remember the day Adel Gutiérrez shot you?"

"I'm not sure if it was the 9th or 11th of December, but that's easy to find out. Mom has the date written down; it was back in 1965."

From where we were sitting, out of the sun, you could see the whole southern expanse of the patio. Several huge rats crept from one side to the other, often scurrying between the thick concrete columns holding up the four floors of the building and the array of metal latticework that blocked the exit to the outside. Some munched eagerly on pieces of discarded bread crusts given them by the prisoners.

"Dude, did you see that? That one is a puff of smoke," exclaimed Oscarito excitedly, when one of the rats attacked three others by surprise, snatching from them a magnificent scrap.

Actually, if one managed to closely observe the rats, the scene evoked sympathy. But the mind is capricious and I not could avoid, at that moment, thinking about the millions of human beings in the world who cry out for a piece of bread. I thought about African children, children of Asia, and children in Latin America who have never held a toy in their hands, nor ever had access to a doctor, nor to a school to teach them to read and write.

"When the chief pointed a gun at your head, do you think that he intended to shoot?"

"Do you doubt it?" José Oscar retorted, eyes widening.

"No, how could I doubt it if he'd already shot you in the thighs? I just wanted to be sure, to find out what you thought."

"Ah, I wondered... Look, if the guys from the block had waited even one second to react, he would have blown my brains out. I'm sure of that," he reiterated. Then he began to trace with his finger, on a little island of sand and soil left on the concrete patio by the previous downpour, a woman's name: Dora.

"Is that your girlfriend?"

"No, my mother. You don't know Mom?"

"Yes, I've seen her on visits, but I've never spoken to her, and I didn't know she was called Dora."

"And Patricio, do you know who Patricio is?" José Oscar asked.

"Of course, man. What prisoner doesn't know Patricio?"

"Poor Dad, thank goodness he has already served his sentence. When he came out of Boniato, he looked like a skeleton."

In 1961, José Oscar's father Patricio was locked inside a Communist dungeon accused of fomenting an uprising. He was condemned to five years in prison, even though State Security investigators could not present any evidence against him during the trial. At the end of his sentence, he was released. However, in August 1970, he was arrested again, and this time sentenced to six years, which, like the previous five, he was forced to serve until the very last day, confined most of the time to the infamous Boniato prison.

José Patricio, another of José Oscar's brothers, became a man before his time by also taking up arms against the dictatorship of traitor Fidel Castro and was captured in combat. At the time of his arrest, he was just 14 years old. The military court condemned him to remain behind bars until he reached adulthood; nearly seven years of deprivation and torture in the hidden bowels of the regime were endured by that wonderful boy before his release.

Harassed even in his dreams by the wolves of the police political, José Patricio had no other option than to seek freedom through the mined fields and multiple barbed wire fences guarded by fierce dogs and armed soldiers surrounding the Guantánamo naval base. He was fortunate to achieve his goal. God rewarded his heroism by granting him the opportunity to live in a free and democratic country *"until the time comes to pick up a shotgun again to save Cuba from this miserable and atheistic communism,"* he later told his brother, José Oscar, in an emotional letter.

The heroic sacrifices of this humble family from the Caujerí Valley of Guantánamo are, in my opinion, among the most impressive and instructive in Cuban history. When the truth is unraveled, knowing in detail about the selflessness and patriotism with which they embraced the cause of freedom, one cannot help feeling admiration and respect, or help being optimistic about the future of our country.

This was not the first time that José Oscar, at my behest, devoted a few minutes to sharing passages from his own life and those of his loved ones. Because of the complications of prison, most of the time, his conversations had been abruptly interrupted at the most interesting points.

# CHAPTER 19

# Confrontation with the Guard on Duty

"Ernesto Díaz, Ernesto Díaz!" a fellow inmate, playing ball while we were out in the courtyard, shouted that someone was asking for me from a cell on the second floor in the middle of the building.

I moved in closer. Indeed, waiting for me was Félix Rafael Vázquez Robles, displaying something the size of a cigarettes pack that he held out to throw down to me.

"Toss it!" I said, after glancing over to make sure that the two soldiers standing guard were distracted observing the prisoners tossing the cloth ball.

After two or three failed attempts, Bibe, the nickname his friends gave Félix Rafael, made a lucky throw toward the vertical openings which formed the outer wall of the building.

Since this was a frequent maneuver, I already knew the angle of the shot and caught the packet directly in my hands.

Then, unexpectedly, at that precise moment, the official on guard entered the courtyard, just in time to see me make the catch. I realized immediately that now it was too late.

"Let me see what you've just caught!" he ordered.

The prisoners, many of whom had witnessed the incident, began to crowd around us. The clamor then faded into deathly silence, *"Look,"* I showed him the packet.

"What's that?"

"Look. Papers... just papers"

"Hand them over!" he ordered curtly.

"Are they yours?"

"Give them to me!" he arrogantly insisted.

"Forget it. Don't waste your time. I won't give you anything."

He became furious, trying to snatch the papers out of my hand, but getting a push instead that left him speechless.

Immediately, I passed the package to Miguel Ángel Alvárez Cardantey. He, in turn, slipped it to another comrade, so quickly that even I myself could not identify the prisoner who actually had it. That further infuriated the official, who snarled angrily:

"Let's go see the captain; there, we are going to solve this matter, you and I."

"Let's go to the director's office, or wherever you like," I replied. "Say no more, let's go!"

We walked out together toward the main office without further discussion. But we had no sooner left the courtyard and one of the custodians had firmly secured the door with chain and padlock, when the guard began to threaten me.

"I'll send you to solitary," he said.

"Go there yourself. I'm not going anywhere."

"You'll be sent to a punishment cell, that's for sure."

"Get that idea out of your head, compadre. You aren't sending me anywhere."

"You'll soon find out," he stubbornly insisted.

Ever since they had tortured us there with loudspeakers, I'd made up my mind not to allow myself to be sent back to "human rights" unless taken there by force. But to do so violently, they would have to beat me and carry me over there, with inevitable adverse consequences for them, because surely that would bring about greater complications.

I held my tongue, letting him chatter on like a parrot. After all, I'd made my decision. I'd already told him, so it made no sense to keep on repeating it. He'd find out when the time came. No use prolonging that fruitless debate. I wouldn't respond in the slightest; unless he offended me, of course.

So, we go into the director's office. Captain Raúl Álvarez was there reclining comfortably behind his desk smoking his perennial cigar, this time at "half-staff." I realized that he wasn't expecting a prisoner visit, otherwise, there would have been a premiere stogy in his mouth, even unlit. Its symbolism was designed to give a magic touch to his personality. He liked to consider himself a faithful imitator of "superior gestures." If the devil had created them with almost the same physical and moral stature, it was perfectly understandable that the fawning captain would try as much as possible to imitate his master.

"So, what happened?" Raúl Álvarez spoke first.

The guard, in a gruff tone, described the incident with the papers. He said that he had surprised me just when they were being thrown from the second floor, and not only had I refused to surrender them but, in addition, that I had pushed him.

"Explain to him that I pushed you because you tried to snatch them out of my hand," I pointed out, seeing that he was only telling part of the story.

The guard officer looked me up and down with a menacing expression. Then, acting disinterested, he continued: "When we came here, I told him that he was going to be sent to solitary and he answered that he wasn't going anywhere."

"I told you I wouldn't go, no," I interrupted him. "I'm not going to the punishment dungeons! Get that out of your head. Before they take me, they'll have to..."

"Who said that you'll be sent to solitary? None of that. We're going to send you to State Security," the captain interjected.

Then, looking at the guard officer he added, "Leave me this to me. G-2 will take charge of him."

Then he immediately ordered. "Go ahead, open the gate to the yard. I don't care to see him anymore."

I realized by his few words that they wouldn't undertake the trouble of sending me to State Security. But the captain had come up with that formula as a face-saving gesture toward the guard officer. It was a solution showing that Captain Raúl Álvarez knew what he was doing. He knew how to avoid a worthless confrontation.

When I turned around to leave, I imagined him sighing in satisfaction behind me, reclining back behind his desk. The meeting was brief and I must confess that this time, I didn't hear the slightest hint of hostility in his voice, not even when, by way of farewell, he said: "Ernesto Díaz, damn it! You never change."

Back as soon I set foot back in the yard, a score of prisoners accosted me with questions, all very concerned and curious about my situation. The storm had blown over, I reassured them, sketching out what was said in the office. Miguel Ángel came up to tell me that the papers were already safe.

"Where?" I asked.

"Up on the fourth floor. As soon you left with the guard officer, we let Mario know and he lowered a small bag and we sent up the letters."

Mario Gavilán had stayed up reading until 3:30 or 4 a.m., so he didn't wake up when they opened the doors for breakfast, or when, an hour later, they opened them to the yard. He woke up, he told me, only after the commotion the prisoners were making when the officer on duty tried to snatch my papers. Miguel Ángel stood next to the gate. Knowing that in 1404 they had a bag tied to a long rope, used mainly to transfer notes clandestinely up from the patio, he signaled to Gavilán to lower it, and in less than a minute, Mario had been entrusted to hide the papers until my return. That avoided the risk of destroying them except if the building director decided to undertake a search of everyone on the fourth floor.

The rest of the morning was spent in absolute calm. After about two hours outside, I went over to American Tony Bryan's cell to collect the letter he had promised.

"Let's wait until another day. I was writing it, but burned it when they took you to the captain's office. I thought you were heading to 'human rights' and wouldn't be seeing us for a while."

"No, Tony, forget about 'human rights.' To those black holes, they'd have to take me in pieces. Or tie me up and carry me over there."

Somehow, we both were moved to comment on the torture that emanated from the loudspeakers there and about the hanging of Rafael del Pino, still an open sore.

Bryan had begun reading to me from one of his lovely poems when the exit door was opened and the duty officer announced the end of recreation.

No inspection followed. Nor did the head captain take repressive measures. The matter was never mentioned to me again. However, Félix Vázquez was called in just to harass him. I was surprised when he told me, but then thought, although very unlikely, that the officer might have seen and identified him from the patio throwing down the packet. It's also possible that they linked us by simple association, since Bibe (his nickname) and I had been convicted previously in the same case, accused of conspiracy by the military tribunal judging us behind closed doors of trying to overthrow the government from prison.

# CHAPTER 20

# General Inspection

One of the few things given to me, that I cherished, was a small rectangular aquarium. It was smuggled in by a fellow prisoner, and in it swam a few small fish he gathered while laboring outside the prison. For several months, to prevent the confiscation of my aquarium whenever a search was underway, I took the trouble of carrying it into the dining room with the help of one of my 1404 roommates. It was not the same to allow it to be taken meekly from our cell as to have it grabbed physically right out of my hands. They could make it disappear in one way or another, of course. Their threats were serious enough, but we were then at a time when our jailers were avoiding confrontations with prisoners, and they had no idea how far I was willing to go to defend my fish. In those days, the American President Jimmy Carter had rolled out his human rights policy and the Cuban government, stifled economically, hoped that by responding to that pressure it might achieve a lifting of the embargo imposed on Fidel Castro by President John F. Kennedy and ratified by all subsequent administrations in that neighboring country. So, my aquarium, and the fish I fed crumbled up hard-boiled eggs, were a beneficiary of this policy.

One morning, we suddenly were notified that more than a hundred guards were on their way upstairs.

"Now they are entering the fourth floor," announced those living in the first cells there, just a minute later.

"Inspection!" boomed voices from one end to the other of the hallway.

"Search!"

"Search!"

That whistleblower cry echoed throughout.

In all Cuban prisons, with very rare exceptions, a prisoner always has something to hide, something to hide in just ten seconds whenever the guards undertake a search. I imagine the same happens in prisons all over the world, especially in the Communist bloc, where those convicted are not entitled to anything, and where —on a mere whim— even a family letter can be considered subversive and a crime punishable by law. No matter how arbitrary, the state is always right.

While I was scrambling to protect my things, almost immediately the guards broke into our cell and ordered us into the dining room, and I forgot to take the fishbowl. I went out with several notebooks in my hand, something noticed by Lieutenant Colonel Raúl O'Farril, who I immediately encountered, along with other officers, standing outside the entrance of 1404.

"Let's see what you've got there," the Lieutenant Colonel interjected.

I pretended not to hear him and continued on, walking quickly toward the dining room.

At that time, the chief captain of the building came into the hallway and O'Farril told him to stop me and examine the notebooks.

I refused to give them up.

The captain told me they had orders not to allow us to remove anything from the cells.

The situation proved risky because in the notebooks, among other things, I had written some rather compromising testimony, detailing the monstrous formula used by the Cuban government to physically eliminate the former army rebel commander César Páez Sánchez, one of the most prestigious and beloved of Cuban political prison leaders.

After protesting vehemently, I let Captain Raúl Alvarez know that

I would only turn over the notebooks if he promised me not to take them away.

"These are the notebooks that you gave me a few days ago. I told you that I wanted them to write down my poems once more, the same ones taken away in the booklet loaned to Dr. Kouri. How can I allow them to be taken again?" I protested. "Stop it. I'm tired of putting up with these indignities."

The captain scratched his head, undecided, looking past my shoulder, perhaps intending to ask O'Farril, but the lieutenant colonel was no longer in sight. He had gone into 1404, apparently to give instructions to the officers scouring our cell.

"Nobody is going to take them away," Raúl Alvarez assured me.

"That's what they always say and then..."

"I give you my word that nobody will take them," he quickly affirmed.

"That's good, because I'm banking on your word," I warned him. "Look, I'm putting them right into your own two hands, and will blame you if they get lost. Then don't come to me complaining about my non-compliance."

The captain tucked the notebooks under his arm. I continued toward the dining room without the slightest hope that he wouldn't turn them into State Security.

The dining room was stifling hot, so I went over to one of the two windows overlooking the courtyard, seeking a breath of fresh air. From there I could see something of corridor A, the entrance to 1403 and all of 1404. From my improvised vantage point, I carefully observed the guards' movements, trying to guess what was happening inside our cell. A while later, I saw Lieutenants Mauricio and Montano take out the fish tank and carefully place it out on the hallway floor. I boiled with rage, stifling the urge to hurl some nasty epithets at them.

During the more than two hours that we remained inside there, crowded, sweaty, everyone shouting to be heard over the din, that dining room had turned into a loony bin. By the time the garrison had finished searching, the prisoners were on edge. This, in turn, evoked tremendous hostility toward the military, at least momentarily, because of the disrespectful way in which we were deprived of a good part of our few belongings. Possibly that same tension, along with other factors –psychological and environmental– drove folks to raise their voices, and speak all at once, as if participating in a chatter fest.

Despite the overcrowding, heat, and noise, I took advantage of those moments of forced inactivity to collect some information about companions whose causes I considered significant, either because of their excessive sentences —many of them completely unwarranted as well—or because of the episodes of extreme cruelty to which they had been subjected during their long years of incarceration.

# CHAPTER 21

# The Hostages of Elbow Key

While the search was still underway, Eleno Oviedo Álvarez took the opportunity to tell me about when he and his companions were abducted by Castro's troops:

"On February 17, 1963, we were sailing off the coast of the Bahamas aboard the vessel White Star, a boat with a fishing license and registration in the State of Florida, when a surprise north wind of considerable intensity made us seek refuge on the south bank of Elbow Key, one of the Bahamas' keys, a British territory at that time.

"At approximately six in the afternoon, quite unexpectedly, three Cuban torpedo boats arrived in the area and began immediately opening fire on our boat, so we were forced to plunge into the water to save our lives.

"With great difficulty and no small amount of agony, we managed to reach the shore by swimming, sheltering in the key.

"A large group of heavily armed men disembarked from the patrol boats, trying to capture us.

"Four of my companions, Juan Reyes, Armando Morales, Agustín Vizcaíno, and Juan Morales, were then all seized by force. The remaining four of us managed to evade the attack, hiding away from the reach of the military, who persisted in strafing and throwing grenades in our direction until 2 a.m. At that time, they decided to withdraw, towing our boat along with them.

"Having no other choice, we remained at the key without food or water, hoping that we might shortly be rescued from that inhospitable rocky point.

"Two days later, on February 19, in the afternoon," Eleno continued, "a couple of MIG-15 jets with Cuban logos buzzed the key several times, firing on us and also on a boat that was sailing to the north of Elbow Key. This vessel apparently had flagged the incident, because a few minutes later, a United States aircraft appeared and the MIG-15, one of those with the number 38, took off again toward Cuba. Then came several aircraft of the U.S. Navy and we lit fires so they would see our position to send a helicopter or boat to rescue us. Later, there appeared on the horizon a ship of medium size, which we thought belonged the U. S. Coast Guard that the next morning would come for us.

"At dawn on February 20, we saw the boat nearing the key. It turned out to be the frigate Antonio Maceo from Cuba. Just as we were able to identify it, a new contingent of soldiers descended and took prisoner the remaining four of us: Eumelio Viera, Domingo Martínez, Rafael Santana, and me," Oviedo Alvarez recalled. "They also used a torpedo boat.

"In the frigate, they took us to Cárdenas Bay. There, we were delivered to the political police (G-2), who transferred us immediately to State Security in Havana.

"The interrogations continued for 125 days. During all that time, we were kept in solitary confinement in enclosed, dark cells, rigorously isolated and subjected to all types of torture and cruelties, hoping to force us to confess to crimes and offenses invented by those in G-2. My health, and that of the rest of my colleagues, were seriously broken by June 25, 1963, when they finally transferred us to the prison fortress of La Cabaña.

"We spent seven years, seven months, and seven days in that prison without ever appearing before a judge, because there was no evidence against us to submit to a legal process. Rather, those interrogations actually proved our innocence. However, on September 26, 1970, without prior notice, we were taken before an improvised military court at La Cabaña.

"The trial lasted barely 20 minutes. We were not allowed to see any lawyers, being subjected instead to the will of an officer who claimed to be the lawyer on duty, a so-called defense lawyer (from G-2) who spoke not a word before or after with any of us, nor showed even the slightest interest in defending us, expressing only that we deserved to be shot, but that he trusted in 'the benevolence and profoundly humanitarian nature of the Revolution,' all that said with a cynical smirk.

"During the trial farce, the officer acknowledged that we had actually been caught on Elbow Key, a British territory. Moreover, that if the Cuban government considered it necessary, they would seek us out not only in the Bahamas, but right there even in Miami, the place where the eight of us who had been kidnapped legally resided."

Eleno Oviedo Álvarez was the only one of the *White Star* crew who, more than two decades later, still remained in the dungeons of the Communist regime serving a 30-year sentence for a crime he did not commit, one of the 610 Cuban political prisoners that dictator Fidel Castro excluded from the pardons program officially decreed by the Cuban government in December 1978. According to prison authorities, although Oviedo had legally left the country in June of 1959 and did not belong to any anti-Castro organization, he was considered "akin to those terrorist groups in exile."

The situation of Oviedo Álvarez has been presented on several opportunities to the UN Human Rights Commission, to the Organization of American States (OAS), and to the prestigious humanitarian institution Amnesty International. Also, formal complaints were made to the government of Britain and the case was reported in detail to former U.S. Presidents Richard Nixon and Jimmy Carter, asking them to submit testimony about the kidnapping, since at the moment that the frigate *Antonio Maceo* had to abandon Elbow Key, there had appeared a U.S. Coast Guard aircraft that made several turns over the Cuban ship, flying over it at a very low altitude. This caused an official to contact the captain of the frigate and, in the presence of the prisoners, say that the Coast Guard was asking them for identification. The captain of the

*Antonio Maceo*, according to what Eleno Oviedo told me, then ordered that no one answer and continued sailing full steam ahead toward Cuba.

In 1973, two similar cases of piracy, carried out by force by dictator Fidel Castro, more than 100 miles off the coast of that same Caribbean island, had astonished the world. Those cases involved the kidnapping of two merchant ships, *Laila Express* and *Johnny Express*. Both were boarded and brought back to Cuba after being subjected to a fierce strafing in which Captain Villa of the *Johnny Express* received five gunshot wounds that left him on the verge of death. Transferred, still convalescing, to State Security, Villa, like his crewmates, was subjected to all kinds of interrogation and torture, to such an extent that in desperation, overwhelmed by his suffering, he tried to commit suicide in a G-2 dungeon.

I met the elderly captain in Gallery 14 of La Cabaña prison. There he showed us his gunshot wounds, some of them in the chest, and told us in detail, how 120 miles off the coast of Cuba, Castro's patrols had intercepted his ship and savagely strafed it before the piracy.

In prison, Villa's psychological state continued to deteriorate. The humiliation and extreme cruelty to which he was subjected by the political police, in a vain attempt to extract from him confessions of crimes he did not commit, affected his nerves so that the idea of suicide persisted in his mind.

*"I cannot stand this,"* he told us over and over again, *"I'm giving up,"* which forced us to maintain constant vigilance, fearful that any neglect might allow the old captain in put an end to his life.

One morning, we surprised him at the very moment when he was putting a noose around his neck inside Gallery 14's bathroom. Those who had taken his words in jest realized that the emotional imbalance of the old man was very serious, so we redoubled our surveillance.

Villa and his comrades from the *Johnny Express* had already spent several months at La Cabaña when, under pressure from President Richard Nixon, who threatened to take drastic measures, and from world public opinion, the terrorist Fidel Castro ordered the hostages released.

# CHAPTER 22

# The General Inspection is Over

An official announced that the inspection, the prison-wide search for contraband, had ended. Immediately, Sergeant Pedro turned on his portable phone during one of the final sweeps through Hall C to communicate with the control board. He had just hung up when we heard a "clack" triggering the release of the dining room door latch.

The first one out of the dining room was Emilio Adolfo Rivero Caro. Emilio Adolfo lived in cell 1403. Perhaps at this moment of relative calm, his immediate concern was for his books, always at risk of being lost during a prison search.

"It infuriates me when they take away my things. I can't stand it. It's the one thing that really freaks me out. Drives me really crazy," my good friend told me more than once, sometimes bitterly, sometimes with a smile. But invariably, I understood it to be a confession of real feeling, something expressed very seriously and frankly. Anyway, his outbursts were mostly just an expression of his temperament, I thought, of his rare dynamism. Emilio Adolfo was not one to be sitting idly around, arms crossed, waiting for sign from heaven or waiting for the sunrise. Long before dawn's early light, he would be pacing around restlessly, staring out at the rising arc as if he'd like to pull dawn up by its hair.

However, on that particular occasion, it wasn't mainly concern about his books, or a matter of his temperament, nothing personal.

I'd gone over by the window to wait for the dining room to empty out and, from there, saw him walking briskly past the entrance to 1403 without even glancing in at his cell. At first, I thought he might be looking for the medicine cabinet, but when he suddenly entered 1404, I changed my mind.

"The old guy is daffy!" I commented to Eleno Oviedo, elbowing him in the ribs. "He must have gotten mixed about his cell."

"What do you mean?"

"He went into 1404."

"I don't believe you; you're kidding," he replied, amused.

I didn't have to prove it. At that moment, Eleno saw him hastily exit from my cell.

"By golly, you're right my friend!" he said, clapping his hands and laughing like a child.

Moments later, I was summoned to the dining room entrance. It was Emilio Adolfo, grinning broadly, his eyes twinkling mischievously.

"You son-of-a-gun," he moved in closer to tell me, "I bring you good tidings: the aquarium is still there."

"Where?"

"In your cell."

I remembered then that Emilio Adolfo had commiserated with me about the possible loss of my fish when Lieutenants Mauricio and Montano had taken them out into the hallway.

"Great news! I had already given them up for lost."

"Sargent Cervantes put them back while you were talking with Eleno. I saw him from the window, but I didn't want to say anything until I made sure."

"Sergeant Cervantes," I thought, he who not so long ago cancelled two of our family visits for no reason. "I just don't understand. Every day, I know even less about these guys."

I still had to find out about another important matter, very important to me: what had happened to my notebooks of poems and the conflicting testimony revealed on any open page, risking sending me right back into the dungeons of State Security?

I didn't find them above my bed or inside the single shelf of a rough cabinet where I kept my books and personal hygiene items.

"It's likely that they took them away," I told myself. I hesitated to claim them since the wiser course would be to give them up for lost, to see if they would be tossed unnoticed into the trash, along with the many books and dishes discarded all over the building during an inspection.

But one doesn't always listen to the voice of reason. Against my better judgement, I went in search of the captain before he left the fourth floor. I immediately planned to berate him for not keeping his promise to protect my notebooks, even after I had delivered them into his hands.

I found him talking with a prisoner at the dining room door. By the angry tone of their conversation, I surmised that it was about something regarding the inspection, another seizure, no doubt.

I held back out of politeness. The captain must have guessed my concern, because as soon as he glanced up and saw me, he signaled for me to wait my turn.

As soon as the other prisoner had left, he asked me: "Tell me, what did they take from you?" Then he whispered to himself, "They're all driving me crazy."

"You already know what they took!"

"They didn't take anything. O'Farril personally assigned me to search 1404, and I was there the whole time."

"What happened to those notebooks I put into your hands?"

"On your bed."

"There's nothing on my bed. I see I can't trust any of you," I protested.

"You're wrong. They have to be there. I left them right on top of your bed. If not on yours, then on someone else's, so go look."

He spoke with such naturalness and firmness that I didn't think it was a trick.

And indeed, back in my cell, I found my notebooks there intact on Zúñiga's bed.

My first impression was that Captain Raúl Alvarez had not looked inside them. Otherwise, he would have delivered them to G-2. I was well acquainted with the machinations of the jailers. Today, analyzing it in more detail, I can imagine other possibilities. Years of experience have taught me to evaluate situations from more than one point of view.

Several days after the general inspection Sergeant Cervantes came over to tell me that Lieutenant Colonel O'Farril was the one who had ordered putting the fishbowl back into 1404.

"You have no idea how surprised he was," he began explaining to me. "When he saw it in the hall, he was astonished. Immediately, he called the captain to ask him how it had gotten up to the fourth floor. Raúl didn't know, and, in turn, asked Mauritius. Mauritius then blamed the guards. He said they were the ones who opened the doors and, apparently, were just fools."

Sometimes Cervantes interrupted himself to imitate the gestures of one or another officer, as if he were a parrot, a clown, or whatever. Actually, I was not amused, but he was having fun, I guess, because he kept on laughing. Maybe at the time, his mind was on a full moon. He might have been mentally unbalanced. It was hard to explain why that man remained a jailer, at times with a rifle on his shoulder, and a gun always within reach. Is the only essential requirement for carrying out that function unconditional loyalty to the Castro police state, never mind about mental health or the tyrant's endangerment of prisoners' lives?

"Finally, O'Farril wondered whose fishes they were," Cervantes continued telling me. "Since I knew they belonged to you, I stepped up and said: 'Colonel, they are Ernesto Diaz's...' He didn't let me finish. Right then and there, he reached out and ordered me to put that fishbowl back in the cell, because otherwise, you were going raise a ruckus."

I wanted him to confirm what he just said: "Are you sure that's what happened?"

"Exactly what I've just told you. He also said that it was better to leave matters alone so you can distract yourself with the fish instead of conspiring against the government."

"I think that you made up that last part. Don't make up stories."

Sergeant Cervantes vigorously rubbed his hands together, letting out a laugh like the bray of a donkey.

"Ernesto Díaz," he told me, "you know too much." Then, this time imitating a parrot, he added, "Never mind that imperialism gets up early because MININT never sleeps."

"Hey, compadre," I interrupted, "leave imperialism out of it; don't start an argument."

He couldn't think of a smart comeback, so he started to leave. If I hadn't been used to his eccentricities, his strange behavior might have surprised me. But knowing him too well, I found his wide repertoire of oddities not particularly amusing.

While he was still facing me, after his brief display of militarism, I said my piece: "Good, based on what you've just told me, from now on, the fishbowl is authorized by one no less than the Lieutenant Colonel! They'd better not try to take it away from me during the next inspection."

"At least, I won't take it."

"Not you, nor anyone else," I warned him. "That is, unless you want a fight on your hands with all twelve of us living here in this cell."

I don't know if Sergeant Cervantes understood that my warning was nothing more than a mere joke. After all, the gesture of Lieutenant Colonel Raúl O'Farril, I imagined, was only a temporary concession reflecting the political whims of Cuban authorities at that time, nothing necessarily to avoid clashes with political prisoners, who actually concerned them very little. (Doesn't the rope usually fray at its weakest point? Didn't the prison system have enough garrisons and sufficient nightsticks and deterrent dungeons?) Rather, it was a reflection of the desperate attempt to improve the impaired image of Cuba's Communist government regarding human rights, one of the preconditions laid down by President Jimmy Carter for lifting the economic embargo imposed by the United States against dictator Fidel Castro.

# CHAPTER 23

# San Ramón and Tres Macíos, Special Torture Chambers

Already for several months we had secretly rewired the electronic door system, allowing us to open the doors at will without the alarm going off in the guards' office. We weren't always able to get to other floors, but some incursions were possible, mainly after six in the afternoon. Movement between the cells within each section of the same floor at any hour of day or night was easy enough. It just required waiting for a guard's carelessness, for errors committed quite often consciously or unconsciously by the prison guard in charge of our custody.

On the eve of visiting day, although the timing for me was quite inopportune, as I needed to write two or three letters to be taken out clandestinely the following morning, José Oscar Rodríguez Terrero paid us a surprise visit in 1404 (he lived in 1405), just to spend a little time with us. It was about 7:00 p.m. when he appeared like a ghost at our front cell door. He struggled to open it, but his short stature prevented him from reaching the trigger lock. Three or four voices rose up together in friendly taunts.

Mario Gavilán opened the door.

José Oscar joked around for a few moments with all of us. He was easy going, at least sometimes. Then he sat down on Húber's bunk and began chatting with the former commander of the Sierra Maestra, reminiscing about the war (during the insurrectionary war against the Batista dictatorship, José Oscar belonged to Column 18 of the Second Eastern Front). Later on, at my insistence, he told us about the many odysseys of his pilgrimages from one prison lockup to another. For the historical record, I'd like to bear witness here on these very pages to his impressive testimony, so that the world and future Cuban generations will know the extent of sadism and cruelty with which Fidel Castro's government treated its political opponents in the prisons of our enslaved island.

"... The journey from Havana to Boniato took seven weeks, because they kept us in prison for many days in Holguín, in jails where we were subjected to torture. We were eight prisoners in total: Jorge Balbuena Calzadilla, Antonio María Rivero Díaz, Gilberto del Río Girón, Alfredo Guevara Sosa, Rodolfo Napoles Miranda, Rafael Trujillo Pacheco, Rolando Nieves Machado, and me. We were moved around in cages, sometimes bound by hands and feet like beasts.

"Our first concentration camp (intended for common prisoners) was Manatí, in Tunas. Then we went on to the prison of Holguín, where we were locked up in a henhouse, tied by hands and feet, always under constant guard. But due to an oversight of the guards, with our teeth, some of us were able to remove the bindings and to shed the blue uniform put onto us by force. Then we were put, barefoot and completely naked, into galleries and dungeons along with common prisoners. It was the middle of December and the cold froze us to the bone. We were kept in those conditions until February, when thanks to a hunger strike that we carried out, after having held several previous ones requesting separation from common prisoners, they decided to move us to Boniato Prison.

"When we finally arrived at Boniato, they locked us up in the cells of the small prison hospital or clinic, again barefoot and completely naked, where we remained several days until they placed us in building 2 C.

"On March 19, 1968, they took thirteen of us to the dungeons of 'La Escalera' (these dungeons were in the same building as the prison headquarters and were the worst at Boniato). That same night of March

19, we were told to get ready to travel, to do our business and gather up our belongings, this last spoken in a sarcastic tone, because we only had the undershorts that we were wearing. Soon, we were again traveling inside a paddy wagon toward an unknown destination.

"At midnight, we arrived at the concentration camp of San Ramón. There, they left José Enrique Vázquez Rosales, Orlando Peña Rodríguez, Alfredo Peña Estrada, Alcides Martínez Calzadilla, Rolando Nieves Machado, and Antonio María Rivero Díaz. The rest of us continued on the journey.

"It was already late morning when we arrived at the concentration camp of Tres Macíos, in the sugarcane region of Bayamo. There, the rest of us were left off: Rafael Trujillo Pacheco, Daniel Morales León, Tomás González Camejo, Silvio Serba Avella, Lázaro Sambrano Cos, Jorge Francisco Valbuena Calzadilla," and, as Jose Oscar called himself, "Oscarito."

"*Special* jail cells had been built for us on the outside of the prison in a paddock: a small rectangle divided into cells 6 feet long by 18 or 19 inches wide. The height was about 2 meters and the roof was perforated, so that when it rained, drops falling down on our bodies became an additional torture. In each of those dungeons, five or six prisoners were crammed together."

"Tell me one thing," I interrupted Oscarito. "How could two or three of you manage to sleep in such a small space? Because only 6 feet long by 18 or 19 inches wide is not much space, it seems to me. More or less like this, right?" I marked a similar rectangle on the floor with my foot.

"Just imagine: while one rested with his legs stretched out and took a snooze, the other two remained standing, if we were three, as in my case at first. Later, they put me alone. We peed," he continued, "by sticking our ding-a-ling out through the bars. I almost peed inside [laughs] and we put shit wrapped in paper up against the door so that urine did not flow back inside. There we saw an eruption of millions of worms that sometimes squeezed in and invaded everything. At the beginning, when we felt a sting, we thought it was from mosquitoes, of which there was a tremendous plague, but then we discovered that the bastard worms were biting us... even on our faces, my friend! There was no light in the cell, so all the time we remained in the dark. The food was terrible and rationed to the maximum, just like water, which was given to us in mere droplets. It was more or less like being on a semi-hunger strike. Also, we were completely bare, because after we arrived at Tres Macíos, they stripped us even of our underwear and shoes. It was a depressing scene: all of us stark naked. But I'd never seen more fortitude and cohesion than was demonstrated by that small group, humble but determined to maintain our dignity and defend our rights as political prisoners, and as human beings, at any price, and even with our fingernails."

Oscarito's eyes said more than all the words in the world. His transparent gaze reflected the admiration and affection he felt for his fellow comrades in misfortune.

"The water given us a drink," continued José Oscar "came from the same trough used by horses and cattle grazing in the surrounding area. We found that out from a common prisoner who sympathized with political prisoners and, in solidarity, passed along that information. We created a tremendous scandal, and from that moment on, they had to leave the hallway door open, so we could monitor them and make sure with our own eyes that we weren't being given water from the cattle trough.

"When distributing our food, the military entered the hallway wearing rubber boots and a scarf or handkerchief over their nose and mouth because of the terrible stench of urine and feces accumulated on the cement floor for weeks on end. One day an old guard wanted to bring us food just out of curiosity," Oscarito recalled. "He wanted to personally witness the experiment, I don't know why. But he failed to cover his nose and mouth and, as soon as he arrived there, started to vomit and vomit. He almost lost his liver. He left in a flash with his shoes all covered with shit and piss.

"Tres Macíos guards are the most uncivilized ones I've ever seen in my whole life, real savages, even worse than those of Isla de Pinos, which is saying a lot. You might see them wearing military boots, all covered with shit, or tennis shoes... or even sandals. But, of course, they always carried a bayonet and a rifle slung over their shoulder.

"Approximately 50 days after we were locked up in those dungeons, seeing that we weren't being broken, they decided to try another tactic. They put me in another lockup identical in size with two common prisoners. They threatened to rape me. Enraged, I reported them to the guards and, in the ensuing struggle, we all wallowed in the shit accumulated in the corridor. In the end, I was overpowered and put back in with the common prisoners. 'Go ahead and rape him,' they were told, and the door was slammed shut behind me.

"You can only imagine the swearing that I let out. I swore on my mother and everything! Something that I don't usually do, but somehow it relieved my powerlessness. I shouted out, calling them fascists, and, indeed, they are worse than Nazis," he paused to revive his memory and continued. "After that, when I explained to the common prisoners that I was a political prisoner and why I was there, they became friendlier. Or they might actually have been terrified, seeing my scuffle with the guards. To reassure them, I tried to soothe them. I explained that it required a strong spirit to resist with dignity those hellish black holes, to be brave. But they had a very different concept of dignity, much less rigorous in their case, perfectly understandable. I also told them our status was different, and that our imprisonment was for different reasons, so regardless of human relations and their willingness receive us, we political prisoners always saw ourselves obliged in principle to reject all coexistence with common prisoners.

"They understood what I meant. That same day, some of my companions and I declared a hunger and thirst strike, demanding an end to that inadmissible violation of privacy and dignity.

"Five days into that situation, the common prisoners locked up with me took matters into their own hands and, early in the morning, they began issuing cries of help, bellows so harrowing that they ended up getting themselves out of there.

"Since that was precisely what we had called for in principle, the Communists thought that by removing the common prisoners, the strike was over. But by then, we had already decided to continue without eating or drinking until we were removed altogether from Tres Macíos.

"Due to the inhumane conditions that we had been enduring for months, especially since arriving at those special dungeons, then with added starvation, our physical condition deteriorated with amazing speed. Even before we'd started the strike, Daniel Morales, because of a gastrointestinal infection, stood on the brink of death.

"When the guards realized its severity, they arrived with a doctor, who proceeded to immediately give him an IV. They hooked it up right there, with his arm strapped to the grille of the gate, above all those droppings.

"At the end of the tenth day without ingesting any water or food, my dehydration was so severe that I became comatose. I went in and out of consciousness. When they found me, they became so alarmed that when they couldn't find the padlock key, they opened up part of the wall (their pounding aroused me) and dragged me out by my feet. It was already night time. I was carried between two soldiers, holding me up by the arms and legs, over to a guard post, and there I was given serum. I heard the doctor say, despite my state of semi-consciousness, 'If I can get half a liter into him, I can save him.' His voice reached me as if from another world, almost in a whisper. As soon as I had taken in 1000 c.c., they took me back the same way to the black hole. After that, they took me to San Ramón.

"My buddies experienced a tactic even crueler: whenever one of them became very ill, they were taken out, and as they refused to receive medical care unless they were removed from Tres Macíos altogether (our request in continuing the strike), they were tied up with ropes on a wooden cross, and kept hanging there until their veins took in the last drop of serum, a torture that usually lasted between six and eight hours.

"Within two or three days after I had arrived at San Ramón, six colleagues were taken first from Tres Macíos and the remaining four who remained on strike at Tres Macíos were transferred in turn to San Ramón." Then José Oscar explained further, "Because of their deplorable health, days before we went on strike, Lázaro Zambrano Cos and Daniel Morales had been sent to Boniato's infirmary.

"At San Ramón, we continued the strike.

"Three weeks later, five of us were taken back to Boniato, but instead of putting us together with the rest of the political prisoners, we were confined to special pavilions near the prison headquarters. To our surprise, after arriving at Boniato, in those pavilions, we found Rolando Nieves, one of the last six who had been sent to Tres Macíos. They also had gone on strike there as soon they were locked in those horrendous dungeons. But because prior conditions had left them all with very broken health, within a few short days, the physical (and psychological) condition of Nieves Machado began deteriorating at an alarming rate. The director of the concentration camp believed that it was preferable that he be sent to die at Boniato. But Rolando had barely survived and so in that prison, we found him tied to a bed, skeletal and half idiotic. He had decided to continue his hunger strike until he found out the status of his comrades. As soon as we got to Boniato, we convinced him to stop his fast, following what had been agreed upon by the initial group at Tres Macíos.

"Our consensus tactic was to go on with the strike until we were moved to a prison for political prisoners. That way, we avoided a sterile stalemate, and at the same time, set an example for those who were unlucky enough to be left behind. So that's what happened. And that meant that everyone came back to Boniato, although in different stages. One group prevailed with only a 21-day strike; others with 37 days or more; and some, like Orlando Peña and Antonio María Rivero were forced to make a greater sacrifice: approximately 70 days was the duration of the martyrdom of their fast." José Oscar paused, then added, "Those two flirted with death. Remember that Rivero was a corpulent man. He weighed over 180 pounds before they took him there and when they joined us at Boniato, I just carried him by myself as if he were a rag doll.

"Another who seemed to be mentally affected was Alfredo Peña, Orlando's cousin. He would only comment about a beautiful woman he had sex with at five years of age. Completely false. His legs and arms seemed to be made of jelly. Someone got a little creosote in the infirmary and put it on his testicles to kill the fungus that was devouring him.

"An indelible image, among many, was when I saw Alcides. He looked like he had escaped from a Nazi extermination camp. All skin and bones, very wild-eyed. His speech was garbled and his smile, a frightening grin.

"Silvio Selva Abella, still on strike, was taken out before me, completely seized up and almost blind. When they tried to straighten him out at the sentry point, the cry that escaped him was heartbreaking. As happened before with Morales, the common prisoners yelled that another political had died. Silvio disappeared. At the end of that horrible way of the cross, we met again in Boniato. Selva had become so disoriented that he knew nothing about the world around him.

"That process left us all like idiots... Tomás, Trujillo, and I, not so much. Mentally, we three were okay. Well, pretty good," he clarified. "Among the rest, some were crazier and others less so, but in the end, all showed a high degree of madness, which, in some cases, persisted for more than five years. For me, Jorge Francisco had proved contagious, since I began to imitate all of his gestures and repeat his words like an echo. I had not even noticed whether the poor guy was crazy as a consequence of the strike and of the torture that he had suffered at Tres Macíos. I realized it when my mental fog lifted and he attacked the guard on duty where we were being held incommunicado. He also punched the director, and, on another occasion, when the post was left unguarded, he escaped and appeared in the office of the prison director, barefoot and in underpants. It gave the officials gathered there with the director a terrific scare when Jorge Francisco pushed the door open and entered. Luckily, they were able to calm him down, and take him back to our pavilion without a major incident. The guard in charge was arrested, of course.

"Days later, Jorge Francisco attempted suicide. I don't know how he had gotten ahold of and hidden away twenty tablets —I don't remember exactly of what– that the nurse had given him on orders of the military doctor, to help treat his mental imbalance.

"He was miraculously saved. We thought he was going to die. From then on, we redoubled our surveillance of him. But crazy people can be very clever. It's incredible the things that he thought up, trying to throw us off. Nonetheless, I was well aware that he was obsessed with killing himself, so the situation was extremely delicate, since any lack of vigilance on our part could result in fatal, unpredictable consequences.

"A few days later, we were sent to the small prison hospital lockup. When we were gathered there together, all of us involved in the strike who were somewhat recovered physically, were moved along with other comrades who had been brought from Havana —altogether about 120 in total —to La Cabaña Prison. It was on August 5, 1968. Those who, as the result of prolonged fasting and torture had become crazy or paralyzed, they sent to Castillo del Príncipe. After two weeks, Jorge Francisco Balbuena Calzadilla, in his suicide obsession, jumped from the top floor of the hospital down to the "Star" (a granite square inside the prison), dying almost instantly. For us, it was a huge blow, very painful news. In this tragic way, that unhappy man had ended his tormented life.

"Colonel Medardo Lemus Otaño, National Chief of Jails and Prisons, in an inspection tour at that time to Castillo del Príncipe, cynically accused the jailers of that eastern province of being 'uncivilized.' He told the inmates that he, Lemus himself, had been shocked when he saw Tres Macíos, to such an extent that he had given the order to demolish it instantly," José Oscar told us, concluding his chilling tale.

But San Ramón and Tres Macíos were not the only experimentation centers used by Cuba's Communist government to annihilate the spirit of Cuban political prisoners and impose, through barbarism and terror, a status identical to that of common prisoners: simply applying the same cruel measures as per the express will of dictator Fidel Castro to all the hundreds of prisons and concentration camps throughout and across the island. Thus, completely naked, barefoot, crushed by hunger and thirst, their flesh lacerated by systematic and brutal beatings, the helpless victims had to rise with renewed stoicism up from the ashes to confront the executioners of the regime and the ironies of fate, heroically salvaging their honor, their most valuable attribute and the only thing that could never be taken away, even in death, by the vilified enemy.

# CHAPTER 24

# Surprise Transfer to a
# Mystery Destination

The night was warm, viscous, dense, like all July nights at the Combinado del Este prison. In cell 1404 of building # 1, some were getting ready to sleep, while others read, joked around, or told stories of their life, real or imagined. The prisoner, like a child, has a prodigious imagination that wanders from reality to fantasy with incredible ease. With his reserves of real experiences depleted, the unfortunate inmate relies on fantasy, not only because he needs to talk, to have something never before told to his companions in misfortune, but because it pleases him. It confirms that his world has not stopped, and so he lets himself get carried away by dreams like a cork floating adrift.

Unexpectedly, a group of officers burst into hall A.

"Macagua! *Here comes the macagua! Right now!*" several voices rang out together (shouting a nickname used by prisoners anticipating a process of pardons).

"The macagua," several prisoners on the list of pardons called out.

The soldiers stopped after arriving in the first cell, 1401. Immediately, the lieutenant marching at the head of the procession proceeded to read off a list of names: Jorge Valls Arango, José Antonio López Muñoz, Roger Reyes Hernández, Víctor Miguel Cantón Gómez, Silvino

Rodríguez Barrientos, Osvaldo Figueroa Gálvez, Reinaldo Figueroa Gálvez, Eduardo Rodríguez Capote, and then, after a pause, he ordered:

"Those inmates, gather up all your belongings!"

"When?" asked Silvino Rodríguez.

"Right away," replied the lieutenant who had just fired off the list of names.

"Okay, but don't rush us," protested Eduardo Rodríguez Capote. "We need some time to collect our stuff."

José Antonio López, protested as well. Truth be told no one was rushing them, but it was normal for them to imagine it. In Cuban prisons, political prisoners have suffered so much humiliation and outrage that the simple presence of a political police officer puts them in a bad mood, makes their hair stand on end.

There was no response. The delegation of military men advanced a few steps up to the door of cell 1402. Total silence ensued.

Then: "Let's see. We now call on the following to also collect their belongings: Miguel Ángel Álvarez Cardentey, Eleno Oviedo Alvárez, Eusebio de Jesús Peñalver Mazorra, Reinaldo López-Lima Rodríguez, and Sturmio Mesa Schutman."

In cell 1403, only two were called out: Ramón Grau Alsina and Alberto Grau Sierra.

Next, they arrived at 1404. Lieutenant Nilo politely greeted those standing gathered behind the bars of the cell door. This officer's mild-mannered appearance adeptly hid his real hypocrisy. His ability to orchestrate reprisals had gained him a privileged position within the prison directorate.

"Jose L. Pujals Mederos, Servando Jiménez, Remberto Zamora Chirino, Gavilán Mario Sánchez, Luis M. Zúñiga Rey, Ernesto Díaz Rodríguez," the lieutenant read aloud and repeated the same refrain as previously, that all must gather up their belongings.

From what I could see, the measure's reach promised to be extensive. As many as 40 prisoners still remained to be called. The officers made their way toward hall B.

"Hmm. This gives me bad vibes!" Húber expressed with his habitual distrust. "And not just a little. I don't like the composition of the group that has been called so far."

"It also gives me some pretty bad vibes," said Remberto Zamora. "Those serpents would like to devour us, always thinking about evil. They don't fool me."

"You're a real scoundrel," interrupted Bacallaito in a mocking tone. "They are just bringing them all to a farm where they can detoxify them a little before pardoning them and still you complain."

"Yes, yes; I'm going to complain a lot," protested Zamorita.

For several weeks, there had been quite insistent rumors about the transfer of *plantado* prisoners to a farm on the outskirts of Havana. No one knew the source of the news, which made us think that it was not more than one of many pitches thrown out by the prison directorate to misinform us. Some of us leaned toward believing it to be true; others, the majority, dismissed the so-called transfer rumors for various reasons. Still, the possibility that the government would include in the pardons program all political prisoners began circulating in those days. In an official bulletin emitted by the Interior Ministry once a month to all prisons on the island, based on an agreement signed in December 1978 by dictator Fidel Castro and members of the "Committee of 75," the Reverend Reyes, chairman of that committee, even claimed that the Cuban government had agreed to release in December 1979 all 610 prisoners who had been excluded. If so, in fact, by the end of year, there would be no political prisoners in Cuban prisons. Therefore, it made little or no sense that the government would carry out a transfer only five months from the date indicated.

On the other hand, more realistically, if the exclusion of the 20% of the damned, announced by Castro at the press conference, was to be the actual position, then sending out to a farm concentration camp those prisoners still in rebellion seemed totally unlikely. However, whether one or the other, now that 60 *plantados* had been called to gather with all their belongings indicated that we would not be staying in Combinado del Este.

Great fanfare was heard throughout the fourth floor. In the north wing, all cell doors had been opened so that prisoners could go to the dining room as soon as they had picked up their belongings, which pleased us greatly, as it allowed us to officially move from one side to another freely, coordinating with our closest friends among those who had been called and to exchange mainly papers that should be saved at all costs, in my case, also saving a small radio and 24 one-and-a-half volt batteries that only a few days before my step-daughter María Isabel had passed to me on a family visit.

The first thing I did was repackage the little radio, about three inches wide, wrapping it with a piece of nylon to protect it from sweat, then planning to tape it with the sticky side out to carry in my underwear. I thought of doing the same with the 24 tiny batteries, but it would have been too much of a load to carry around on my body, so instead, I hid them inside a packet of powdered milk. I tested it out and found they were well camouflaged there, not detectable by simple touch. The only risk I faced was a search by one of those super-extremists who would open up the packet and dig out the milk by hand or empty it onto a paper on the floor. The odds of that occurring were 50% or less, so to lighten the load that seemed like a worthwhile venture.

Now we faced a future transfer without having the faintest idea about our fate, and the worst thing was uncertainty about the thoroughness of the search to which we would be subjected. Faced with this situation, to avoid excessive risk, I coordinated with Miguel Ángel Álvarez Cardentey to take care of the radio, while I would be responsible for an important manuscript. Having confronted this main stumbling block, I breathed a little easier and patiently took on the task of collecting my few belongings. To make handling easier for me, I divided everything between two sacks. I ended up with plenty of time and space, lots of space. As for the fish (as mentioned before, I had been given some pet fish, along with a fishbowl, by a common prisoner allowed to work outside), I had my doubts about whether to take them. Finally, I decided to try to take them, considering also that possibly not everyone was being called to make the transfer. Of the twelve *plantado* prisoners in our cell, half of us were going out that night. Some would be excluded, according to all indications. Of the six remaining in 1404, Húber Matos was the only one I had confidence would care properly for the fish (as he done so before in my absence). However, his punishment of 20 years would end on October 21 of that same year, that is, three months hence. Although the tyrant had stated in his press conference that Matos would not be included in the pardons program, we knew that our esteemed colleague had received international solidarity for years as an anti-Communist leader, in particular from Costa Rican President Rodrigo Carazo, so Castro would have no choice but to order his immediate release as soon as his conviction had expired. Tony Lamas, on the other hand, would be completing his 20 years on April 17, 1981, only a short time away, and, despite his vertical attitude and pointed rebelliousness, we imagined that he could be one of the next to be pardoned. As for the others, Gustavo Areces, Heriberto Bacallao, and Argelio Aparicio, it was hoped that they would not be excluded, and the release of Jesús Silva Pontigo had already been officially decreed.

Remembering the globs of transparent plastic material that previously Pedro González had inflated by immersing them in boiling water and blowing them up like balloons, I immediately discarded the idea of taking the fish bowl itself with me. We all put our heads together, anticipating that, inevitably, I would lose the fish bowl in the inspection despite my strong objections, and secondly, that even if the fish were not taken away, only a miracle would save that glass bowl's arrival in one piece to our new destination.

When Areces saw me tossing the fish into the two plastic receptacles that I had created, he cried out to the sky: "Look at him, look at him! Didn't I tell you that this guy was a phony?"

And after a long pull on the tiny stub of his cigar, he shouted, "There were those who actually believed you! Who believed you saying that the fish belonged to everyone in the cell."

"Be quiet, my friend," I interrupted him. "Stop all this fussing. You know very well that the fish belong to us all… It just so happens that I am responsible for their care and custody."

Heriberto Bacallao joined in the fun: "Listen, this guy really knows a world about psychology!"

Feeling supported, Areces returned to the attack: "So the fish belong to everyone," he repeated, and then yelling at me full in my face, "Scoundrel!"

"Go ahead, damn it, this guy is really good, itching for a fight, a tremendous fight! Come on, you want me to leave them with you? Just let me know; now's the time to speak up."

"Hear, hear! Don't you dare–break his arm," Servando joked.

"And you're going to believe his farce?" inquired Gustavo Areces.

"Why not?"

"Because this guy is telling stories, nothing more."

"None of that. What happened is that you are biased against him, because he didn't want to pass the electrical current on to you," Servando argued.

And turning to Matos, he asked: "Húber, what do you think about this controversy?

Matos shrugged his shoulders, smiling, instantly reaffirming his decision to stay out of the fray, saying, "I pass," then "knocking on wood" using these terms popular among Cuban domino players to mean, "I don't know anything" or *I don't have a dog in this fight.*"

"Pepe, what do you think of that?" Now Servando addressed José Pujals, trying to getting someone to back up his efforts to make Areces look foolish.

"Never mind, I'm Chinese!" said Pepe, who had just filled up his third or fourth bag of possessions.

"I am Chinese," and "I pass," mean more or less the same in Cuba —*"No comment."*

That night had been tremendous fun, like many other nights in our little cell universe, but the need to get our things together hastily, the uncertainty of a journey to an unknown destination, and regret about having to leave behind some valuable companions in 1404, all of them our true brothers, cast a shadow.

Long after we had already collected our belongings, they came for us. From the dining room of the fourth floor, they sent us down to the dining room on the ground floor, where we stayed half an hour until they began to call us out, this time in groups of twenty.

I was on the first list. We had not yet been searched and when they told us that the bus was waiting for us in front of the main gate of building #1, I had a sudden flash of optimism. Never before had I been transported from one prison to another by bus. If it was happening now, that wasn't a bad sign, on the contrary, a magnificent one.

"So far everything is going well," I dared to think, maybe a good star was shining down on me that night, because, most fortuitously, I got a window seat. After so many years without having the slightest access to the outside, suddenly I was given a magnificent opportunity to look out, painful as it would be to see a deteriorating and bleak Havana landscape. I imagine that my colleagues were equally optimistic, as indicated by their joyful faces and lively chatter. For the first time, we began to breathe easier after having been commanded to pack up so urgently without the slightest explanation of our next destination.

The first bus started moving out. Since the fourth-floor cells had remained open, hundreds of arms protruded through the vertical openings in the building's façade, all waving excitedly. All our comrades left behind shouted at the same time in a beautiful gesture of fraternity, voicing friendly phrases, familiar words, and, until we said goodbye, emitting a familiar whistle through which we were able to identify a friend.

The bus slowly advanced about fifty meters until it passed into the inside lane bordering the double fence with sentry towers and dogs comprising the prison security cordon. Almost without stopping, it took a left turn and continued on slowly. Another left turn, after about a hundred meters, and we found ourselves opposite the visiting room. Finally, the bus stopped opposite the main gate to the exit, where a guard with a paper in his hands came inside to verify we were 20 prisoners, a rather routine operation, then we traveled outside the prison compound accompanied by the officers in charge of the operation and various guards armed with automatic rifles.

Before us lay the road that linked the prison with Monumental Road, the highway leading to the city of Havana. The driver was authorized to continue and immediately resumed. However, instead of moving forward, as soon we reached the gate, the bus turned right and stopped between the buildings of the prison directorate, 50 meters from Post No. 1.

There a considerable number of officers had gathered, including the director and about 20 very young guards, boys conscripted into obligatory military service (S.M.O.), who lined up on both sides of a narrow corridor through which we were led, each of us carrying our belongings to the inside of a theater used by the military. We were not told why we were there, but were commanded to take a seat. As we were allowed to sit wherever we wanted, almost all of us, being suspicious, went to sit up in the last row, where we had a fuller picture.

Fifteen minutes passed before the second group arrived and a while later the last 60 showed up with all the crates, occupying more than half the seats. Above, on the stage, sat a wooden table and, behind it, a single chair, a puzzling development that captured our attention. The only thing that occurred to me was that someone would show up to lead us in worship. I imagined that many others might think the same. This idea gained force when I observed that Captain Andrés Rodríguez went up to the podium accompanied by a G-2 Lieutenant, whom the prisoners knew by the name of Roberto.

Captain Andrés remained standing for a few seconds watching the show. Then he sat down in the chair. He was dressed in civilian clothes. His companion, standing at his side, leaned over to him, whispering something in his ear. Because of the distance, it was impossible for us prisoners to hear anything unless spoken aloud. Both men smiled and looked up toward the side aisle where a platoon of guards had just burst in, preceded by several officers of the political police. Altogether, they totaled about 15 and took up positions around the theater. We were then ordered to approach them so they could search our belongings.

As usual, the first group went up and each prisoner tried to commandeer the guard that most suited him. I preferred to wait to make sure, first, what type of search would be taking place and, next, which guard appeared least demanding. A while later, already convinced, I took my things to a young recruit. While higher authorities working with political prisoners were carefully vetted, the vast majority of young people in compulsory military service were sympathetic toward us. At the beginning, due to the widespread repression in the country, a goodly proportion of them ran a little scared. But, as they became more aware of our treatment, our moral terms, they sought to approach us in one way or another to subtly manifest their dissatisfaction with the regime of misery and slavery imposed on them by the tyrant now taking his turn in office.

That one of those boys might be standing there with a bayonet in his hands or a rifle pointed at us, did not mean at all that he supported the Communist dictatorship. These young men did not belong to the breed of the privileged; they were simply part of the oppressed people, subject to all kinds of humiliation, hunger, and blackmail. Victims of terror, they only pretended to escape reprisal from others who perhaps were pretending also.

"I think I'm going to come out of this better than I expected," I thought with satisfaction when the recruit took one of my crates of books that I had placed on top, and gave them back to me without even looking inside. Then he extracted the two plastic containers holding the fish without even opening them.

"Water?" He just asked me.

"Water," I meant to affirm, but without thinking, I replied: "Fish."

The youthful guard smiled with the craftiness of unbelievers, imagining safely that it was a joke. He shook his head a couple of times and handed me the two containers. But, seeing the pack of books in my hands, before giving me time to set them down, he placed the containers on the floor as if anxious to finish an unpleasant job. Then he took the plastic bag of powdered milk with the batteries inside.

That was a difficult moment. My pulse raced and I couldn't help a grimace of annoyance when I saw him untying the bag, or rather pretending to untie it, because he had decided not to open it, also placing it on the floor next to the two temporary fish tanks.

After only about five minutes, the recruit gave a nod to all of my belongings. But when I was about to return to the last row of seats where I'd been sitting before to observe the rest of the show, feeling now out of danger, Captain Andrés and Lieutenant Roberto invited me to go up on the stage.

"Bring the crates also," the captain ordered, seeing that I had left them in a corner in a vain attempt to evade a second search that I imagined might be carried it out with greater meticulousness by those two sinister characters of counterintelligence.

"They have already been searched," I said, trying to prevent them from falling into their hands.

"We know," the captain replied, "but anyway, we want to check them out to give us something to entertain us."

Lieutenant Roberto gave me a cynical smile.

I went up onto the stage.

As might be expected, their "entertainment" focused on everything that smelled of paper and writing. Each book was examined page by page and, after the printed books, they passed on to my handwritten notebooks. Among them were a collection of my most recent poems, most unpublished and written during the last hunger strike, a copy of my book *An Urgent Testimony,* published in 1977, and another of *Carousel.*

After reading 10 or 12 poems, Lieutenant Roberto asked, "They're yours, right?"

He knew very well they were mine.

"I don't know what you mean," I replied, acting puzzled.

"I mean, did you write them?"

"Ah, yes... you mean what you just read, right?"

"And what about the others in the agenda?"

"What agenda?"

"Notebook."

"Yes."

The conversation had turned into an ironic wordplay.

"So, are you also a poet?" the lieutenant asked sarcastically.

"Not me, and what about you?"

"What, you are not a poet?"

"Not really."

"What's the point? Didn't you just say you wrote those poems?"

"Agreed, but someone who writes verse is not necessarily a poet. I, for example, am not."

"So why was your book published?"

"What book?"

"An Urgent Testimony."

"Oh, it was published? I never knew."

"Published by Alpha 66."

"Thank goodness. I was already thinking that you were going to tell me the CIA."

"Alpha and the CIA are the same thing."

"Leave that to fools!"

Captain Andrés, determined to discover the formula of the neutron bomb within any of my books, kept scrutinizing them page by page only occasionally looking up for brief periods. Moreover, upon hearing my words refuting the stupid argument of his officemate, he intervened only to insinuate that it was a waste of time to discuss such nonsense with me.

"When were you taken prisoner, Ernesto?" Lieutenant Roberto asked, changing the subject.

"I've been around for a few years."

"How many?"

"I can't tell you if it's been 10 or 15; I've not been paying attention."

"Your family is in the United States, right?"

"I think so."

"How many children do you have?"

"If only you knew; now you've got me thinking. I'm not quite sure if there are two or three."

"What would you do if you were reprieved?"

"Uf! I have so many plans. One of them is to travel around the world on a palm trunk. I'm thinking of setting out from the coast of Baja California for a first stop in Hawaii."

"Stop it, stop," Lieutenant Roberto interrupted.

Most of the guys had already returned to their seats with their inspected belongings.

Again, Lieutenant Roberto spoke up: "Returning to your poems:

I actually found some very interesting. I'd like to be able to read them more calmly. If I borrowed your notebook, would you care?" There was an undertone of malice in his words.

"No problem, but let's define our terms; if you are going to keep it, you can just tell me now outright and I will give it up for lost. But if you tell me that it's just borrowed and still keep it, I'll ask to have it back. Note that I am telling you now so that later when the problem arises, there will be no lamentations accusing me of being argumentative."

The officer affirmed that he only wanted to borrow it, as a private matter between him and me. This would be an exception, he explained, taking into account that G-2 already had made copies of all those poems, thanks to my notebook taken months before by Dr. Kouri. The rest of my books and notebooks, including a testimony about the murder of the former revolutionary commander and leader of Alpha 66, César Páez Sánchez, had been confiscated by Captain Andrés Rodríguez.

"All this must be sent to State Security. They will look at it and decide whether it can be returned," he told me while I protested the outrage of this new looting.

I was well aware that the books and manuscripts, including the notebook of poems that Lieutenant Roberto said he wanted me to lend him, would go on to swell the political police files. The measure wasn't surprising. I knew their methods. It was not the first time that I was the victim of indiscriminate repressive dispossession, nor would it be the last. It was part of a pattern of punishing me. About the rest of my things, they showed no special interest. Most were not even taken out of the crate, making me pretty happy regarding the batteries and fish. However, just when I'd thought that I had finally escaped those leeches, Lieutenant Roberto then asked me to leave all my property there on the table, and to follow him.

Soon I found myself walking behind him along a narrow corridor behind the stage. When we got to the area of the bathrooms, the officer stopped. "Go inside," he ordered "and take off your clothes please."

The bathroom was illuminated. Through the only window, you could see the director's office. The officer closed the blinds and stood facing the door two steps away from me.

"What is all this about?" I ask harshly.

"You know very well."

"All I know very well is that if you think I would be foolish enough to be wearing something on my body, you screwed up," I replied while unbuttoning my shirt, pretending to be very angry. "You're wasting your time."

"You think so?"

"Here," I said dryly, putting my clothes in his hands.

Of the 60 prisoners, I was the only one who had been ordered to undress. I did not refuse to abide by the order, considering that my refusal might lead to a generalization of the measure, and that was precisely to be avoided at all costs. If, for some reason, I'd had the misfortune of falling into the hands of these two counter-intelligence officers, the fair and intelligent option was to bear my cross. The official checked the shirt thoroughly, seam by seam, fold by fold. Then he did the same thing with the pants, until, convinced that he was plowing in the sea, he decided to end the search.

"Could this be interpreted as a privilege that you wanted to have with me?" I asked sarcastically, while I got dressed.

"You may interpret it anyway you like, Ernesto Díaz, but no one knows better than you that we dare not take our eyes off you," he said, and, after looking me up and down, with an arrogant gesture, he indicated that I should follow him.

It must have been 2 a.m. when, at last, I was freed from the nuisance harassment of the political police. I could finally relax in one of the theater seats. Very few inmates still remained to be searched, about 8 or 10 who had waited until the very last minute. Among them was Silvino Rodríguez, whom the counter-intelligence officers never let out of their sight. He seemed to be having trouble with his papers. Among other things, he was stripped of all his family correspondence retained to keep alive the memory of his loved ones, although he had been allowed to bring it all into the prison to begin with, according to official policy.

The rest of the morning went by without incident. From time to time, I remembered the fish and checked to see if they were okay. Sometimes, I left them uncovered to make sure they were getting enough oxygen. But, shortly after, the guppies began jumping up and falling out, forcing me to cover them up again to save them from suicide.

"Behave yourselves, all right? Let's see how we get out of here," I told them sternly before putting them back into the water.

Certainly, given the frequency with which the fish relapsed, it was fair to assume that my words to them went in one ear and out the other, just as with any other naughty guy, my younger self included, as when my mother had told me not to throw any more stones at the church bell, or to stop dissecting lizards.

Already at dawn, two soldiers began giving each of us a bread roll with cheese. Although it was the first time in prison that we had been offered such an exquisite breakfast, we were still angry about our bad night and the prior incident with Silvino, so we began rejecting the sandwich and the others, with few exceptions, followed suit, an irrational act, if you will, but perfectly understandable by those familiar with prisoners' reactions.

Around six in the morning, with an empty stomach, I was loaded onto a prison bus, along with 19 others, into one of the so-called "kennels," divided into two fully enclosed chambers locking ten of us inside each. As we could barely fit into such a small space, the crates with our belongings were piled into the compartment for the custodians, leaving only enough room on the seats for them to sit. We immediately began to sweat profusely. After 40 minutes of an agonizing wait, the motor began to purr. A few seconds later, the cage was on its way. We were kept in the dark about our destination.

During the first hour of the trip, we made multiple guesses.

"Now we must be close," someone said.

"Surely, it has to be a new farm prison camp," opined another.

From time to time, we heard the harsh hooting sirens of patrol cars and motorcycles escorting us. In Cuba, transfers of prisoners tend to be carried out under strong police custody which includes, among other vehicles, a number of the G-2's alfitas [Alfa Romeo police cars] because those sinister characters had to be present for everything to do with repression and the security of Castro's hostages. The deployment of security forces, apparently exaggerated to a ridiculous extent, was also due to the need to maintain a climate of terror among the civilian population. In our country, frequent dramatic movements of inmates from one a prison to another are organized with the main objective being to destabilize prisoners, but, in turn, to remind the citizens of that enslaved island of the price to pay by those not resigned to always live down on their knees.

Several hours passed while we were being transported like animals, leaving behind Combinado del Este, indicating that we were traveling well beyond the boundaries of Havana province. Some dozed off after a night of insomnia and stress fatigue. Others chatted or told old stories to a captive audience since it was impossible for us to avoid even the most mundane conversations. From time to time, someone would speculate on our destination, mostly as a joke, as our disorientation was total.

At approximately 2:00 p.m., we stopped at an uninhabited concentration camp in the central part of the island, near the city of Santa Clara. There they ordered us out of the cages, still policed by a cordon of heavily armed guards and a dozen German Shepherd dogs. Some prisoners who knew the area explained that the name of that detention center was Preprensado. High walls surrounded a huge warehouse designed for constructing pre-fab wall boards and pre-cast concrete columns and a single dining hall remained still standing, blocking the view to the outside. In the courtyard, the grass was very overgrown.

Our stay in Preprensado was very brief, just time to use the restroom and consume a spam sandwich and a lemon soda. Mario Gavilán refused to eat anything for fear of vomiting when we started out again, as the swaying of the cage tends to produce terrible dizziness, so he gave me his sandwich. Guillermo Rivas Porta, who at that moment was talking with me, looked at me enviously, but when I gave him half, his eyes gleamed and he embraced me joyfully.

Our next stop was in Camagüey, at Kilo 7 prison. It must have been between nine and ten in the evening when we arrived at that prison. There we were given a meal of macaroni and a boiled egg. To our surprise, we were told that we would be spending the night there and would continue the journey at dawn. This was good news because it would give us time to rest after our very tiring, cramped travels. The 60 prisoners were divided between two adjacent halls apparently intended to be a dining room with multiple tables inside, which many used for sleeping. Others of us, less fortunate, had to lie down on the floor, which, thanks to our extreme physical exhaustion was not an obstacle as we slept there with legs outstretched.

It was still dark when we woke up for breakfast. When they returned us to the cages half an hour later, it was daybreak.

At 1:30 in the afternoon, we arrived at to our destination, the dark eastern prison of Boniato. It was July 24, 1979. During the 950 km of travel between Havana and Boniato prison, most of us were carrying at least 5 or 6 pounds of weight, and some, such as Rivas Porta, much more. Maybe this can convey a better sense of the effects of the stifling heat that we were forced to endure, something truly inhuman, not to mention the agony of being crammed together more than 25 hours pressed up against each other without room to extend our legs to avoid cramps and swelling. After we were submitted to another rigorous search (this time nobody escaped the humiliation of having to take off our clothes), we were sent to Pavilion A of building 5, consisting of a small dining room and 40 cells 2.5 meters by 1.5 meters.

As might be expected, as soon as we entered the cell, I uncovered the first fish container, but found them all floating belly up, making a terrible stink. When I had earlier asked a Boniato guard if they were still alive, he had rushed to cover up the tank, responding slyly: *"Yes, yes, all are alive."*

I rarely miss an opportunity to voice an objection, but this time, I did not respond to the mockery of our jailer because I had been focused on salvaging an essential document of Gutiérrez Menoyo's. The guard had failed to look into the second container, telling me in a confidential tone that although it was forbidden to have animals in prison, since I had made such an effort to bring them from Havana, he was going to "turn a blind eye."

The ill-intentioned goon could not have imagined that he was the one being mocked this time, not the prisoner. By one of those whims of fate, the guppies in the second container had miraculously survived.

This time, we were lucky to be able to choose our cellmates and our cells. Mario Gavilán, Miguel Ángel Álvarez Cardentey, my fish and I were imprisoned in number 29.

A few days later, Gavilán moved to number 32, taking advantage that it was empty and was almost opposite 29, since the cells were divided into two rows of odd and even numbers facing each other, separated by a corridor approximately 2.5 meters wide.

# CHAPTER 25

# Second Group of Political Prisoners Arrives at Boniato

The day after our arrival at Boniato we were surprised by another convoy coming from Combinado del Este prison. The bulk of these new prisoners was also from the fourth floor, but from the south wing of the so-called "underpants" unit, comrades who in the summer of 1968, when the government had agreed, after a mass hunger strike, to restore the yellow uniforms of *plantado* political prisoners, had nonetheless refused to accept that in a gesture of admirable sacrifice. This new group also included ten *plantados* from the second floor of the north wing, and some 15 mostly young people, who, although they belonged to the re-education plan, still maintained a rebellious attitude. These last were sent to building 1A, designated for rehabilitation plan inmates. The rest were installed in hall 4A, separated from us by a courtyard about 40 meters wide set with stone slabs. Above 4A were the punishment dungeons, 40 in total.

We could not avoid clashes with the prison's wardens starting from the very first day of our arrived at Boniato. Since the inspection had stripped us of the aluminum tins we had used to receive food, on the morning of our arrival at the new center we were each given another aluminum plate, but Lieutenant Modesto, in charge of the four halls of building 5, told us to return the receptacle after every meal. After a long discussion where all logical reasoning proved in vain, official intransigence and the prisoners' tempers clashed. The result was a collection of the plates, cell-by-cell, by the guards. I broke mine into small pieces that I threw out the window onto the patio. That same afternoon we decided not to accept any type of prison food, as we informed Lieutenant Modesto who had passed along the order, until the director agreed to allow each of us to have our own plate, as in all prisons on the island. Our comrades in 4A, with whom we regularly communicated in sign language, similar to that used by the deaf, agreed to join us. In fact, although seemingly insignificant, with our resistance we were expressing our unwillingness to accept even the slightest disciplinary action, much less if it accorded us a status parallel to that of common prisoners.

Modesto subsequently informed us that those in 4A would not have a right to medical assistance because of our refusal to wear the yellow uniforms, nor would we be allowed the monthly family visits which had been granted to *plantado* prisoners. To cover their nakedness, by then, those in the "underpants" unit usually came to the visits in shorts fashioned by the prisoners themselves from pieces of their sheets, and wearing white sweaters. In this same clothing, they attended dental and medical appointments at Combinado del Este. But with his promised release of 3,600 prisoners now in its final stages, dictator Fidel Castro had enjoyed symbolic applause and indulgence from many philanthropic institutions and respected Western leaders, absolving him for a while for committing atrocities against the remaining Cuban political prisoners.

Anticipating that the rejection of prison food could be prolonged, we gathered together all the powdered milk and sugar that we had managed to salvage from the searches to ensure an equitable and rationed distribution, allowing us all to resist for the longest possible time with the least physical deterioration. The quota we agreed on was of three portions per day, at breakfast, lunch, and dinner. So, I found myself forced to give up my powdered milk. Because of my stomach problems, I then preferred to confine myself to taking only water with sugar.

After a little more than a week in this situation, as we had kept up our strong defiant attitude, the director received an order from the High Command allowing us to keep the plates in our personal possession and, in turn, authorizing the "underpants" prisoners to continue receiving visitors once a month and also restoring the right to medical care. Satisfied that the demands that we had originally raised had been met, both pavilions considered it appropriate to put an end to the rejection of food. However, ten of us in 5A, plus eleven more in 4A, agreed to continue the semi-fast indefinitely to protest the repressive measure of moving us nearly 1,000 kilometers away from our relatives.

Eloy Gutiérrez Menoyo, Juan Evelio Hernández Ramírez, Onofre Pérez Hernández, Rolando García Fuentes, Santos Orlando Mirabal Rodríguez, Alfredo Mustelier Nuevo, Rodolfo Suárez Cruz, José M. Barco Gómez, Manuel Tailor Crespo, Pedro Flores Pino, and Guillermo Casasús Toledo were in the 4A group.

Then in 5A, we were Julio de las Nieves Ruiz Pitaluga, Ramón Méndez Pimentel, Sergio Montes de Oca Gil, Miguel Ángel Álvarez Cardentey, Mario Gavilán Sánchez, Ignacio Leal Denis, Gerardo Martínez Pérez, Isnaldo Fernández Guerra, Guillermo Rivas Porta, and I.

The first family visit scheduled for us in Boniato was for August 15. Already facing the possibility of getting news into exile via our families to detail our new repressive escalation, the 21 of us who were continuing to reject prison food decided on an even more vigorous protest, declaring ourselves on a complete hunger strike on that same date. This meant considerable sacrifice because our health was not optimal due to the terrible food we had been eating for years and years and to having received insufficient medical care, continued physical abuse, long periods in punishment dungeons, and, in addition to all this, the inhospitable torment of our cells, where we were regularly forced to survive living with rats, bedbugs, cockroaches, flies, and mosquitoes, just to name a few of the plagues swarming Cuban prisons.

Two weeks before the designated date of the family visit we were authorized write to our loved ones to let them know that we were in Boniato prison and that they could visit us on the 15th, but most of the letters got lost or would not arrive on time at their destination, so only a score of prisoners were lucky enough to be able to meet their relatives during the three designated hours on that bleak August morning.

Among the wide range of diabolical measures Fidel Castro pursued by transferring us to a more secure and more repressive prison at the eastern end of the country, solitary detention was a main objective. The tyrant wanted to make sure that our indignant voices did not transcend the iron curtain, that our echo of rebellion and dignity would be muffled by the thick, high walls of Boniato. And he intended at the same time that we should become living fossils, that our ears would not encounter any breath of fresh air, or any sign of encouragement or stimulus. To his sick mind, a political prisoner, his opponent being held behind bars, not only had lost his status as a human being, but had to be treated as a beast or a nasty bug, and neither beasts nor disgusting insects have the right to defend themselves or to receive information.

But the torturers are not always able to satisfy the wishes of their master. Two detailed general inspections could not prevent the sagacity and firm resolve of prisoners subjected to the unscrupulous will of our jailers. Only 72 hours after our arrival at Boniato, the first edition of our Pony Express was happily circulating. Using as a receiver the small Sanyo radio that my step-daughter María Isabel had given me on her February visit to Combinado del Este, José Pujals and Luis Manuel Zúñiga were tasked every evening with copying verbatim the full broadcast of the Voice of America. Then, starting at 10:30 p.m., Ángel De Fana and I transcribed in writing the most important news from BBC, Radio Netherlands, Radio Germany, and Spain's Radio Exterior. Then, between midnight and 1:00 a.m., it was Colombia's Caracol chain, Radio Sucatensa of Venezuela, or one of the stations from the Dominican Republic. As you can see, the international information that we received clandestinely was extensive and valuable.

Despite my hunger strike I kept up with my modest collaboration while I still had strength to do the work. With great regret, when I could no longer stand up, it was Ángel himself who recommended that I resign from our joint task. De Fana, working alone, was very adept at correctly copying news commentaries, usually transmitted only once.

Despite the modest improvements, we had managed to achieve during massive rejections of food, gradually, by the first week of August, we had concluded that we needed to organize a more energetic protest. Both in 4A and 5A, private discussions were held on a "hall" level. We held assemblies of everyone gathered along the corridor running from one end to the other between the two rows of cells. Whenever possible, the head of each hall was selected through a secret ballot to serve a two-month term as moderator and as disciplinarian when tempers got out of hand.

As a result of our shared concerns in both pavilions, we agreed to carry out a hunger strike during the celebration in Havana of the Sixth Summit of Non-Aligned Nations. Differences of opinion emerged about when to start fasting, so it was left to each individual to participate according to his health and willingness to sacrifice. However, despite the serious physical impairments of many, produced by the calamities of an imprisonment as long and ruthless as our own, almost the entire group joined in the strike on August 22, the starting day advocated by those supporting a longer fast. This time, no demands were made to prison authorities. Our action was undertaken as a vigorous protest against the appointment to the three-year chairmanship of Non-Aligned Nations of the most abject and unconditional ally of the marshals of the Kremlin since his seizure of power, the very inappropriate choice of dictator Fidel Castro. Overlooked were his warmongering services to Moscow in sending more than 45,000 troops to Angola and Ethiopia to implement through destruction, terror, and death a totalitarian system similar to Cuba's. Fortunately, the complicit silence of this natural satellite of the Russians, when Moscow troops invaded one of the non-aligned member countries in a desperate attempt to crush the desire for freedom of this heroic people, ripped off Castro's mask.

# Interrogations Over: Back to La Cabaña

A little more than a month after my meeting with a High Command official at the G-2 residence in Bocaciega, State Security in Havana sent for me with all my belongings. "All my belongings" meant a toothbrush and paste and a sliver of soap, all that was allowed to us in the dungeons of State Security.

Moments later I heard that they had given Felipe and Emilio the same order. So, only remaining there, in addition to us three, were César Páez and Eloy Gutiérrez Menoyo. The rest of the political prisoners accused of conspiracy had left, each according to his alleged responsibility, in different groups since the end of November.

The first-floor guards put me in handcuffs. Then we boarded the G-2 "alfita" vehicle. Up front with the driver sat the officer in charge of our transfer. I sat in the middle of the back seat. On each side was a guard holding a special AK rifle with a folding butt.

After only about 50 meters, the guard on my right and I got into a short discussion because he wanted to stop me from looking out the window. I thought that was silly. But they tend to apply coercion to everyone without realizing that there is a huge difference between any citizen who enjoys freedom–we'll call it "freedom" figuratively, as in

Cuba, no one is really free —or one who has just been arrested, and a man who has already spent several years in prison and from whom already everything has been taken away, making him fully aware that he has nothing left to lose. So, I kept on looking out of the vehicle which zoomed on at breakneck speed, undeterred by the guard's continuing recriminations and stupid threats. (After all, I was curious about the outside world, which for me had not been visible for six years.)

I thought that at last, he had given up after not speaking for 8 or 10 blocks, even if, from time to time, he gave me a withering look, and shifted uncomfortably in his seat. However, while we waited for the green light at the traffic signal at the intersection of Vía Blanca and Calzada 10 de Octubre, he warned me for the fifteenth time to keep looking down at my feet.

"What you want is impossible," it occurred to me to tell him, "unless I take my shoes off."

I guess that he took that as a joke, judging by his acid response. I was surprised that he didn't actually utter a swear word.

We were at Avenida del Puerto, not far from the entrance to the tunnel that crosses Havana Bay. The G-2 car we were riding in had stopped briefly because of traffic caused by a minor accident. Several young boys, although supposedly "shitting in their pants" (I don't know if all youth were meant to be included in that interesting observation by the officer of the High Command), approached the patrol car to catch a glimpse from the sidewalk of the victim. Taking advantage of their interest, I scratched my ear so they would see that I was handcuffed. At that moment, the ornery guard was lighting a cigarette and didn't notice. But when we started up again, I was surprised to see one of the boys imitating my gesture, waving goodbye as he pretended to scratch his ear.

Next came our most violent and final dispute. We exchanged strong words. I let the guard know that the only way that he could prevent me from looking where I wanted would be to take out my eyes with his bayonet. At that point, the officer intervened: "Let's stop this," he asked me in a conciliatory tone, and then told the contentious guard, "Let him look out wherever he wants."

The soldier haughtily answered that he was just following the rules. But the lieutenant reminded him that *he* was in charge of the escort mission and that reprimand proved effective.

Five minutes later we arrived at La Cabaña prison. It would have been about 10:30 pm. At the warden's office, my name and routine data were taken before I was sent to Gallery 18, where I found Adolfo Borges, Emilio Nazario, Felipe, Vicente Manso, and some other friends. Vicente was one of the most enthusiastic members of our organization. He, Desiderio Quintero Acosta, and Oscar Tey Tur were the first to be sentenced in Cuba at the beginning of 1960's for organizing clandestine cells of Alpha 66 within the island. Tey Tur had died in 1973 due to a mysterious cancer. Only a very few days before his death did the authorities begin to offer him medical assistance. I managed to see him in the Cabaña infirmary 15 minutes before they took him away in an ambulance and he no longer recognized me. Viewing him there on the stretcher, I realized sadly that the hefty and energetic man I knew had been reduced to a symbol, to a memory. What remained of Oscar Tey Tur was no more than bones and wrinkled skin. Desiderio Quintero, meanwhile, had been freed in 1972, months after the well-known surgeon José Ángel Suárez Gayol, also a political prisoner and holder at the same time of ID number 232 of Alpha 66, performed successful surgery at the Castillo del Príncipe hospital to remove his stomach cancer. According to the last news about Desiderio Quintero, before our family visits had been suspended and we were put under more rigorous isolation a little more than three years ago, he was living with his wife and son in New York City and enjoying excellent health.

On that first night after my return to La Cabaña, we stayed up talking until daybreak, exchanging impressions about our just-concluded experiences in State Security. We were surprised by the sunrise. It was perfectly understandable after three months of solitude and silence, in reconnecting with good friends and engaging in lively conversation, that some of us would lose track of time. From the others, I learned that in December the rest of those remaining in Guanajay Prison had been moved to La Cabaña. Previously, on September 21, 1972, about 200 *plantado* prisoners from that same prison had also been transferred to La Cabaña after several days of rioting and clashes with the prison garrison.

They had arrived without any belongings, almost all of them bruised and injured because of excessive beatings by prison authorities. This criminal assault has gone down in Cuban political prison history as "Black September."

I also found out in private conversation with Borges that on the day after Emilio, Felipe, and I were taken to State Security, he had burned several documents that I had buried and covered up with cement and paint inside a wall of Gallery 14. With the exception of Emilio and Felipe, Adolfo Borges was the only person who had known about this burial.

"They could have stayed there a hundred years without the slightest risk," Adolfo said. "You cannot imagine how much of that wall I had to destroy to find them when only two months before you had shown where they were buried."

In fact, I had absolute certainty that there was only the remotest possibility that the political police would ever find them. However, to make sure, I had charged Borges, in case I was taken to G-2—something for which we were waiting due to insinuations about the Alpha 66 conspiracy sweeping through prisons of the island– if after 24 hours, I still had not returned, he was to dig up the very important documents about our conspiracy plans and incinerate them. He should only try to keep at all costs, because of its extreme importance for the organization, one doubly encrypted document also buried in the same gallery, but in a lower corner of the wall. No one else knew of this second burial.

About mid-morning on February 3, taking advantage that the halls had opened for recreation, I went to the hiding place on the pretext of greeting some friends and, at a glance, confirmed with satisfaction that the seal and paint remained intact. A week later, while Gallery 14's residents were in the dining room, I removed all the documents from the wall.

# Summoned to a New Interview

The days went by in relative calm until mid-March when I faced the first new setback with the authorities. That morning, I was sharing three precious visiting hours with my aunt Graciela and step-daughter María Isabel when a sergeant appeared with the untimely news that I was being summoned to the prison office for an interview.

I refused to go. My visit was only three hours once a month, I explained to him, and therefore I was unwilling to sacrifice any part of it under any circumstances. If higher authorities wanted to talk to me, they would have to wait until the visit was over.

The sergeant insisted, but given my repeated refusal, he was left with a shrug. "I'll ask again," he said, and departed.

He reappeared five minutes later. This time he warned me that in any case, I would have to go with him as those were his orders.

"They told me to tell you that it won't take more than twenty minutes," the Sergeant assured me and, probably thinking that it would impress me, he added: "Two G-2 officers are the ones looking for you."

The soldier was greatly miffed when I reaffirmed that I wouldn't talk with anyone until my visit was over.

My aunt grew very nervous when the sergeant's impertinence inevitably turned into an argument and I let him know, already quite irritated, that to get me out of the room, he would have to take me by force. I well knew that they would not want to create such a spectacle in front of some 100 political prisoners and around 300 family members. In addition, they had no justification for choosing such an inappropriate moment. Finally, as much as my attitude bothered them, if, in fact, the G-2 operatives were so interested in holding an interview with me, they had no choice but to patiently wait two hours for the visit to be over. Although the sergeant left and did not return to bother me, my aunt Chela as well as María Isabel spent the rest of the time with their nerves on edge.

Back in the gallery, I learned that on the same morning, intelligence officers had also called for interviews with César Páez Sánchez, Eloy Gutiérrez Menoyo, and former rebel army commander Ramón Guin Díaz. Nothing of particular importance, they told me.

With Eloy Gutiérrez Menoyo they had used a different tactic. While the G-2 officers interviewed César Páez, and then Ramón Guin, Eloy was kept locked up in one of the guard corps' dungeons. A few hours later they sent him back to his floor without anyone having spoken a single word to him, showing —rather confirming, I would say– that it was not by chance that the so-called interview had been scheduled on the day of my visit.

With Gutiérrez Menoyo and César Páez Sánchez there was a return to extreme security measures, and on April 6 of that same year, 1974, both were held incommunicado in an underground bunker, number 23, along with Húber Matos, Lauro Blanco, José Pujals Mederos, Silvino Rodríguez Barriento, Antonio Lamas de la Torre (Tony), Osvaldo Figueroa Gálvez, and the poet Jorge Valls Arango, who had shared with them a fierce solitary status in Castillo del Príncipe from late 1970 until November 1, 1973, when César and Eloy were taken to State Security to be processed for the Alpha 66 conspiracy. Those aforementioned seven colleagues had previously been transferred from Castillo del Príncipe to Gallery 23 of the military fortress of La Cabaña on the night of December 21, 1973. After that, around a week after having met with the others, Gutiérrez Menoyo and César Páez were joined in that infernal isolation bunker by Sergio Montes de Oca Gil, Jesús Silva Pontigo, José Manuel Martínez Fernández, Enrique Fernández

Ruiz de la Torre, Sergio Rámirez Hernández, Alberto Ordaz Acosta, and Reinaldo López-Lima Rodríguez.

Although I don't know the exact date, I think that it was early in May of 1973 when Ernesto Valdés, the official of counter-intelligence– by then chief of G-2 at La Cabaña– and I had a violent argument. It was on a morning when, accompanied by two other officers of the political police, he had entered the outdoor courtyard where some 300 prisoners were taking in the sun and began to repeat to me, like a good parrot, the same slanders that were used against Andrés Nazario Sargén, orchestrated by the official of the High Command during the interview we underwent at the G-2 residence in Bocaciega.

It's worth mentioning that this repugnant Castro henchman had a rather shameful record, as do all opportunists.

As the island's youth struggled heroically underground and in the mountains to regain the national dignity and democracy violated by the cunning military coup led by Fulgencio Batista, the current G-2 agent, Ernesto Valdés, enrolled in the navy under the command of the famous Emilio Lauren to combat the Cuban revolutionaries. Shortly after the triumph of the Revolution, in his eagerness to perpetuate himself on the throne, the unscrupulous Fidel Castro opted to implement in the name of democracy, justice, and the right of his people to be free, a communist dictatorship in the style of his idol Joseph Stalin, so then the disinherited Ernesto Valdés joined the thousands of revolutionaries who pledged themselves to the tyrant next in line. Those who had conspired with him at that time and had the fortune to escape the firing squad, could not specify with accuracy if it was by a twist of fate, or due to his background of services rendered to the dictatorship of Fulgencio Batista, that put Castro's goons on the track of Ernesto Valdés, detecting his subversive qualities. Then, according to the testimony of my prison comrades, the offer of State Security to the ex-confidant of Lauren had been made: choose between prison or infiltration of conspiracy groups in order to spy on their activities, thus leading to his incorporation as an official member of G-2 and to his services on behalf of the Revolution.

For a man of unyielding self-regard, with the morals of an animal, the tempting offer meant the culmination of his greatest longing, resulting in the achievement of his new career as a henchman. He had been born for this; this was his horizon, his sky, his universe. Ernesto Valdés embraced the flag of opportunism and gave over his soul to the devil by moving over into his enemy's column. Among his greatest feats, to mention just one, is that of having betrayed the comrades of the 30th of August, Cause 455/62, leading to the deaths of several hundred Cuban patriots –as previously mentioned—all vilely murdered by firing squad.

After my heated discussion with the chief of counter-intelligence of La Cabaña, penal authorities intensified their review of the supposed sentence which, months before, during the process of interrogation, G-2 had imposed on me. It could have been a coincidence, and a matter of chance, that those repressive measures were taken against me when I had suffered a dislocation of my left arm two weeks after the incident with Ernesto Valdés. The doctor attending to me in the Orthopedic Hospital, perhaps through negligence, immobilized my arm without even taking X-rays, leaving it dislocated. So, 45 minutes later, I was back in prison. Evening had begun to fall and I was in terrible pain all night long, despite the many painkillers I was taking.

The next morning, as the pain had not abated, I asked to be taken to the prison infirmary. There I was seen by Dr. Álvarez Tejeiro, a political prisoner, who was amazed to see that they had left my bone out of place.

"This is unconscionable," he exclaimed, very irritated. He immediately called in Dr. Valero. This doctor was serving time for a criminal offense and had been appointed by the prison's administration to attend to military prisoners, who lived on a separate floor in a different area, but who received medical attention in the same infirmary as Section No. 2.

Dr. Valero was also outraged. He said the case required my urgent return to the hospital, and without further delay he proceeded to write a note to the orthopedist and another to the prison administration requesting my transfer there.

Using a procedure rare in urgent cases, after a prolonged wait, the duty officer appeared in the infirmary to communicate to Álvarez Tejeiro and Valero that he had superior orders to not authorize my drive to a hospital until I was seen by Dr. Torres Prieto, a political police officer and the medical director of La Cabaña.

The nurse injected me with a tranquilizer and I returned to my floor. It was already noon when Dr. Torres Prieto sent for me. He glanced at the injured area, as if repulsed, and cynically argued that it was fine and that I wouldn't be going anywhere. In vain were my protests and those of the Dr. Álvarez Tejeiro. No doubt, the medical director acted in this miserable way following orders of the High Command.

I had no choice but to resign myself to my fate. When the date arrived that the orthopedist had set for my appointment three weeks later to remove the bandage that had immobilized my arm, they invented a pretext to postpone the trip to the hospital: that the paddy wagon was out of gas. After several days of fruitless efforts, I took off the bandage myself.

I still had to wait another week before being taken to the hospital. When we got there, we found ourselves with a new obstacle in that my appointment, of course, had expired, and it was also a different doctor than the one I had seen before now giving that morning's consultations. That fact actually pleased me, because it turned out that this specialist served me well with the enthusiasm and delicacy of a true professional. I cannot forget his gesture of disapproval when he took off my shirt and saw that the bone was still out of place. I explained how I had battled to be taken back to the hospital and the negligence of La Cabaña's medical director trying to convince me that the arm was well. The doctor wiggled the arm from side to side exclaiming: "Incredible! Incredible! This is criminal."

Of the three guards assigned to me, one was left outside the small room where I was being examined, standing right next to the door, wielding an automatic rifle. The other two had accompanied me inside, each one with his AK slung over his back.

The doctor dragged a metal chair to the center of the room and asked me to sit down. "Although I fear that it is already too late," he lamented, "I'm going to try to see if I can put it back in place." And he warned me that it "was going to hurt a little."

A little?... I don't know how I endured it without fainting. The pain felt like the horn of a rhinoceros thrust into my shoulder.

I returned to La Cabaña with my arm in a sling and an order to report to Fructuoso Rodríguez Orthopedic Hospital to undergo surgery 10 days later. That specialist's interest in repairing the damage done by another doctor, whether intentional or not, his love for his profession, his pure humanism, were met with serious opposition from my jailers. Not satisfied even with new repressive measures, when the specified date approached, Lieutenant Barrios told me that higher authorities had refused to grant me permission. I hotly disputed this decision demanding respect for my right as a political prisoner–and as a human being–to receive required medical care, but despite my injured arm, I was sent me to the punishment dungeons indefinitely. That was on May 10, 1974.

Due to the subhuman conditions prevailing in those black holes, an inmate was allowed to remain there a maximum of 21 days. However, in my case, the section chief, Lieutenant Ibrahim, kept renewing my punishment. Nor was this the first time use of such an arbitrary action. My comrades Roberto Azcuy Cruz and Pedro Ortiz Anaya also were subjected to this torture regiment for an indefinite period. For the former, it was for five months, and around two months for the latter.

Not until September 7, a week after we had sent a strong protest in writing to then Interior Minister Sergio del Valle Jiménez, were the three of us finally sent back among other *plantado* prisoners, putting a halt to that form of excessive punishment.

Also victims of similar retaliation at that time were José Agustín López Rodríguez and Julio Acosta Lozada, who shared the same dungeon area with me, but with each of us in a solitary cell, during all the time they spent there, some two months approximately.

I won't dwell in detail on all the calamities we were forced to endure, sleeping crammed up on the floor among rats, bugs, cockroaches, silverfish, and infernal swarms of mosquitoes, without being able to stretch our legs or to bathe, except every few days when a guard granted us the privilege of removing the grime in a two-minute shower. After all, that experience belongs to an already remote past and is not among the worst suffered by the immense majority of Cuban political prisoners. However, my left shoulder never recovered from that medical neglect, and to this day testifies to their indifferent cruelty.

# CHAPTER 28

# Back to Military Court

Right there at La Cabaña, a judicial prosecution of the alleged Alpha 66 conspiracy got underway on October 9, 1974. We learned that same morning that we were to be tried when we saw some 100 agents of the political police, almost all high-ranking officials, crowded together in the garrison's small theater-auditorium. Likewise cited was Eloy Gutiérrez Menoyo, who minutes later joined us in the dock. Two or three days before, the sheriff had visited us to communicate officially that we would be processed for a crime against state power, but the date of the trial or its location had not been revealed.

On the theater platform, standing about two feet high, there were comfortably seated the president of the court and four jurists, among them a woman. The prosecutor and the secretary were very close to us on the left. On the opposite side was another woman who turned out to be the court reporter and also the appointed counsel, as we were to learn later.

I was the first one ordered to stand, immediately after the secretary read out the indictment, where the prosecutor had proposed a 25-year sentence.

I was ordered to step forward, which put me some 4 or 5 meters away from the judges.

The first question was whether I wished to make a statement. My

166

immediate answer was "Yes." I was determined to confront the court, to become a prosecutor of tyranny in front of those one hundred officers. I wasn't going to miss the opportunity that the enemy had made the mistake of giving me.

"Defendant, respond to the questions of the prosecutor," the president of the court intoned authoritatively.

"First, I'd like you to clarify something. According to the act from which the secretary just read, this is a public trial. And if it's a public trial, why are only military present? Where are our relatives? Where are our friends?"

"Limit your answers to what you are asked," the court president curtly advised,

"I have the right to be informed as to why my family has been prevented from witnessing the trial."

"You are not entitled to anything. Just answer the questions," repeated the president of the court, raising his voice, maybe to hide his embarrassment.

It was not an open trial, but a grotesque farce. That's why the arrogant judge chose to avoid answering my uncomfortable questions.

The prosecutor took the floor: "Accused, can you tell me what date you left the country?"

"March 13, 1961."

"Keep facing the president of the court," the prosecutor ordered when I turned to the left to respond to the question.

Of course, I paid no attention.

"How did you do it, legally or illegally?"

"How could I have done it? Illegally," I said, and added, "in a small boat."

"Where were you going?"

"North. To the United States."

"Well!" exclaimed the prosecutor and, after a brief pause, "You say that you were headed toward the United States. That's to be expected. And it is also to be assumed that upon arriving in that country, you immediately joined one of those counterrevolutionary organizations. Right?"

"No sir. I did not join any counterrevolutionary organization."

The prosecutor turned in his seat. To my right, the young woman court reporter was taking furious notes because of the rapid-fire exchange. I occasionally shot her a glance.

"Did you not join Alpha 66?"

"Yes sir: in the middle of 1961, when it was created."

"Then?"

"Then what?"

"Isn't Alpha 66 a counterrevolutionary organization?"

That was the question I was waiting for.

"No sir. You are the counterrevolutionaries. Alpha 66 is a *revolutionary* organization."

I immediately felt the murmur of the spectators and the persistent ring of the president shaking the bell, angrily warning me that they would not allow me to express disrespect.

Neither was I willing, I told them, to allow them to show me disrespect.

After an exchange of harsh words, there was silence. Then the prosecutor continued with his questions: "Accused, as a member of Alpha 66, did you participate in hostile actions against Cuba?"

"What you mean by hostile actions?"

"Armed attacks."

"If you know the answer is 'yes,' why are you asking?"

The prosecutor took notes, whenever, apparently, any of my answers interested him. This time, he scribbled something, smiling, making me think he was preparing a rebuttal. Since I thought I had nothing to lose —or at least thought so at the time—I didn't pay much attention.

"We know that in 1964," he continued, "you moved with a group of Alpha 66 to Santo Domingo, and there underwent training."

"No sir, you're wrong."

"Weren't you in the Dominican Republic that year?" he asked, a little surprised.

"Yes sir."

Communists get very annoyed at being called "sir," so then only to fluster him, I repeated it over and over again. When I let out the first "No sir," I had observed that, but he pretended not to notice and probably wrote me off as incorrigible.

"And you're saying you weren't training?"

"No sir, I was not training.

"What were you doing then?"

"Going through training."

"That's the same thing!" he sputtered, upset, thinking that I was trying to make fun of him. Perhaps he was right.

"For you it might the same, but for me, it's one thing to train and another go through training."

"Okay, whatever you say."

He paused briefly, then regaining his composure, asked: "We're there many of you going through training?"

"Some."

"Eloy Gutiérrez Menoyo was there with you?"

"Possibly."

"Was Eloy Gutiérrez Menoyo in the camp with you? Yes or no?"

Because of his insistence, I turned to the defendants' bench and pointed toward Eloy. Immediately, Eloy nodded, indicating that I should respond affirmatively. However, I opted for something simpler.

"There you have Gutiérrez Menoyo," I said. "Ask him if you are so interested in knowing."

The prosecutor's face contorted into an angry grimace. His eyes sizzled with fury. I also noticed the five judges with their scowling faces.

"Where were you captured by our revolutionary forces?" the prosecutor asked, giving up the previous question.

"This henchman of tyranny continues to pretend that they are revolutionaries," I thought, but responded: "Around Morrillo, Pinar del Río province."

The prosecutor began tapping his fingers on the file of papers in front of him. "Do you recall the date?"

"I think it was on December 4, 1968."

"Was there an armed confrontation?"

"Yes sir."

"And what sentence was imposed for that crime?"

"Fifteen years of deprivation of liberty."

"So, the Revolution showed you mercy on that occasion, right?"

"Mercy? Merciful with me? Not at all," I protested angrily, "Mercy was shown by those who judged Fidel Castro for the Moncada barracks assault."

My words produced a tremendous uproar in that room full of officers. The court president stood up, livid, shaking the bell, shouting angrily: "That's far too much! An insolence, a lack of respect that we cannot allow to be tolerated!"

"It's not a lack of respect; it's the truth, "I replied energetically. "Already I've served almost four times the sentence imposed on Fidel Castro and I have not assaulted any military fortress or murdered anybody."

"Either shut up or get expelled from the room," the president of the court threatened, unable to control his overflowing fury.

"You may expel me right now if you feel like it!"

"Did I tell you to shut up?" the president roared again.

I replied anyway, just to undermine his authoritarian demand.

The prosecutor resumed. He spent five minutes asking me questions of little importance. Nothing was asked that had any direct relationship to the crime of conspiracy for which we were being judged in this new case. However, it was part of the show that State Security wanted to present to the "select" audience gathered that morning in the improvised trial hall in the military fortress of La Cabaña. And who knows how long that intentionally prolonged and ill-considered interrogation might have gone on if I had not protested so vehemently: "How many times will I be judged to belong to Alpha 66? How many times will I be condemned for the same offense?"

These and other questions that put the court on the defensive went unanswered. The prosecutor decided to put an end to that game of bringing up my previous activities as a member of that powerful organization of Cuban exiles already judged and sanctioned.

At the prosecutor's behest, the secretary handed me the typed file of my statements in State Security. I was supposed to verify the signature, supposedly mine, stamped at the end of the document. But without knowing the prior text, I could not risk either affirming or denying, so limited my response to: "Looks like it."

The prosecutor, dissatisfied, tried to press me into giving a categorical response.

"No, I cannot assure you if it is or is not my signature. I cannot be sure because you falsify signatures and falsify our statements."

"Not true," he declared defensively. "We aren't accustomed to doing that, nor do we need to."

"I can prove it," I insisted, convinced I could.

Before this, right after my return from State Security in early February of that same year, 1974, my comrade Armaranto Cabrera Álvarez, who had developed a clever way of organizing clandestine cells, informed me that the officer investigating his case, during the interrogation process, had given him a statement to read, purported to be mine. That statement, according to what Amaranto told me, was a silly trap concocted by the dunderhead officials of G-2, that spared no effort legal and illegal, honest or perverse, to try to confuse their victims. They thought this trick could pave the way for them to extract confessions from those who, because of low intelligence or confused emotions, were incapable of discerning the subtle difference between reality and an elaborate scam. Certainly, G-2 investigators believed in their full right to use any method to destabilize and extract confessions from their opponents, having chosen to be repressive agents and proceeding to shed all dignity, all qualms, and act with impunity. They knew that no one would call them to account, that "Communist legality" is pure farce, a dead letter. Perhaps they relied on article 58 of the Constitution of the Cuban Socialist Republic? "No one can be prosecuted or punished except by a competent court, according to laws in effect prior to the offense and with the requirements and guarantees that these establish."

What guarantees?

"Every defendant has the right to a defense."

What defense?

"No violence or coercion of any type may be imposed on persons to force them to confess."

Physical torture at times has caused a victim's death; mental torture on more than a few occasions has caused serious psychological disorders, even delusions. Doesn't that constitute violence or coercion?

Finally, article 58 says: "Any statement obtained by breach of this precept shall be void and those responsible shall incur sanctions as prescribed by law."

Can someone please cite even one case of any G-2 agent judged and sanctioned for breach of this precept? Where are the murderers of Marcelo Díaz, the killers of José Antonio Campos, the assassins of so many other prisoners who have lost their life in the black torture holes of State Security? I would like to know the case of a single sanction that has been overturned by the violation of this article.

"We are not accustomed to falsifying statements, nor have we any need to do so," repeated the prosecutor, without particularly raising his voice, but visibly upset.

I admired that I was not called out for "lacking respect."

"I have evidence that you do that and much more. You folks are masters of fakery. You falsified my statements in State Security and forged my signature to try to confuse some of my colleagues. You should be ashamed to be forced to resort to such unscrupulous and mediocre methods, given all the means at your disposal and such a repressive system as you have created, with absolute impunity to torture your adversaries as much as you like for as long as you like..."

The president of the court interrupted me, choleric, in one of his fits of hysteria. I thought they would expel me from the courtroom for expressing myself so crudely. But they did not. Then, this time in a leisurely tone, I added: "I'd like to have the document read. Only then will I be able to tell if that is my signature or not."

After receiving the prosecutor's order, the secretary, who had returned to her seat, proceeded to read the typescript file. As soon as she had finished, without waiting to be asked, I affirmed: "Yes, that is my statement. That's my signature."

I returned to the defendants' dock seeking the eye of Amaranto Cabrera. I hoped at that moment that he would seek to testify that my supposed statements, given to him to read by his interrogator at State

Security, were false. But Amaranto remained inexplicably silent, a complicit silence, perhaps involuntary, which greatly disappointed me because he would thus lose a great opportunity to unmask those who had mocked him by trying to trap him with grotesque falsehoods like a fly entangled in a viscose web.

"Amaranto doesn't want to expose them to ridicule," I thought. "Or he may not want to face the court so as not to complicate his situation. He knows that irritating them will make his sanction more severe and he's apparently not willing to pay such a high price."

Just one question that I could ask him at that moment would force him to reveal them as phonies. But might not my good friend, my courageous comrade, reproach me later for having put him in such a difficult situation unnecessarily? After all, had not my speech already more than clarified the stupidity of G-2's professional spies in trying to forge my signature and my statements? Had not the boomerang, either due to their inability or perversion, already fallen on their heads—and on their ridiculous robes—unmasking the Machiavellianism of their sterile sleepwalking?

Eloy Gutiérrez Menoyo was the second one to be called to give statements to the court. With a firm step, he walked to stand on the platform opposite the five military judges.

Before he had even uttered the first word, I anticipated a red-hot debate. And indeed, in the twinkling of an eye, a raucous discussion had already begun between Gutiérrez Menoyo and the prosecutor. The latter had been bothered when, responding to a question of his, Eloy had argued that he did not know what he was accused of, based on the fact that he had not agreed to accept any responsibility during interrogations in State Security, nor was he provided with any statement regarding the alleged crime of conspiracy of which we were accused.

"Didn't you just hear the indictment read by the secretary?" the prosecutor asked him, a little irritated by Eloy's ironic response, indicating indifference and contempt for the farce of the trial.

"I wasn't paying attention," was the justification given by Gutiérrez Menoyo, not deterred in the least.

"Would you then like the indictment to be read again?" proposed the prosecutor, or at least that was the implication of his questioning tone.

Menoyo shrugged. "As far as I'm concerned, you can do whatever you want," he sighed. "That's up to you."

The secretary once again started reading the act of the indictment. As soon as she had finished, Eloy Gutiérrez Menoyo jumped up to defend himself from certain cowardly epithets applied to him. "Counterrevolutionary" was the first qualification that he rejected with energy and no small amount of irritation. "Traitor" caused the former commander of the II National Escambray Front to erupt with righteous fire, a raging blaze, while his fragile body shook and quaked. Although without solid defense arguments and somewhat demoralized, the prosecutor interrupted constantly to try to explain Castro's reasons for implanting in Cuba a Communist dictatorship along the lines of Joseph Stalin's.

Seeing the prosecutor in constant trouble, and to avoid making him appear ridiculous before the audience of so many officers, the president of the court intervened again and again to try to quell the bitter controversy.

"I forbid continuance of this type of dialogue between the prosecutor and the accused!" the president ordered desperately, without getting Gutiérrez Menoyo to pay attention.

Then the court president violently pounded on the metal bell with his gavel, sometimes hitting the table. Occasionally a word, a challenging phrase from Eloy Gutiérrez Menoyo, evoked a hum of indignation behind him, because the immense majority of those officials invited to witness the trial were, as I said, G-2 agents, unconditional Castro lackeys who didn't care who was right. Their eyes were fixed in only one direction. Their minds had become rotten, swollen, trained only to obey and to do evil, providing with them psychological compensation for the multiple frustrations of their abject and miserable lives.

"I cannot be accused of being a traitor, nor I can be charged as a counterrevolutionary," Gutiérrez Menoyo repeated loudly when the prosecutor, unable to refute the truths being thrown in his face like gusts, wielded once again the magical epithets manufactured in the laboratories of State Security against everyone who, in one way or another, has had the courage to confront the regime of carrion and prey imposed with the barrel of a gun.

And Gutiérrez Menoyo continued:

"You are the counterrevolutionaries. I am fighting by those same principles for which I took up arms against the dictatorship of Batista. The traitor is Fidel Castro, Fidel Castro, who betrayed the Revolution by implementing, by deceptive means, a Communist dictatorship a thousand times more cruel and bloody than the military dictatorship of Fulgencio Batista."

"Get out! Leave the courtroom!" thundered hysterically the president of the court, interrupting Eloy's speech, "you have been ejected from the trial for lack of respect."

Eloy replied with vehemence. The lord president then shouted: "Security! Guards! Remove the accused immediately from the room."

Several agents of the political police, wielding Soviet sub-machine guns with bayonets, rushed towards Eloy Gutiérrez Menoyo, gesturing with their arms in the air and pronouncing phrases that nobody could really understand in the general disorder that reigned all over the auditorium theater, improvised for the great show.

I couldn't help smiling with satisfaction when I saw his honorable exit, being escorted by rifles held by demoralized gendarmes.

After a call to order, the president asked Amaranto Cabrera Álvarez to testify. To my surprise, the secretary introduced a typed file asking him to verify the authenticity of his signature. During the eight months between the interrogation process and the date of the trial, Amaranto insisted that he had not signed any State Security documents. Once an interrogation was over, whether a defendant had stamped his signature acknowledging his statements was of no importance to us. What was important was not if he accepted or denied, but the ability to avoid making embarrassing statements and to keep from implicating third parties needlessly according to the moral principle of fellowship among those accused in the same cause of defending the freedom of their homeland. Whether Amaranto Cabrera had signed or not was not a matter of great significance. Instead, his lack of sincerity, the unnecessary deception maintained for eight months was reason enough for us to feel a regrettable loss of confidence in him.

"Accused, would you recognize this signature as yours?" the secretary inquired, following the ritual used by state puppets to provide a veneer of legality to the grotesque comedy of the trial.

"Well... I would say the same thing that's already been said, that it looks like it," Amaranto Cabrera affirmed, pointing toward me with his left index finger.

The prosecutor roughly rebuked him: "It doesn't matter what anyone else has said! Answer: is this your signature or not?"

Never had I seen a person more easily irritated (a wonderful actor, a great comedian).

"This... Yes, yes, that is my signature," Amaranto Cabrera affirmed after a quick glance at the typed document.

The prosecutor smiled with perfidious arrogance when she began reading the document. Nothing spectacular. In his statement, Amaranto, among other things, dedicated a beautiful paragraph to highlighting my activities as leader of Alpha 66. However, I recognize that he had avoided mentioning for himself and for me any truly sensitive secrets.

After the reading, Amaranto responded to the prosecutor's questions for ten minutes. Then he returned, a little shaken, to the docket of the accused.

Félix Rafael Vázquez Robles was the fourth and last defendant to provide a statement. The fact that "Bibe," as we his friends affectionately called him, was included in responding to the crime of conspiracy in Cause Number 405 of 1974, when so many other prominent figures with greater involvement in the clandestine activities of Alpha 66 –including ex-Commander César Páez Sánchez, a member of the national directorate –had been dismissed from the judicial process, was something impossible to fathom, and less so was the prosecutor's request for his 20-year sentence.

The accusation against Félix Rafael was limited to two alleged offenses. To support the first, the court asked for a statement from Lieutenant Ferreira, head of the garrison at Castillo del Príncipe during the time that Eloy Gutiérrez Menoyo, along with eight other leaders of Cuban political prisoners, was in a special isolation unit at that facility.

In his accusatory testimony, Lieutenant Ferreiro declared that on the occasion of a family visit granted to Eloy Gutiérrez Menoyo, Félix Rafael had appeared at the front door of the prison accompanying Dr. Isabel Rodríguez, who was authorized by the superior authorities to visit Gutiérrez Menoyo. According to Lieutenant Ferreiro, he asked Vázquez Robles if he also was planning to enter the visitors' room, but he replied that he only wanted to help Isabel bring in a heavy crate of food for Eloy, although he'd like to have the opportunity to see him, if the criminal authorities would allow it, since he considered him a brother due to the strong ties of fraternity forged during their many years together.

"Permission denied," had concluded the former head of the garrison of Castillo del Príncipe, claiming that when he went to consult with his superiors, they had ordered him not let Vázquez Robles inside, since, with the exception of Dr. Isabel Rodríguez and Dr. Carlos Gutiérrez Zabaleta, Eloy's father, it was strictly forbidden by the High Command to allow anyone else to visit Menoyo.

The second argument tried to demonstrate "the criminal responsibility" of the accused, Félix Rafael Vázquez Robles, which consisted of an alleged table of encryption keys found during a search carried out by the political police. No proof of conspiracy against him, no clandestine note, not even a simple compromising conversation. Nothing, absolutely nothing, that justified his presence before the military tribunal rendering judgement on us, so at the end of the process of interrogation, the G-2 investigator assigned to his case didn't even bother to ask if he had signed his statement, also failing to ask Vázquez Robles if the official had left a written report.

I must confess that because of the prosecutor's fragile accusations against Félix Rafael, I experienced a childish enthusiasm, thinking that because of lack of evidence, this meant he would be freed as soon as the court handed down his sentence. Despite my vast direct experience as a victim of the Castro dictatorship, it was hard for me to believe that this man would be condemned to prison without any convincing proof of his conspiratorial activity. It is that the human being tends to easily forget, or at least I forgot at that moment, perhaps caught up in wishful thinking that with Vázquez Robles, such an unfortunate injustice would not be committed. Faith moves mountains. It prompts us to walk on brambles and over the sea. It is a beautiful star shining for us in the darkest night sky. But it is also a blinding light. So, it is no wonder that in the moment, I departed from reality in thinking of a chimeric legality, a legality that does not exist nor ever will under a totalitarian regime, under a regime of booby traps and immorality as shameful as the Castro dictatorship.

As had occurred before with me, in the cases both of Amaranto Cabrera and Vázquez Robles, the assigned lawyer was limited to a few routine questions. So, when the session was adjourned to allow the members of the court to fill their Jurassic bellies – after their hour and a half of "strenuous" work –the official designated by the police for our defense had invested exactly 44 words on behalf of his four defendants.

The trial resumed around 1:30 p.m. Soldier Eusebio Dubet, a jailer at Guanajay prison, was called as a prosecution witness. His appearance was brief. His testimony was limited to an occasion when the prisoners returned to their cells after a family visit; meanwhile in carrying out a rigorous search, he had found a "balita"—a rolled up ball of papers—containing clandestine correspondence, which he immediately delivered to the top prison authorities. Dubet also said that, as far as he knew, it concerned matters related to the conspiratorial movements of Alpha 66. But he avoided specifying to whom it was given, perhaps because he had actually forgotten, or perhaps for some other reason, although I'm not inclined to believe that it was out of sympathy with us, since on more than one occasion, this same soldier had participated in massive beatings of political prisoners.

Finally, at the prosecutor's insistence, Eusebio Dubet agreed that said correspondence could have belonged to one of the Bayolo brothers (Santiago and Alberto Bayolo), but that given that a little more than two years had elapsed since, it was impossible to accurately recall that detail.

# CHAPTER 29

# The Final Witness

The last witness to provide testimony was Emelina Pérez, the mother of a young man who I fought beside, who was captured with me. Her older son had already been executed four years ago. She was escorted by a G-2 patrol, almost as if she were a prisoner herself. Nonetheless, my feeling when I saw her, after we were brought back from our lockup during the trial break, was one of pure joy. It had been eleven months since I had laid eyes on her. The political police had forbidden her to have any contact with me. The only contact with her was through clandestine letters that we exchanged through María Isabel once a month, when she came to visit me before I was sent to the punishment dungeons. Thanks to that miraculous exchange, I was kept informed of her situation, of the psychological pressures placed upon her by the political police right after she returned home following the monstrous process of torture she endured at the hands of State Security.

"Emelina tried to commit suicide," I was told by my aunt Chela with tears in her eyes, when we again saw each other a few days before the trial, after my four months of isolation in the enclosed cells of La Cabaña's death row.

That same morning, María Isabel had given me a letter from our heroic friend where she confessed in a dispirited tone that she was unable to go on any longer. "The cross crushes my soul," she wrote. "I cannot bear this heavy load. It's too much weight for this silly old soul, already a good-for-nothing because I'm beginning to feel so cowardly." And, later on "Do you know what those miserable SOBs want now? Nothing less than that I should agree to testify against you. When I was told that, I began to fret a lot, so much so that..." The letter went on and in the last paragraphs, became a little incoherent. While Emelina confessed that she was going through a very intense nervous crisis, she avoided telling me that G-2 officials had threatened not just her, but had vowed retaliation against her son Emilito, the only fruit of her life, its unique breath, her only hope, so in her crazed despair, she had tried to kill herself.

That unhappy woman didn't know that my sentence had already been issued some time before. In a camouflaged State Security residence, not far from the peaceful beaches of Santa María del Mar, my fate had been decided nine months earlier. The trial was nothing more than a legalistic varnish to justify the official farce being orchestrated to impress a hundred uniformed sheep.

Right away, I started writing a few quick lines to Emelina, explaining that there was no significance to the fact that they wanted to force her to appear as a witness at our trial. "Don't worry about us. You have no way of harming us. You know what you can say and when you should keep quiet."

I remember that Lieutenant Mauricio had just entered the visiting room then, and since I wasn't sure if he had had seen me writing, I feared that my family might be strip-searched and the letter found, so I gave up the idea. "Isabelita," I said, "rather than giving you a piece of paper, it's best you give Emelina my verbal message."

"And what if I forget?"

"You won't forget; this is not child's play."

María Isabel nudged me with her elbow, "Boy, you're becoming such an old grump."

"Me, old?"

"Old in spirit. All you do is fight."

"No one is fighting. I just told you that..."

"This is not child's play," she said, rushing to get in the last word.

"By the way, Ileana says that she and you plan to enter the dance contest of the Guaracheros de Regla. Is that true?" I asked.

"We'd like to, but Mima doesn't want to. The Guaracheros is also the best troupe in Cuba, and so to be accepted, you have to know how to dance phenomenally well," she paused and added, "Ileana does dance well, but I still know very little."

"So why not ask aunt Chela to teach you? She's a terrific dancer. For 40 years, she was soloist for the Chancleteras of Cojímar."

This time it was my aunt who poked me in the ribs. I had to catch my breath.

"Darn you!" she grumbled, bringing her fist threateningly to my nose. "What are you talking about? Are you crazy?" And turning toward María Isabel, "Pay no attention, Aly. He's making that up. Ridiculous! I do believe that this boy is missing a few screws."

María Isabel giggled.

"So, are you gonna me teach, auntie?" Isabelita asked.

"I told you that's a crazy lie. Lies...lies. He's always inventing crazy things."

A kiss on each cheek calmed my good-natured aunt. She gave me a gentle smile exposing her naked gums.

Oh, I thought, luckily Aunt Chela wasn't born in that land of long shadows, where old women were left to die in the snow when their teeth, already worn down by so much work, became useless tools to tame the furs worn by their demanding husbands.

As the visit was about to end, I made Aly repeat for me for the third time everything she should convey to Emelina. I wanted to make sure that she had understood and would not forget any of the essential details.

Standing subsequently in front of the judges' podium, with a voice muffled by anguish, Emelina began to answer questions from the prosecutor.

"Witness, who gave you the documents that you had in your possession?"

"Well... Ernesto gave them to me. Ernesto and my son Emilito," She added, as if wanting to mitigate my responsibility by including her son.

"Did you know what was in the documents?"

"No, I never read them. They always warned me not to read anything of what they asked me to keep. Besides, how was I able to read them when they were sealed?

"Way to go," I told myself. "That's right."

"But you must have been aware that to receive those papers clandestinely was committing a crime," the prosecutor continued, trying to coach her.

"Well, not such a crime," Emelina defended herself.

"But, you knew that it was forbidden to secretly take papers out of the prison!"

Emelina nodded, murmuring an almost imperceptible, "Yes."

"So then, why did you do it?"

"How can a mother deny her child?"

"Ernesto is not your son," the prosecutor insisted.

"No, he's not my son. But he's like a son to me. In addition, as I've already told you, these things were also given to my son Emilito."

"Never mind Emilito," the prosecutor rebuked her. "What we want now is to clarify the case of Ernesto Díaz."

The interrogation lasted five more minutes. From time to time the president of the court interrupted with his usual arrogance. The officials, one by one, started ganging up on Emelina to box her in. Hurt by her anguish, I had to bite my tongue to avoid uttering a swear word against those Pharisees with their leopard claws who had assumed the right to bully and humiliate a defenseless old lady in the name of a false justice and of a government corrupted to its core, a government of crows and vultures.

Soon, I was moved by a mental image of the execution of Luis Aurelio (Yeyito), my courageous friend, a brother from our painful banishment together, the older son of that sainted woman now trembling a few meters away like the leaves of an almond tree in the wind. Enraged from head to toe, and without power to contain myself, I exclaimed in a voice that carried to the most distant ear of that hall:

"What barbarians you are! What barbarians! First you murder her son. And now the same killers attack her with blackmail and threats."

That's all I could say. The court president, the director of that caricature of a Roman circus, let out a shattering scream that all but cracked the walls and shook the portrait of Vladimir Ilyich Lenin that adorned that room, installed there in a symbolic gesture to "honesty, freedom and justice."

Immediately, I was ordered expelled.

With the fury of offended demons, the political police rushed toward the dock, and in less than a minute I was being escorted out the door, surrounded by bayonets and rifles. I smiled in satisfaction. Finally, for me, the curtains had closed on that grotesque spectacle. I had left behind a fragment, a tiny fragment, of the poignant history of the political prison in Cuba.

Three days later a bailiff arrived at La Cabaña to deliver to us the decisions on our cases, in the presence of Lieutenant Mauricio Nodarse, head of the political prisoners' section, I was sentenced to another TWENTY-FIVE YEARS!

# CHAPTER 30

# The 1980'S Begin

The new decade and year of 1980 began amid the same atmosphere of hope and despair as during the previous few months. Except for reading, without many options, and writing some verses now and then, life went on with its usual rhythm of shadows and chimeras.

In February, I received a visit from my aunt Graciela for the second time since our arrival at Boniato. Her welcome company was enjoyable as usual, though I encouraged her to spread out her visits a little more to avoid those terrible travels from one end of the island to the other. But aunt Chela was determined.

Once the program of pardons of *plantado* political prisoners from Oriente province was over —mostly of soldiers— only 25 of us were left, so in April 1980, the inmates of Pavilion 5A were transferred to building 4D. Once again, I was to share the same cell as Miguel Ángel Álvárez Cardentey and Mario Gavilán, cell #7 at the time. As in Hall 5A, if cells were inside a gallery, during the whole time there we were allowed to have open doors, allowing us greater internal mobility. We even had access to the dining room from 6:00 a.m. until about 10:30 p.m., the time the third and last count of the day was carried out.

Despite the small cluster of ex-servicemen still remaining from the easternmost region of the country, who were older and held a different view of their rights, living together for us was good. There was above all understanding and respect. To avoid friction, we established mutually agreed upon norms. That is, while we all lived on the same floor, in practice, those from Havana as well as those from the eastern provinces maintained complete independence. This was true especially concerning collective attitudes toward the achievement of an objective or toward demonstrating something to the enemy, since we were unwilling to resign ourselves to accepting all the prison staff's whims, reprisals, and arbitrary orders.

Food, the poor quality of the food, was a sensitive issue. Already, I've said that the authorities used food to leverage systematic pressure and blackmail. Unfortunately, adequate access to food as an indispensable right kept us in constant conflict and diverted our attention partly away from matters of greater significance. But hunger is bad advisor, no big secret there.

Health care was another serious obstacle that we faced after our arrival at Boniato. After they had wanted to suspend medical care for us indefinitely a few weeks after our transfer to building 4D; instead, Lieutenant Lestapí, chief of internal order in those days, demanded that medical consultations at the prison clinic require us to submit to a strip search, that is, one carried out while we were completely naked. Apparently, this requirement for medical and dental assistance was directed exclusively at Havana inmates, since the small Oriente corps was still allowed to continue attending the clinic without being required to undress to be searched. The Boniato prison brigade was displaying its vertical regionalism, and viscerally, too, it might be added.

# CHAPTER 31

# Mariel and the Peruvian Embassy

Following events at the Embassy of Peru in Havana, when more than 10,000 Cubans invaded the diplomatic headquarters of that nation seeking political asylum, something unprecedented in history –as much in terms of its drama as in its magnitude– all of the island's prisons and concentration camps began to experience a tremendous upheaval with massive releases of common prisoners, more than 20,000 in all, who were then sent to the United States, mixed in with 100,000 other desperate Cubans who, in that spring of 1980, left via the port of Mariel in small boats sent by Miami relatives eager to achieve freedom for their kin back in Cuba.

Paradoxically, this wily unscrupulous measure to rid the government of thousands of common prisoners, including not a few renowned murderers, habitual rapists, people who in our own prisons had committed multiple bloody acts, did not benefit even one of those youth sanctioned for trying to leave the country clandestinely, even though many of them requested that the authorities grant them a chance to take advantage of this favorable situation, believing naively that they would be able to break free of their chains to be reunited with relatives in the United States. They forgot, perhaps, that in reducing the burden on the prisons, the tyrant of Cuba was very far from being motivated by any humanist feelings, rather, quite to the contrary, by a perverse instinct to discredit the 100,000 other victims of the system who were leaving the country in such a dramatic fashion to escape the oppression, hunger, and moral degradation imposed by a dictatorship so corrupt and vile.

No doubt this Machiavellian, as well as quixotic measure, undertaken by dictator Fidel Castro might have provoked a serious incident with the U.S. government, but the bearded patricide understood very well the peaceful character of President Jimmy Carter. The kidnapping of officials at the U.S. Embassy in Tehran had shown him that. Castro knew, no doubt, that this matter would not go beyond a traditional threat, or would be simply limited to a formal protest. I cannot help thinking that if instead of Jimmy Carter, Ronald Reagan had been in the White House at the time, Castro would not have dared to send to the United States more than 20,000 prisoners serving time for common crimes.

Many of these common prisoners, as mentioned, had committed countless violent acts in prison. We knew several cases of those released from Boniato who had raped teenagers, almost children, slashing them afterwards wildly to finish the deed. We know that Castro will never be condemned for this act of piracy, vandalism, and immorality. Tyrants of the extreme left may indulge and even applaud accomplices of other dictators in the forums of international agencies responsible for monitoring the enforcement of justice and the respect for human dignity. The powerful tentacles of international Communism hover dangerously over the globe. It's time to leave aside petty interests and understand that political corruption is harmful not only to the moral fabric but also to the cause of freedom. If those representing true democracy do not rise up indignantly to condemn the dirty tricks of the enslavers (of any tendency or political philosophy), we—the intellectuals, poets, artists, students, workers, ordinary people– in short, all of us, must raise our voices in protest. It is an unavoidable duty if we want to block the path of shame and outrage from all those would-be dictators.

# CHAPTER 32

# Repressive Surge

We spent the summer of 1980 in Boniato prison in relative calm. Still, group members found that many families residing in Havana were unable to make the authorized monthly visits, mainly because of money problems —travel expenses had risen to 100 pesos per person– though clandestine correspondence did allow us a narrow, yet satisfying, means of maintaining contact. Those rare visiting days were almost considered celebrations.

In September of that same year, we began to notice the first signs that the government was preparing a new repressive escalation against us. Among other things, that month we heard that G-2 officials had visited several of our families to inform them of rumors related to a so-called mutiny of *plantado* prisoners at Boniato. The rumors concerned some deaths and numerous injuries, all unconfirmed, but "from a reliable source," according to the version propagated by the political police. The launch of that false alarm by G-2 agents was an effort to make sure that the rumor would be spread from mouth to mouth and would reach over to exiles, where the press would immediately echo it. Aware that at the first family visit, prisoners themselves would take care to deny the news, the very Cuban government had orchestrated this hoax to confuse public opinion, which otherwise might later react with skepticism if there was a new mass shooting of political prisoners, as had happened at that same prison on September 1, 1975.

Immediately I wrote a long letter to the secretary general of Alpha 66, Andrés Nazario Sargén, informing him of the steps being taken by State Security to create conditions conducive to carrying out a new massacre at Boniato. Especially notable, I mentioned, was that G-2 agents visiting the families had presented themselves as being "disaffected" regarding the regime and, to make matters worse, were still wearing official olive green uniforms.

At the October 16 visit, special security measures were invoked. Instead of all of us being taken out together as a group, as was usual, which allowed us to enter the small search chamber all at once and to choose, with some exceptions, the soldier who best suited us among the searchers, we were being called out four or five at a time by G-2 personnel, who practically took us by the arm to escort us to be searched.

As we were being taken out in alphabetical order, I was in the third group. Given this situation, logic invited prudence, especially since we were in the habit of carrying something without much risk of being detected. By then, most of us had added a double lining and inside pockets into our underwear used for hiding correspondence of relatively minor importance. However, the presence of those G-2 officials made me suspect that we were on the threshold of a conflict, that the three hours shared each month with our families might end soon, perhaps that very morning, so I needed to take advantage of that opportunity.

I decided to take the risk.

Among other things, I had hidden inside the double lining of my underpants some dozen letters, each already stamped, showing the addresses of recipients and alleged senders, the latter taken from local magazines and newspapers, to more easily evade the G-2 censorship installed in all the island's post offices. We also never used to send unauthorized correspondence to the addresses of our own family members, whether inside or outside the country, whom State Security could have located and blacklisted

In addition to the above dozen letters, I had a notebook of poems by Jorge Valls Arango, "The Cricket's Song," about 15 by 10 centimeters, whose beautiful verses Valls had dedicated to President José López Portillo in a gesture of gratitude to the noble and sensitive people of our sister Mexican nation. I also wore taped in the crotch, photos that an official had filched from Boniato's files and given me in a gesture of goodwill, as well as several letters squeezed into a plastic ball ("balita") – the most important and compromising for me if found– and a miniature of my book of children's poems *The Carousel,* destined for a great friend, fervent admirer, and passionate defender of Cuban political prisoners, Fernando Arrabal.

They returned from G-2 to get five more of us. Ángel de Fana came just before me on the list. So, we were called out in the same group. Ángel, although he usually was carrying something too, was very generous with me and always let me take the place I wanted in the inspection. "Let me have the strictest one," he told me, referring to the most extremist soldier. "I'm going in lighter than you."

We were so in sync that a subtle look or simple gesture was enough to let him know which guard I thought was going to let me go free. Anticipating that I might need extra time, I had left a bootlace untied. That would have given me a justification, if necessary, to stop to tie it when the five of us entered the inspection room. From a practical and logical standpoint, stopping to tie a bootlace, when immediately afterward we would have remove both boots, might seem absurd, but we prisoners were used to doing absurd things. A good part of our jailers considered that after so many years of isolation and torments the majority of *plantado* prisoners would have become a bit mentally unbalanced. They considered us pretty crazy to have assumed certain political stances. Maintaining intransigence by renouncing the "fabulous benefits" of the reeducation plan simply as a matter of principle was something that made no sense to them. To Communists, principles are meaningless.

"You guys are not so smart," I was once told by First Lieutenant Ismael Bell, Boniato's supply chief and a member of the prison's administration. "'If you were in power and we were your prisoners, we would get down on our knees, prostrate ourselves on the floor, do whatever we had to do without any kind of complex or remorse, so that you would treat us better and we would be freed in the shortest time possible, because being in jail doesn't solve anything. We Communists are practical. You are too romantic; you don't know anything about real life."

Similar remarks could be heard from our jailers on multiple occasions during my long years of enclosure in Cuba's dungeons under the Communist regime, and those same arguments were preached by State Security interrogators. "The end justifies the means" was the motto adopted by those Pharisees. "The means" to which they referred to, of course, are limitless, including everything from the worst moral degradation to the most abject submission to grisly genocide.

I wasn't required to rely on the strategy of the untied lace. I was lucky to find a clear path and did not go to be searched where a G-2 official had indicated, but rather with a guard in a corner who seemed to offer greater security. He was a young soldier and somewhat timid, but not as much as I would have wanted – or needed – him to be to get away unscathed.

When, after having thoroughly searched my pants, shirt, and boots, he ordered me to pull down my underpants, I did so very quickly with my thighs held together so that he wouldn't have time to see the load distributed in the inside pockets of the double lining.

Immediately, I started buttoning up, but that old trick, used successfully many times before, failed on this occasion. No doubt, G-2 agents had been giving special instructions to be more cautious and distrustful than usual that morning.

The guard, although a little awkward and with subtle delicacy, ordered me to pull down my underpants a second time.

I protested, feigning anger, in a desperate attempt to deter him.

Not so. Apparently, it was not my lucky day, or maybe I just had worn out my lucky star. Fortunately enough, I had followed Jorge's good advice not to risk his book of poems. The fact was that despite how much I was carrying my usual success in circumventing the inspection was a factor contributing to my ill-timed decision, which risked losing everything, including the visit from my family members, who had traveled more than 1000 kilometers on an arduous trip.

Resigned, I repeated the same operation.

Already I had begun to button up the briefs again when the guard asked me to pull them down a third time.

"Forget it!" I replied energetically, showing that I was unwilling to compromise.

The guard stubbornly insisted, claiming that he thought he saw something hidden in the underwear.

At that point in the inspection Lieutenant Fabá, head of the Boniato garrison, came into the room, a repressive military officer and sly old fox with vast experience in conducting searches. As he was approaching us I raised my voice so he couldn't understand what the guard was saying, while with the sharp anger of a victim, I continued getting dressed.

"Enough already of this shit," I protested. "If to see our families we have to put up with so much humiliation, best to return me back to the gallery and let the visit go to hell."

I also said some other swear words.

Not far away, Reinaldo Figueroa Gálvez and his brother Osvaldo, also being searched at that time, began to vehemently protest. And so did Ángel De Fana in gesture of solidarity, to divert the attention of Lieutenant Fabá and the other military.

The impetuous disturbance so impressed the guard searching me that he only managed to articulate, with his face very pale and in an almost imperceptible tone:

"Excuse me..." And repeated: "I thought I saw something in the back of your underpants."

Although my initial impulse was to return back to the hall —perhaps the safest choice— I took advantage of the confusion of the military's entrance to leave with a group who had already been searched and join others waiting for the doors to the visiting area to open.

Later that afternoon we found out from our family members that several ambulances had been parked outside the main prison office; along with 100 members of Santiago's special police and a dozen German shepherd dogs.

The rumor had it of a mutiny by political prisoners.

It was not so difficult to understand that such an ostentatious deployment of force was due to something directly related to us.

A while later, from the dining room of building 1C, communicating to us by sign language through window openings, common prisoners let us know that Boniato's prison squad was searching our two pavilions (4A and 4D), and that the corridor was swarming with Santiago riot police searching with dogs, shotguns, and wearing tear gas masks. They also warned us not to take back anything, because, according to them, it was rumored that upon our return, we would have to strip.

With great uncertainty, we each bid goodbye to our own family. We were concerned primarily that they might be under threat of having to undress as well. It was not the first time that would happen. In the mid-1960's, this immoral practice was used at the Isle of Pines prison, and later at the very same Boniato prison with those visiting *plantado* prisoners wearing yellow uniforms. The so-called "naked," after having been stripped in July of 1967 —in a gesture of admirable rebellion— refused to accept it again. Then thirteen months later, after the interior minister had reversed the measure, they were kept more than seven years locked up in enclosed dungeons, subjected to a regime of fierce torture all that time, without allowing them to see their loved ones even once, or to even to write a letter to them.

Although over the last few years the ruthless repression against us and against our families had decreased considerably, now soldiers were roaming all over the prison, armed to the teeth with rods and sticks, the whole Boniato garrison, reinforced by the Santiago special police with their savage dogs and their blackjacks, shotguns, and gas masks. And outside beyond, as a symbol of the disaster that awaited us, was an impressive array of ambulances.

As we had been warned, as soon as we returned from the visit the search began and the first conflict arose, provoked by the attitude of some of the soldiers. Little by little the dispute escalated and shoving began. Instead of imposing his authority to calm things down, the garrison chief cried out to the guards of Post #1 —all the posts had been reinforced that day—to bring out the 30-caliber to mow us all down. He immediately ordered his men back inside the inspection room to avoid being hit. At this critical juncture, the warden appeared, breathless and very alarmed, and loudly commanded the removal of the 30-caliber. He then spoke to us in a conciliatory tone to avoid, he said, useless bloodshed. Then several of our comrades spoke —among other things—making sure the warden knew that we were unwilling to allow them to undress us completely. We agreed to lower our underpants only to the knees, at most, and not accept anything else, whatever the price.

After many arguments, the warden agreed to our demands and, although the atmosphere remained tense, very tense, the search was carried out without any other setback. Luckily there was no bloodshed at all, a true miracle, except that all that cumbersome mobilization, all that show of police riot gear, blackjacks, clubs, nightsticks, tear gas, guns, dogs, and ambulances, turned out to be no more than a simple drill to panic our relatives and try, in turn, to upset us emotionally. I don't dare to speculate which of those two objectives was mostly behind the deployment of such a show of force. Knowing the methods habitually used by Castro's jailers, even after a profound analysis based on lived experiences accumulated during years and years in the prisons and concentration camps of Cuba's tyrant, it's still very difficult to arrive at a categorical conclusion. Only one thing is very clear: whatever had been the motivation, it was not an isolated incident but part of a carefully orchestrated plan launched several weeks before when the G-2 agents had visited several of our families to let them know that at Boniato, *plantado* political prisoners were in a mutinous mood.

# CHAPTER 33

# Escape Attempt and New Wave of Repression

In the face of the new repressive escalation that clearly was assaulting us, we had no choice but to assume a firm, assertive attitude to resist somewhat the government's treacherous plans. Among the available options, although our health was quite impaired because of prolonged fasts and many years of enclosure, the hunger strike as a tactic was gaining increasing support within the group of *plantado* political prisoners now transferred to Boniato. On the one hand, Silvino Rodríguez Barriento, Alejandro Novo Álvarez, Alberto Azcuy Cruz, Luis M. Zúñiga Rey, Wilfredo Martínez Echevarría, Servando Infante Jiménez, José Oscar Rodríguez Terrero, and many other esteemed companions began to work on their own to launch a hunger strike at a not-so-distant date, as soon as they could prepare the minimum necessary conditions.

Likewise, there were Eloy Gutiérrez Menoyo, Evelio Hernández Ramírez, Onofre Pérez Hernández, Julio Ruiz Pitaluga, Sergio Montes de Oca Gil, Ramón Méndez Pimentel, Guillermo Rivas Porta, Mario Gavilán Sánchez, Isnaldo Fernández Guerra, Miguel Ángel Álvarez Cardentey, and several others from our group who had remained on an almost two months' fast already, demanding that the authorities return us to Havana. So then, we agreed to restart the hunger strike on December 15.

Given this favorable coincidence, we undertook the task of combining both efforts to try to all engage together in the new protest, starting, if possible, before Christmas. However, an unexpected event intervened on November 9, 1980.

That day had passed normally. The 10:30 p.m. count had just taken place and as Negro Cardentey used to go to bed early, I took my quilt out into the hallway outside the cell, and stretched out to read Cronin's *The Green Years* that a friend had loaned me on condition that I return it the next morning, as he had several other borrowers pending before giving it back to its original owner in Hall 4A. About five years earlier, I had adopted the habit of reading into the early morning hours, most of the time until dawn. Then I would throw myself down on my bunk and sleep 5 or 6 hours at most, regardless of noise. That was sufficient for me to recover my energy and feel fine.

Someone approached to tell me in confidence that Adolfo Vinent Bonis (el "Paisa") had cut through, with a hacksaw blade, the bars of his cell number 18 and was preparing to escape that night along with Alfredo Mustelier Nuevo and Samuel Tejera Milián. The situation was complicated, since Samuel lived in 4A, meaning they needed to undertake a coordinated operation to arrive together in the courtyard between buildings 3 and 4 before climbing the west wall of pavilions 3A and 3C. Even if they achieved this first step successfully, they needed to cross the alley surrounding the prison and the double security cordon, fully lit and with numerous high-rise checkpoints, where guards armed with rifles kept a constant watch.

But for Adolfo Vinent, no escape, however difficult or far-fetched, was deemed impossible. And if anyone questioned it, it was enough for him to give a brief account of all the times he had successfully escaped for the listener to be convinced of the capabilities of this modest, simple man, brave to the point of recklessness, and sly, very sly.

The first escape that Adolfo Vinent undertook was nothing less than from the quarry of the Isle of Pines on November 2, 1966, where he was sentenced to forced labor. He knew that if he failed, he would be mercilessly machine-gunned down. This was during the time when so-called "bosses" commanded gangs of political prisoners forced to work from dawn to dusk, not only subjecting their victims to brutal beatings and to bayonet stabbings rendering their flesh raw, but they even actually killed defenseless men for any trivial reason with complete impunity.

I don't know what magic tricks Adolfo Vinent used to escape the boss's surveillance and to cross the security cordon undetected. Both in the quarry and the forced labor fields, each block's prisoners remained at all times surrounded by a cordon of guards, well-armed and always ready to shoot.

Nine days later, due to a stroke of bad luck, Vinent was re-captured when he tried to leave the island. After receiving a fierce beating, he was sent to the punishment pavilion of the old model prison for an indefinite period.

Moved months later to Boniato prison, Vinent was confined in a special dungeon known as "the staircase," facing the guard corps office within the same building as the prison headquarters.

One morning the perplexed guards discovered that Adolfo Vinent's cell was empty. "El Paisa," as we called him, to everyone's amazement, had managed to escape from Boniato's infamous "staircase." That was on June 8, 1967. This time, Adolfo stayed out on the street for a month. They captured him as he was trying to leave the country illegally, subjecting him to an additional six-year sentence.

The third occasion on which Adolfo Vinent Bonis managed to escape from jail was on March 1, 1969, alongside Edmundo (Mundito) Torres —a psychology student sanctioned for standing up to the Communist regime— this time, escaping from Pavilion 5B of Boniato. They unfortunately ran into some infiltrators among the highlands militia mobilized within a group of regime opponents who, in those days, carried out armed actions in the area, and who surprised the two fugitives and captured them only six hours after their escape.

But El Paisa was not intimidated. Let's see how he described his fourth prison escape:

"The June 8, 1969 escape was carried out from cell #29 of building

5C. Since several times a day, each bar of my cell was thoroughly examined, I cut out a square below the window so that a piece of the wall could be pulled out and replaced, that is, an opening where I could pass through and, immediately after, the boys would take charge of sealing and painting it, so the escape route would remain a mystery.

"So, we did it.

"The opening came out onto the yard, and I climbed up to the second-floor roof by cell #1. Once there, I jumped onto the roof connected to the kitchen galley, and went inching toward the back where I slid down without difficulty into the ditch.

"At that time, there was no fence and it was all very easy."

It was a great escape and, yet, Adolfo Vinent tells me about it in just four sentences, with tremendous modesty, without any drama or spectacle.

On that occasion, Vinent managed to arrive as far as Havana, but had no luck trying to secretly leave the country, and three months later, the political police again had sunk their claws into this unfortunate fugitive. El Paisa, down but not out, was once again submitted to the dungeons. As might be expected, the authorities there tightened their surveillance and took special security measures.

Nine years passed before Adolfo Vinent Bonis had a chance to try to escape again, nine years of solitary confinement most of the time, locked up in a cell with its window and door covered by double steel plates.

Here is one of his many anecdotes:

"I was transferred," Vinent told me, "to a dreadful dungeon, plunging me into total darkness with moisture permeating my very bones. And, at certain times of day, the heat was so intense, it was hard to breathe.

"When I protested about my inhumane living conditions," he recalled, smiling somewhat impishly, "they told me that was how it had to be, by order of the High Command, to prevent my escape. I answered them that they were trying to leave me blind in the darkness and that I was going to prove that this particular black hole was no more secure than the cells from which I had escaped before."

The next morning, when the guard opened the double doors of Vinent's dungeon to make the count, he found a hole in the wall where a man could fit perfectly. But Vinent was still there; he had not yet made his escape. So, then they decided to build him a tiger cage held inside a covered black hole, reinforced everywhere with thick steel bars. This took place in September of 1975, a few days after the squadron at Boniato had machine-gunned down the *plantado* political prisoners in pavilions 4C and 4D.

Vinent remained confined there in the tiger cage almost two years until the summer of 1977, when he was transferred to Combinado del Este prison in Havana.

"You can imagine how happy I was to get out of that tiger cage. A month before being taken to Havana, I had cut all the bars and was looking out for a good opportunity to escape," El Paisa confessed to me.

The last time that Adolfo Vinent Bonis had managed to escape was on May 24, 1978. As a result of an incident related to the search during a Combinado del Este family visit, Vinent had been prosecuted by the authorities and appeared for trial at the courthouse in Guanabacoa. After the judge had found him not guilty, the soldiers guarding him made the mistake of locking him up in a regular cell while waiting for the paddy wagon to come for him, and neglected to keep him under watch, allowing El Paisa to cut the padlock with a piece of blade that he kept hidden, as someone carries a charm, always waiting for a lucky break. (He was like Houdini!)

Again, rapid police mobilization frustrated his desire to leave the country to permanently escape the bars. Twenty-four hours later, Vinent was recaptured, and after a brief stay in State Security, he paid for his thirst for freedom in the punishment cells of Combinado del Este.

Excluded from the pardons of 1978 and 1979, Vinent was part of our contingent of imprisoned rebels who, in July 1979, were transferred to Boniato prison.

At the news that El Paisa and Mustelier had chopped through the bars of cell 18 and Samuel Tejera had done the same in Pavilion 4A, and all three were now trying to escape, put the rest of us on high alert. The suspense lasted some 30 minutes, giving them time to descend to the patio by shimmying down a rope made of sheets. Since Pavilion 4A was located on the ground floor of the north wing, for Samuel, this first step was much simpler. To exit the courtyard, he only had to exit through the previously cut bars. Nonetheless, Vinent and Mustelier had gotten ahead of Samuel —that may have been their plan— and after stretching out on the grass so as not to expose themselves to the perhaps indiscreet view of common prisoners, they climbed onto the roof between buildings 3 and 4, scaling up via side meshes installed there. Very soon, both were at the edge of the corridor at its east end, trying to get onto the roof of building 3. Samuel Tejera, in turn, had progressed through the patio, snaking along— as Mustelier and El Paisa had done two minutes before– over the sparse grass.

Soon enough, the night air was pierced with the chilling wail of a siren. The alarm had been given and the powerful reflector of post #1 began to sweep all the buildings and the double gate near the security cordon.

Immediately the whole garrison mobilized. The corridor and courtyard of the north wing between buildings 3 and 4 filled up almost instantly with guards. Soon, surrounded by automatic rifles and with their arms held high, the three compadres were escorted to the warden's office. Once there, they were stripped naked and were forced to endure all kinds of threats, harassment, and abuse. One hour later, they were transferred to State Security in Santiago de Cuba, where they underwent a prolonged process of interrogations, solitary confinement, and torture.

Meanwhile, aware of the inevitable repression that would result from this escape attempt, we prisoners in pavilions 4A and 4D were bracing for the onslaught.

At approximately 1:30 a.m., the squadron burst into the corridor of our building. In the lead came Sergeant Noaldo Pérez, who since mid-August had replaced Lieutenant Lestapí as Chief of Internal Order. Noaldo already had a reputation due to the frightful cruelty with which he treated common prisoners. Not only did he beat them bloody, but often left them unconscious lying on the floor on a pool of blood, and he practiced sexual savagery. He used to deliver terrified teenagers to thugs condemned to death for them to rape in their punishment cells for any infractions they had committed. From our cells, we could often hear the heart-rending screams of those victims, since, so as to limit their resistance, the rapists carried out their horrendous moral crime at knife point. One case that most affected me was of a young man, practically still a child, named Luis Pérez.

Luisito was locked up in a 4C dungeon in a punishment pavilion. Lieutenant Banderas —because Noaldo was not the only one who used this "disciplinary method"— took out two condemned murderers in that same pavilion, two vermin among the cruelest, mentally damaged products of the indolence of the prison system in Castro's Cuba, known by the nicknames "Tuti" and "Polito," and gave them the keys to open up the boy's cell and violate their new victim to their hearts' content.

The unfortunate adolescent spent the whole early morning crying out for mercy. He begged the guards to take him out. He called out for his mother over and over again in a shaky voice, as if to find salvation by invoking his dearest loved one.

His tenacious resistance was useless. His anguished pleas fell on deaf ears. I will never forget, should I live for another hundred years, that chilling plea so often repeated: "Polito, please, do not disgrace me. See that I am a man. Just between my legs nothing more, nothing more..."

Monsters!!

When something like that occurred, a violation enabled by the jailers, the next morning Sergeant Noaldo appeared and with the greatest cynicism ordered the victim: "Get up, you have to go to the hold, because now you are already queer. Last night they split your ass." And he was then locked up in a section of the prison used to segregate homosexuals.

Even though morally devastated, they usually resisted going to that special holding place, so Sergeant Noaldo and several guards administered a savage beating and after kicking them, even in their face, they were dragged inside that den of iniquity.

# CHAPTER 34

# Devastating New Search and Beatings

Before the garrison began its blundering repressive inspection, they had locked the prisoners of Pavilion 4D —around a hundred in all—into the dining room and chained and padlocked the door. From there, we saw one after another of our belongings raining down into the hallway, even old crusts of bread were thrown down! Old bread that we had kept for days, mainly for times when by its terrible quality, we were forced to reject the food, or to make a pudding when we got ahold of a little powdered milk and sugar.

The pre-dawn morning seemed to us to last longer than usual. Inside the dining room, the overcrowding almost kept us from even taking a forward step. Some stretched out on the two long granite tables or on the floor, trying to rest if at all possible, although it was something of a fantasy to expect any shut-eye where dozens and dozens of voices were rising, all simultaneously, struggling to be heard over the din. In addition, the uncertainty about what might come next —our past experience proved worrisome— prevented any hint of sleep.

Even before sunrise, a gallon-sized can appeared —imagine if you will why and for what purpose it was placed in the dining room— and more by imitative instinct that by urgent physiological need, folks began to take turns urinating, and soon the stench became unbearable.

When the sun's first rays finally rose, the garrison began to withdraw, indicating that the search was over. Usually, immediately after a search, the dining room door would have been opened and we each would be frisked before leaving for our cells, but sometimes we would be called out in groups of 10 or 12 to submit to an examination of our underpants, similar to that before a visit. However, this time, long after the last guards had left, we remained still locked inside the dining room.

Breakfast was not served that morning. As the day progressed, the heat started becoming unbearable. We still hadn't slept and began feeling physically exhausted. Since the space was so cramped, only a few more anxious guys ventured over to the area around the door, gathering there beginning in the early morning hours, becoming an impenetrable human knot, some only distracted by observing the guards' in their plundering, others waiting for the search to end to return to their cells. These latter guys usually did not have any illegal papers, or any tiny radios, or so many other things that many of us might have left behind, yet they carefully observed what each guard was seizing and which guards had found out that we "were doing nothing at all," including those who showed a complete disinterest in what prisoners might have hidden. Those were the guards whom we tried to have search us and, invariably, with rare exceptions, we got them. Generally speaking, "not doing anything" was applied much more frequently by those boys who were completing their obligatory military service. Among officials at Boniato, according to what I could observe throughout the years, those who carried out their functions in a limited way were relatively few: Modesto, Laudelino, Enrique, Salvador... At the opposite extreme were lieutenants Fabá, Lestapí, Banderas, Escalona, Julio, Taquechel, Tomás, Estable, Zamora (that true bastard, Zamora!), and several others of the same ilk not worth mentioning.

Shortly before noon, the squadron returned. There were more than a hundred soldiers in all, wielding thick rods of corrugated steel, sticks, bayonets, machetes, and some, even baseball bats, and of course, not missing in a situation like this, were a pack of police dogs and several tear gas canisters.

Common prisoners in Pavilion 3D were the first to the sound the alarm just as soon they saw the vanguard marching through the corridor between buildings 2 and 3. Heading up the shock troops was provincial officer Lieutenant Cobo, followed by all of Boniato's officialdom. All except one, Lieutenant Silva, who had been sleeping the night before when the escape had occurred and was then awakened by Pedro, the unit's Commissioner of Communist Youth, who had informed him abruptly that *plantado* political prisoners were escaping "en masse," shocking him so much that he suffered a cardiac arrest, dying almost instantly. Although he was the officer who usually made the count, that night he had had guard duty, so when the Youth Commissioner ran to wake him up so dramatically, his heart just couldn't take it.

For the Communists, a death on their side has always resulted in a call for revenge, whatever the actual cause. In this case, "counterrevolutionary prisoners," (all of *us!*) shared in that responsibility, so the warning was made to all of us equally, even when they might be prevented from actually murdering us en masse.

The argument chosen this time was that before returning to our cells, we all needed a haircut and a shave, but not just among ourselves, as we normally did it, but with common prisoners as our barbers, which the authorities mostly knew we would not accept, not only on principle but for logical security reasons. No one dares to meekly expose his neck to someone of questionable scruples (except, certainly, for those few honorable souls who had been unavoidably integrated with common prisoners by the injustice and arbitrariness of the police regime in Cuba). Nobody wants to entrust his head to a murderer, a vulgar rapist, a man without morals able to sell out even his own mother without the slightest remorse. Might not one of these be capable of committing the worst sort of wrongdoing in exchange for a promise of release from prison, or even for some drug, or other enticement in the case of the mentally ill? What were our adversaries making this grotesque offer unable to do? What else can be expected from those who betray their homeland for love of their own visceral needs, unconditionally supporting a tyrant who enslaves his own people and makes everyone live their life groveling on their knees?

The garrison began trotting up the stairs, divided into two groups. Those carrying tear gas stood next to the dining room entrance, along with about 30 or 40 guards who occupied positions in front of the cells all along the hallway. The rest of the military had not entered into our gallery, remaining clustered in the small lobby separating pavilions 4C and 4D, where four benches had been placed so that the common prisoners could clip us without needing to take each of us out individually.

Alejandro Novo Álvarez was ready to exit as soon as the dining room door opened. Alejandro Novo, a very capable and brave comrade, was at that time head of our gallery and, as such, came out first to represent us among the authorities, to defend us fearlessly against the powerful and bloodthirsty enemy by asserting our inalienable rights as political prisoners. And right beside Alejandro, ready to help him deal with the situation were Luis Manuel Zúñiga Rey, Servando Infante Jiménez, and Roger Reyes Hernández. Raúl del Valle Vilardel and Clemente Rodríguez Isla also formed part of that first group.

What happened next wasn't surprising either. While Alejandro was inside one cell arguing with Noaldo Pérez, the head of internal order, Lieutenant Cobo was outside in the lobby directing the guards there, who began ruthlessly hitting Zúñiga Rey, Roger Reyes, and Servando Infante Jiménez with dowels, sticks, and chains for flatly refusing to be shaven and shorn by common prisoners.

As might be expected, the rest of us still locked up in the dining room began bursting forth with pent up fury and raising our voices, shouting loud, aggressive epithets against the military.

Tear gas guns were pointed toward the barred door to the dining room, which was being shaken almost off its hinges by the prisoners. At my right, Antonio López Muñoz was clinging to the door's bars and had to leap back to dodge the tip of a bayonet being thrust at him by Lieutenant Escalona. It almost hit him in the stomach. Muñoz yelled "you miserable lackey," "son of a bitch," and a handful of other insults. The least offensive was "Communist pig," as Escalona apparently didn't care because he just smiled cynically.

The head of Interior Order, when the blows began and he saw the prisoners' violent reactions, got very nervous. He ordered the guards not to fire their weapons or to release the tear gas.

"Novo, this has to stop… Novo, we need this to stop. Help me. Tell your people to calm down. I'm going to find a solution to this," Sergeant Noaldo appealed to him, as Alejandro Novo would tell us later. "You should have seen his eyes: he looked like a terrified madman…"

The beatings endured by our three comrades were tremendous. Luis Manuel Zúñiga had his head split cleanly in three places; his skin was ripped open over his ribs and back; his body was blackened by terrible bruises. For several days, he could hardly breathe because of a savage blow to his left lung. Servando Infante was crushed until he could endure no more. Roger Reyes became a semi-conscious tattered rag doll, held up by his arms and kicked by one of the military several times in the belly with the heel of his boot. All three were taken to the prison hospital because of the multiple injuries they had sustained. However, despite their critical condition, before providing them with any medical care, their hair was cut, taking advantage of their inability to resist.

As for the rest of us, an explosive situation had been created, with unforeseen consequences if the authorities insisted on having us shorn by common prisoners, since the beatings of our three comrades, far from scaring us, only energized us further. Finally, the penal administration agreed to let us have our own barbers as usual. Once again, we had won a moral battle, thanks to the blood spilled by our three brave fellows, and to our energetic response to the proposed humiliatingly repressive measures and cruel violence of the regime's jailers.

We had not eaten breakfast that day nor lunch or supper, not only because the food was filthy crap, but to demonstrate our disgust at the indiscriminate way in which we were being deprived of almost all of our belongings, including, believe it or not, eyeglasses and dental prostheses, and more seriously even, because of the savage beating administered to our three brothers.

As is customary among the arrogant military of Boniato, our coordinated action to reject food was met with a new retaliation. That same afternoon, we were informed that from that moment on, the diets of the sick were being suspended. This, obviously, irritated our people even more, and so the next day we boycotted breakfast, lunch, and dinner.

A new inspection began at dawn on the 12th, done obviously to irritate us and make us feel police pressure. There was nothing to worry about, with all that had been removed by the previous inspection, we had little concern for our remaining property. If anyone had anything left, rather unlikely, experience had shown that the prisoner should never feel very attached to anything material, not even to his own skin.

Only one very significant fact came to our attention: while the seizure was underway and we remained still locked up in the dining room, there had been an order for the immediate relocation of the homosexuals of 4B ("The Boat") to another pavilion. After the last of them had been removed from the building, our cell doors were being sealed off by welding on thick steel plates.

Half an hour later, we confirmed what everyone had already imagined. With the solder still hot, whenever a cell in 4B was sealed up with metal planks, the military would take three 4A cellmates and pushed them inside, closing it with lock and padlock. When they had finished with those wearing only underpants, because of their refusal to wear common prisoners' uniforms and their resistance to other arbitrary rules, they began to summon the rest. Then Sergeant Noaldo, adopting a Nazi-like stance while standing next to the door of the 4D dining room, began calling us out in small groups —four or five at most— without allowing us to collect more than a bar of soap, toothpaste, toothbrush, and a towel (in many cases, only theoretically, because most had been lost in the previous inspection), next, we were escorted by the guards to an improvised punishment cell where we awaited an uncertain fate.

From 4D, besides a cluster of easterners, there were 15 or 20 guys from Havana still left in the dining room when Lieutenant Milet, prison vice-director, told us that by order of the High Command, that we would be considered to be on hunger strike after 72 hours of rejecting food if we persisted. We were being offered —he informed us— the opportunity of choosing between two options: a gallery where we could stay as before, with cell doors open 24 hours, or a walled dungeon in 4B for those choosing the hunger strike.

Only a few Havana comrades, who for various reasons were unwilling to accept the challenge of the hunger strike, opted for the first choice, going with the eastern cohort to building 2C. The rest of us decided to share the fate of those already locked up in 4B without previously having been given a choice.

I was assigned to cell #22, together with Sergio Montes de Oca Gil and the poet Guillermo Rivas Porta. We were already locked inside the cell while welders were still finishing affixing the steel plate covering the front steel bars, and the electrical sparking of their welding forced us to take refuge in a corner, protecting ourselves with a sack given us by a common prisoner working to seal up our cell. The heat was terrible, nothing short of suffocating. Prison authorities apparently considered it would take too long —or perhaps would coddle us too much— to have us wait, as they had been allowing at first, so that the door would be ready before inserting its victims into the cell.

It was also our visiting day.

During that first night of being locked inside that dark, enclosed hole, plenty of gray thoughts crossed my mind, but nothing hurt as much as the painful picture of our elderly mothers returning to Havana with the anguish of not having been able to even embrace their sons. Likewise, my health was not optimal for resisting our situation. For several months, I had been suffering from a brutal form of cystitis, and my duodenal ulcer gave me no respite. But there was no time for lamentations; duty called, and there was no choice but to subordinate the miseries of the body to the strength of the spirit.

The next morning, communication was re-established. Access to our hall was authorized for three or four comrades who, although not on strike, had decided to remain with us in those enclosures. Among them was Dr. Alberto Fibla, who generously offered to provide medical attention, although severely limited, since he had no drugs or instruments of any kind. Thanks to these fellow prisoners, we could exchange notes among us, limited also because very few of us were able to salvage a pencil stub or spare pen. I always carried these two "weapons" with me when I foresaw a repressive inspection. A spare pen can easily be hidden on any part of the body, even in the hair, and during prolonged isolation it proves to be very useful, especially for us poets. I'd had that experience and Rivas Porta as well. So, we both made sure that during our confinement, as long as the strike lasted, we would not be hampered by a lack of ink. I was then writing my poetry collections, *Upwind,* and *The Bell of the Dawn,* the latter dedicated to children, and even though the occasion was not very conducive to poetic creativity, I needed to be prepared in case a favorable emotional state arose.

Since there was no water in the cells and the containers we had were small jugs, our colleagues who had volunteered to help us out provided a tremendous service. Luckily for us, they had come forward and the prison's administration had agreed to allow them access to our hall.

During the first week, Rivas, Montes de Oca, and I did nothing more than tell old stories, reminiscing about our adventures, significant events, and mostly pleasant experiences; then, already a little weary from the fast, our talks became shorter and the hours longer. Occasionally, my ulcer kicked up for a while. Whenever the pain got intense, I squeezed a fist against the sore area, lying face down, and even if it might be only a psychological effect, occasionally I felt some relief.

On the ninth day of fasting, around 2 p.m., I began to feel an acidity sometimes rising up into my throat. However, I paid no attention, since for me it was something usual, a simple notice that my stomach craved a sip of antacid. But I had none and tried to make do with a jug of water.

The rest of the afternoon I was quite well. However, just at dusk, the acidity arose again, moderate at first..., but as nightfall progressed, around 7:30, the acid rose full up into my throat. The ulcer also hurt intensely and I felt a tremendous nausea.

I sat on the edge of my bunk, leaning over the service hole, expecting to vomit, and I did eject a little acid and bile by sticking my finger down my throat. Then I was overcome by an immense fatigue. Montes de Oca and Rivas Porta grabbed me on either side and helped me to lie down. In a few minutes, I got even worse. I completely lost strength, and cold sweat soaked my body.

For a few seconds, I lost consciousness.

Rivas and Montes de Oca might have thought that I had died, because when I came to, the former was crying out for a stretcher to take me to the hospital.

I tried to downplay my situation as simply a matter of having fainted, when I felt a sudden urge to vomit and felt a strong taste of blood. My memory of what happened next is vague; renewed cries from Rivas pressing the guards, cursing from Montes de Oca and his fist banging violently against the metal plank covering the door, then the noise of many metal planks being hit at the same time... Again, vomiting, the taste of blood, and passing out.

When I returned to consciousness, I was lying on a canvas stretcher set down on the floor in front of the guard post at Boniato's medical clinic.

I tried instinctively to get up, but unbearable pain in my stomach forced me to fall back down on my side before turning face up again. Several officers surrounded me, among them Lieutenant Marrero, who, with his usual despotism, advised me that I would not receive attention as long as I did not jettison my current attitude.

"So, it's your choice," he said, "either you agree to stop the strike or we'll take you back to your cell right now."

"That's just blackmail. I never asked for medical assistance nor am I going to abandon the strike," I replied, trying to summon up all my strength. "And we are already talking about doing more. Take me back to my cell."

The officials exchanged glances, a little surprised. Marrero himself instructed the orderlies, two muscular common prisoners, "Get going. Take him back to 4B!"

Left to my fate, I closed my eyes in exhaustion as soon as we got underway. Only one thing concerned me: the angry reaction of my comrades on seeing me being returned in such critical condition without any treatment whatsoever. It might end up unleashing a conflict, given the solidarity and strong ties of brotherhood among the men of the political prison, consolidated by our shared pain of the flesh and by our common goal of obtaining freedom for our people enslaved by the totalitarianism of a tyrant hatched from the egg of a snake.

To my surprise, I was not taken back to Pavilion 4B. Instead, I was taken to a medical cell-cubicle (3.5 meters square) where fellow prisoner Luis Arroyo Ramos had been for a little more than two weeks, also on hunger strike. Facing this "special" cell, separated by two bathrooms and a small vestibule, was another similar cell. Both cells had metal planks to cover them, but both remained open all the time so we had access to the bathrooms.

As soon as I was deposited in the bed, the orderlies and officers retreated. A post official affixed the chain and locked the padlock around the barred door and also withdrew. Arroyo approached my bed in a friendly manner and we exchanged a few words before I again experienced vomiting and fatigue. When he saw blood, he got pretty frightened, but not as much as I was. Antonio López Muñoz, "The Bone," who had been admitted days earlier and occupied the opposite cubicle, when he heard me vomiting, quickly came over to help me. Meanwhile, Arroyo was already putting a cotton ball soaked in alcohol under my nose, then he sat down at the foot of my bed doing nothing more than watching me, quite worried, I imagine, about my deplorable physical condition.

A few minutes later, seeing that time had gone by and the nurse had not yet arrived, Arroyo went over to the door of the vestibule and started shouting out angrily.

On duty was Luisito, a civilian nurse from Santiago de Cuba. He was kind to political prisoners. He arrived almost instantly, but did not enter the cubicle. He merely informed Arroyo that they had been given strict orders not to offer me any kind of medical care unless the doctor had seen me first. "Furthermore," Luisito explained, "they forbade me to even enter the cubicle. No one can approach his bed."

Arroyo's arguments proved useless. The nurse knew I was vomiting blood, and that my condition was serious, but the order had been given by the penal administration and he wasn't willing to risk violating a military order. He didn't want, as he said, "to go up in flames."

At that time, Dr. Dalmau had already been freed and the only doctor attending the Boniato infirmary was Dr. Nelson Stanley (whose name might have been owed to forbearers in the English-speaking Caribbean). In the morning, he would make rounds from cubicle to cubicle noting the condition of each patient admitted. Then he treated some 20 prisoner cases and left at 4:30 p.m., leaving the prison without medical care until 8:00 a.m. the next morning, Monday through Saturday. On Sunday, none of the two or three thousand prisoners, sometimes more—the figure varied according to the frequency with which common prisoners were taken out to concentration camps— were entitled to get sick, with the exception of stabbing victims, who, in the case of very serious injuries requiring urgent surgical intervention, were referred to the Provincial Hospital in Santiago. Only in very exceptional cases, when someone was gravely ill, was Dr. Stanley allowed to come in on an emergency basis.

"They may be looking for Stanley," Arroyo told me, something I already knew, because from my bed I had overheard his conversation with the nurse, and also the angry words which Muñoz had hurled at Luisito, blaming the warden for what could happen to me because of their "shamefulness," and other rather strong swear words that defined what he considered, rightly, to be a repressive measure of the higher authorities.

Shortly after midnight, the frequency of my vomiting began to increase and the pain in the pit of my stomach made me bite the pillow. I don't remember experiencing any greater physical suffering in my life. At that moment, I just wanted to die as quickly as possible to escape that horrible agony once and for all.

# CHAPTER 35

# On the Brink of Death

It dawned... what felt like several centuries later. Two hours would pass before Dr. Nelson Stanley showed up, two hours at a minimum, which for me meant an eternity. It was amazing to me that I was still alive. Since childhood, I've always been drawn to the story of the so-called seven lives of the cat, imagining that I might have some kitty ancestry myself.

Around 8:00 a.m. came the sound of keys in the vestibule door, then the click of a squeaky lock opening.

"Finally, it's the doctor!" I nearly exclaimed in shock and joy, like a castaway just spotting on the horizon a rescue ship approaching him at full speed. But I kept quiet, lacking enough energy to make even the slightest sound.

It was not Stanley.

An official of medium stature, with gray hair and an expressionless face came over to my bed to ask me if I had reconsidered my attitude toward the hunger strike.

I replied gruffly that I had nothing to reconsider, that my position had not changed. As with Lieutenant Marrero, I indicated that I didn't want to discuss the matter further.

The official tried to convince me that it was senseless to die "simply on a whim," especially for a young person like me who had "a world ahead." I won't repeat the compliments he gave me, hypocritical and undeserved.

As he was leaving, he said he was very sorry to inform me that as long as I refused to stop the strike, he would authorize no type of medical assistance, "not even an aspirin." That was an order from the interior minister, according to him, because the government did not accept "being force-fed." As I also recall, in a "magnanimous" gesture, he told me that I seemed to have a perforated ulcer, so might have only a few more hours left to live.

"With any luck," I replied, so as to leave no doubt about my firm determination not to abandon the strike, whatever the consequences.

The man shrugged his shoulders in apparent indifference and left, while I began vomiting once again.

That morning, Dr. Nelson Stanley did not go from cubicle to cubicle, visiting patients. Because of his unusual absence, at 9:00 a.m., Arroyo Ramos investigated, and the nurse Elia informed him that the doctor was making rounds among common prisoners. Given the cases he still needed to see, she estimated that Stanley should be finished around 10:30 a.m.

Vomiting and more vomiting ensued, and to add insult to injury, a tremendous bout of hiccups followed. The pain already could not become more devastating; it had already reached its peak. I realized that because of our shared desperation, López Muñoz and Arroyo were suffering as much as I. Since midnight, when the nurse had said that he had been forbidden to approach my bed, both of them were making a supreme effort to contain their anger, hoping to be able to persuade someone to give me a tranquilizer shot to calm my agony.

Knowing the explosive character of "The Bone" and the dynamic and fraternal fellowship that both he and Luis Arroyo had demonstrated at so many difficult times over the years, I had asked them both to calm down. However, since it was already 11:00 and the doctor had not appeared, their tempers flared and, via the same nurse, they sent an ultimatum to Dr. Stanley, announcing that if he did not show up in ten minutes to assist me, they would set fire to the mattresses and anything flammable inside the two cubicles. Elia was so scared and left so fast that she seemed to have wings on her feet and was back almost instantly to inform them that Dr. Stanley was already consulting with the last patient and would be there without delay to assist me.

In less than five minutes, he was at my cubicle. He lamented my deplorable physical condition and tried to make excuses, saying he had been given absolutely no information about my case, which was hard to believe.

I don't know if it was the bloody vomit already spilled on the floor or my pitiful appearance that moved his sensitivity, so that he could not avoid a gesture of compassion and voiced a very harsh rebuke for those who had withheld information about my grave condition.

"I can only guess what you must be going through," he said, "but you have to endure a little more before we can inject a pain reliever. We need to take an image to determine the cause of the bleeding first. It would be best to take you to the provincial hospital..."

Stanley was about to say something else, but was interrupted when Cusa entered pushing a wheeled stretcher to take me for X-rays. Cusa was a common prisoner, an excellent person, who often was assigned to clean up at the prison. When we arrived at radiology, Pucho was already waiting for us, also a political prisoner since 1959, who had gone over to the re-education plan and now worked as a radiology technician. While we had known each other for only about a year, there was a strong bond between us. It was a miracle that I could retain in my stomach the barium sulfate that I had to swallow before four or five X-rays could be taken.

Back in the cubicle, already Elia had prepared an IV of dextrose and other ingredients. "Stanley told me to prepare a serum strong enough to knock out a bull. You're going to sleep like a baby," joked the nurse, perhaps to lift my mood.

But after an hour, the pain had not abated and the vomiting continued with the same frequency. Around 3:00 p.m., the doctor returned and asked that I try to take, in small sips, as much as possible, of a gluco-physiological serum mixed with aluminum hydroxide and also belladonna. Before leaving, Stanley wished me good luck.

Thanks to Pucho, that same afternoon I was unofficially informed of my X-ray results. My plates had been sent to the radiologist at the Santiago Provincial Hospital with whom Pucho had maintained good relations. The specialist had diagnosed a cardiac lesion at the entrance to the stomach. That same diagnosis was ratified by Dr. Stanley the next morning. Stanley then ordered new X-rays.

Again, I found myself being carried by stretcher to the radiology chamber... and again the serum that supposedly would "knock out a bull," according to Elia, was waiting for me on my return.

The next nurse on duty, Dolores, had only begun working recently at Boniato. She was left-handed and her hands were small, and also slightly rough, apparently because of the work she had to do during her childhood and adolescence, since, as she confessed to me later, she came from a humble peasant family. She displayed a rustic beauty and a strong-willed spirit. But at first glance, her eyes displayed the diaphanous tenderness of all women. Few females, even those who strive to be businesslike, can avoid showing such tenderness and an exquisite sensitivity.

Dolores was not at her best when searching for a vein in my arm. After her second attempt had failed, she began to decry her bad luck, becoming very nervous. I tried to give her confidence by downplaying each useless stick. But I actually felt like wringing her darn neck...; unfairly, perhaps, because her ninth attempt finally succeeded. Although my bleeding had already diminished, even three days after the crisis, the vomiting was not over.

I was soon joined by Félix Piña Proto with complications from diabetes, Jesús Nazer Fraga ("The Moor") with a serious renal colic, and Manuel Hernández Cruz, suffering from several conditions, including Ménière's Syndrome. Because of the overcrowding, Hernández Cruz was installed in the small vestibule facing the two bathrooms.

After 72 hours of uninterrupted IV infusions without any cessation in my vomiting, which, although it seems incredible, occurred 200 to 250 times a day, Dr. Stanley was stumped. "Thanks to your extraordinary physical strength, you have managed to survive so far," he said after taking my blood pressure, "but I fear that your body may not be able to resist much more if this vomiting persists."

Then, to my astonishment, he asked me: "What do you think I should do that might bring any better luck?"

This question from a medical professional to a sick patient might seem absurd. But in light of both the IV and intra-muscular treatment I was getting, especially gravinol (a medication to combat dizziness and vomiting), I had subtly questioned whether I wasn't being over-medicated. I recalled a one-year-old relative who actually had died after an overdose of injected gravinol.

But Dr. Stanley had decided the amount that I was being given would not be considered excessive. It so happened that shortly before midnight, the nurse, Carmona, had injected me with a second dose of intramuscular gravinol and, just as I had anticipated to Stanley beforehand, I went into anaphylactic shock. Perhaps that simple coincidence led him to think that I had some knowledge of medicine, or else some propensity for prophecy, so he was asking for my help.

"I would try," I decided to tell him, "suspending everything being given orally and keep only the IV as you have had it, adding, a couple of chlorpromazine capsules to see if I can sleep awhile."

Sleep. Four consecutive days I had already gone without sleeping even a single second as a result of that damn vomiting. In addition to my terrible physical exhaustion, the forced insomnia had put my nerves on edge, making me tremble from head to toe. If with the chlorpromazine, I could manage to sleep at least a couple of hours, it was even possible that my stomach could be calmed somewhat. So far, I had vomited all oral medications and even sips of water, so I considered it best to put absolutely nothing at all into my stomach for a while.

Stanley accepted my suggestion. By afternoon, the frequency of my vomiting became progressively reduced and...

I have no precise idea of the moment when I fell asleep, especially given my extreme physical exhaustion, but I think it happened during evening twilight.

When I woke up, it was already dawn. Three hours later, the doctor gave a great sigh of satisfaction and surprise since, for more than 15 hours, my vomiting had disappeared and my pain was slight.

The rest of the day passed without major setbacks, so before Stanley left that afternoon, I asked him to discharge me. I wanted to return as soon as possible to my enclosed cell in 4B to join my companions there and to share with them the uncertain outcome of our hunger strike.

Stanley expressed amazement at the prospect of my returning to the dungeons.

"Impossible!" he exclaimed. "That would be crazy."

And after a brief pause, he added, "Furthermore, I advise you to quit the strike."

It was not the first time the doctor had suggested that I abandon the strike. Directly or indirectly, he had asked me to do so, despite my implacable negativity.

"With what you've just been through," he continued, "and given your body's condition, I won't be responsible for signing your discharge. And much less with that lesion in your stomach which, although it seems to have evolved well, remains a delicate issue."

There was no way to convince him. So, I decided to wait until the next day. In any case, it was better to stay in the hospital few more hours before making an issue of returning to my cell in Pavilion 4B.

That day my stomach tolerated a solution of gluco-physiologic, aluminum hydroxide, and citrobelladona without difficulty. Shortly after Dr. Stanley left, I was joined by Julio Ruiz Pitaluga, suffering from a tremendous eye infection. He could barely see. No beds were available and, so that he wouldn't have to sleep on the floor, I offered him half of mine. But Cusa later got him a pad for the floor and so Ruiz Pitaluga, in order not to disturb me, chose to lie down in a corner of the cubicle.

The next morning, we learned that four or five compatriots who had been admitted to the cubicles of the opposite medical wing had decided to abandon the strike. Apparently, they were not prepared mentally to sustain a fast under such difficult conditions and perhaps considered it not worth the sacrifice. We found this out from Orlando Molina Contreras. Molina, taking advantage of an oversight at the post, had escaped to the bars of the vestibule to where Manuel Hernández Cruz's cot was located to inform that him that he also was forced to abandon the strike because of a pulmonary injury, detected through X-rays the day before, he explained. He was so affected emotionally, that when he told us that he was abandoning the strike, he could not hold back tears and began crying like a baby. For some —I would say only a tiny minority— a step of this kind is no reason for any type of remorse, even without a reasonable justification. Instead, for the overwhelming majority, giving up a hunger strike midway hits the prisoner very hard, causing even a mental trauma which lasts for a long time, sometimes even for a lifetime.

A good example is the case of the hunger strike carried out by a little more than 800 *plantado* political prisoners at La Cabaña in the summer of 1969. Since that fast lasted 35 days and the authorities radically forbade anything beyond the most minimal medical assistance unless food was accepted, about 250 men who for different reasons could not hold out until the very last moment, abandoned the strike and were morally devastated by having waived their status as *plantados* by accepting the so-called "re-education plan." Many of these men were valuable fellows with a very beautiful history of resistance and tremendous combativeness sustained through long years of prison. Many of them had spilled their own blood in prison and in the fields of forced labor at Isle of Pines in an exemplary attitude of heroic rebellion.

I tried to lift Molina's spirits with supportive words. In reality, he was a partner who was very beloved by all. It seemed that when he withdrew from our cubicle, under pressure from the ill-humored guard arriving in search of him, his spirit had been somewhat calmed.

# CHAPTER 36

# Back Again to Pavilion 4B

Stanley reappeared around 9:00 a.m. He had been consulting, he told us, from very early, on other urgent cases. The situation was getting complicated for the doctor and for the authorities, and for us, too, of course. Suffice it to say that the strikers got the worst part, enduring the greater physical and psychological burden.

The first case that Stanley attended in our cubicle was that of Julio Ruiz Pitaluga. Pitaluga told him about the unsanitary conditions of our cells in 4B. Previously, our section had been occupied by homosexuals who were not given any means by which to clean the human waste from the floor and walls.

More than just our cells seemed genuine filthy. It would be difficult to find in any part of the human world more abandoned than the homosexuals at Boniato. Seen from the outside through the railings overlooking the lobby, "La Patera" looked clean and adorned with decorations and flags of all colors strung from one end to another of the hall, with a ping-pong table at the center, a television, and an organized library. However, inside the cells, not visible from outside, was a veritable sewer, unclean, a smelly pigsty, that at first glance, churned your guts and raised your hair from head to toe. And this was without mentioning the many cases that existed there, according to Stanley himself, of syphilis, gonorrhea, and tuberculosis.

The doctor prescribed for Pitaluga some antibiotic eye drops and advised him to no longer use contact lenses. He was authorized to stay with us for a couple of days.

Taking advantage that Jesús Nazer had already recovered from his renal colic and was returning to his cell that morning, Julio Ruiz could have his bed, but the latter didn't want to stay in the dispensary any longer than necessary for Stanley to see him and provide him the right medication.

As soon as he finished with Pitaluga, the doctor approached my bed to take my blood pressure and investigate how I had spent the night. In the absence of any setback, I wanted to take the opportunity to be released.

No, Stanley insisted that I should remain for at least four or five more days. Since he refused to be swayed with reasoning, I let him know that I was determined to not stay in the dispensary beyond noon. I finally overcame his obstinacy and he agreed to let me go at my request, but making sure to note that it was under my full responsibility.

Around 11:00 a.m., Julio Ruiz Pitaluga and I returned together to 4B, escorted by Lieutenant Laudelino and another officer.

We had to walk some 200 meters and our physical condition was quite deplorable, mainly mine at that moment—so our progress was slow. When we arrived at the top of building 1A, we found waiting there to greet us, our esteemed friend Ángel Cuadra and several others.

We embraced each other through the bars.

Already in pavilion 4B, since my friends had not expected me to return for some time, Evelio Hernández, who had been sharing cell 24 with Nelson Rodríguez and Roberto Martín Pérez the night I was taken to the infirmary, were now living in number 22 along with Rivas Porta and Sergio Montes de Oca. Because of this change, I took up residence in cell number 12 along with Pitaluga and Víctor Miguel Cantón.

The first exchange between the gallery captains (Alejandro Novo and Ángel Luis Argüelles Garrido) and the prison's administration was held 18 days into the strike. The prison's deputy warden had sent for them, informing our representatives that the "Command" had asked for attention to our concerns. Milhet received them at the office of

Internal Order, together with Sergeant Noaldo. During more than two hours, Novo and Argüelles discussed the embarrassing situation created by the prison authorities following instructions from the High Command. Over two hours were spent in a fruitless exchange, because according to the issues raised by the deputy and the Chief of Internal Order, any possible agreement could not be considered until we had first put an end to the strike, which our people were unwilling to do under any circumstances.

As soon they returned from the meeting, both Argüelles and Novo asked for silence while all of us listened, and in loud, slow voices recounted the interview with Lieutenant Milhet and Sergeant Noaldo Pérez.

The decision to continue with the strike was unanimous, with the exception of Víctor Miguel Cantón, who told Pitaluga and me that from the beginning, he had understood that the fast would cease as soon the prison authorities received our leaders, regardless of the outcome of their meeting, and so Miguel decided to end his hunger strike.

The following morning Víctor Miguel was allowed to move to cell number 8, with Roger Reyes and Raúl del Valle, taking advantage that these companions, while not accepting the fast, were among those who had decided to share our same fate by staying with us in the dungeons of pavilion 4B.

"If they don't take me to cell 8 cell, I will continue rejecting food," Miguel had told us, "because I'm not going to eat in front of you." In that gesture of friendship and humanism, Víctor Miguel Cantón had put our situation even above his personal decision.

Two or three days later, Eloy Gutiérrez Menoyo, who had been sharing cell 35 with Ángel Luis Argüelles and Roberto Perdomo Díaz, was able to get a transfer to number 12 together with Pitaluga and me. Previously he had sent us a note that his cell was a disaster, due to walls impregnated with fungus, crusted blood, and grime, and the bunks stained with excrement. All that, of course, was the result of someone actually crazy who had occupied that cell before the prior inhabitants of 4B were evacuated in order to close us up in that pavilion. Instead of sending those people to a psychiatric hospital, Boniato's mentally ill were also confined in the "patera." Some homosexuals loathed that forced coexistence with them, and others cheered it. For most of the gay prisoners, the crazy ones were objects, simple objects, of entertainment, of singular fun. They performed wonders for just a crust of old bread or a cigarette butt! Such was the hunger and longing for a smoke suffered by these wretched souls, imposed on them by the will of the "humanist' jailers of the regime. Every few weeks, Cause, the chief of the "patera," allowed them outside for a while to take some sun between buildings 2 and 3, and then we used to give them cigarettes and something to eat that they devoured instantly before going out to cavort around the patio. Usually, they were wearing only ragged and filthy underwear. The spectacle was very depressing, depressing for any sensible person who understood the tremendous scale of this human tragedy. Chief Cause, of course, could not understand it. He couldn't understand it because he suffered from the same degree of mental alienation, being as much a prisoner as they were, giving them ruthless beatings and depriving them systematically of a good part of their meager food rations.

After 25 days of fasting, the spirit of the strikers was magnificent. Most admirable was the stoic sacrifice of those comrades who suffered from serious health conditions, but maintained an upright attitude, at great risk to their very lives. Specific cases were those of Dr. José Enrique Velasco Santa Cruz and Justo Guerra Remedio (Guerrita), both very ill, with chronic diabetes, and both over 60, who were in my opinion the most exemplary. Also deserving mention were Mario Gavilán Sánchez, Isidro Rodríguez, José Oscar Rodríguez Terrero, Eduardo Capote Rodríguez, José Miguel Barco Gómez, Sergio Montes de Oca Gil, Pedro Santana Camejo, Julio Acosta Lozada, Pedro González Rodríguez, Ángel De Fana Serrano, Ernesto Palomeque Bussiel, Armando Yong Martínez, Pedro M. Montey Hernández, Manuel Hernández Cruz, Julián Domínguez, Adolfo Duque Favelo, Roberto Azcuy Cruz, Servando Infante Jiménez, and many others, who in a worthy response to the challenges coming from the prison's administration accepted without hesitation, joining in our hunger strike even though very few months remained on their sentences —almost all, 20 years— well aware that the authorities could in retaliation impose additional sanctions to prevent their release. The very same Alejandro Miguel Novo Álvarez was one of those close to completing his sentence and, despite this, accepted with enthusiasm the harsh responsibility of representing us to the prison leadership and, like Ángel Luis Argüelles Garrido, with a dignified fortitude, defended our rights as human beings and as political prisoners.

Because of physical deterioration, over twenty of our associates had to be transferred to the prison infirmary. Except for my own incident, there was no attempt to condition medical assistance on someone's renunciation of the strike. Others, because they were stronger in body or perhaps in spirit, refused any medical care whatsoever. As in all human assemblages, apart from individual needs, different ideas and different criteria were expressed.

On about the 28th day of fasting, Eloy Gutiérrez Menoyo was hit with a severe pain in his head and chest. At nightfall, seeing that his pain was increasing and he had suffered from frequent fainting spells, I communicated to Dr. Alberto Fibla (a *plantado* prisoner who ended up completing a 25-year sentence) and to Dr. Velasco about the clinical picture that Eloy presented. Both agreed that he should be transferred immediately to the infirmary. Eloy was reluctant, but Pitaluga and I convinced him to go, fearing it could be a heart attack.

It was about 9:30 p.m. when a stretcher arrived for him. His stay at the clinic was short. The next morning, the stretcher-bearers brought Eloy back to 4B. Since the pain had gone away, he told us, after the nurse had administered an IV solution containing a tranquilizer, as soon as the second liter had finished, he asked the doctor to let him go. Stanley, as in my case days before, had disagreed, but yielded to Eloy's insistence, making a note in his medical record that he was being discharged under his own responsibility.

Recalling setbacks during his brief stay in the hospital, Eloy told us about an incident that made us smile. The nurse on duty that night was Dolores. She was very willing —syringe in hand— to try to find a vein. But Eloy, forewarned by me about my nine punctures from the "golden lefty," flatly refused to deliver his arm in sacrifice to the lady.

Three days after Eloy had returned from the infirmary, two new doctors arrived at Pavilion 4B, accompanied by nurse Marcos Campos and a couple of officers. Already, several comrades had been admitted in fairly serious condition. The doctors visited cell-by-cell to check for themselves on the deteriorating physical status of each of the strikers. The result was that 15 were admitted immediately to be administered IVs. Since the clinic capacity was very limited, beds were set up in the hallways and in the small lounge where common prisoners received visitors.

December 11 saw great activity. The higher authorities were eager to bring a prompt end to the strike, if nothing else, I think, because of the risk that a man might die, even more than one, at any moment. They knew that at La Cabaña, eleven years earlier, of the 800 or so prisoners who had gone on strike, at least 600 resisted for 35 days; and a few, including, Húber Matos, Tony Lamas, and Silvino Rodríguez Barriento, had fasted one week longer without any deaths, although many were paralyzed for a while. There were other cases, such as that of Domingo Ortega Acosta, who completely lost his balance, unable to coordinate movements of his legs for more than three years. And most serious and most poignant was the case of Federico Hernández González, who, as a result of the long fast, suffered irreversible injury to his spinal cord that also affected his cerebellum, preventing him from coordinating his movements, but unlike Ortega Acosta, he was condemned to suffer from it for the rest of his life.

But, now almost on the eve of 1981, those same men, who in the summer of 1969 had resisted without major setbacks after 35 days of rigorous fasting, now older and with a longer time in prison, no longer had the same strength. Their uninterrupted tenure behind bars, subjected to a regime of deprivation and appalling cruelties, had taken their toll after 17 years, and the higher authorities knew it. In addition, during their visits to the enclosed cells of 4B, the doctors had observed the general dehydration and the severity of symptoms among some of the strikers. Certainly, some reports to those higher up, by them and by Stanley (as the prison's medical director), would have reflected a situation that was very critical, if not alarming. It was imagined this influenced the dynamic mobilization of Boniato's officialdom and their haste to admit the most serious cases for treatment. It was not too hard to see that the boat had begun to fill with up water in their desperate attempt to get to shore.

Shortly after dark, an official came for Novo and Argüelles. The deputy director had sent for them, a soldier told them, to discuss with them for a second time what conditions our people needed to end the strike. Since their extreme weakness prevented them from walking to the prison office, they were transported on stretchers.

At this second meeting, as previously, Lieutenant Milhet and Sergeant Noaldo received them. The result was an official promise that after our fasting stopped, then immediately, the walled enclosed cells would be opened, allowing us access, as before, to the interior hall 24 hours a day, and the dining room from dawn until the 10:00 p.m. count. Similarly, visits from our families (four people maximum for each prisoner) would be restored, as well as the right to take two hours of sun and air out on the patio for two hours three times per week, and medical and dental care guaranteed without the imposition of a humiliating strip search.

Novo and Argüelles returned, speaking from the hall to report on what had been discussed with the top brass. As was expected, the widespread view, with a few exceptions, was that what Milhet and Noaldo had offered, representing the High Command, would satisfy our main needs. However, it wasn't until the next afternoon, on December 12, when it was agreed to definitively put an end to the hunger strike.

As promised, an hour later, the jailers went cell to cell, removing the locks and lifting off the bolts. The doors were opened to all cells, except #12, at our request. That is because we, the residents of that cell, Eloy Gutiérrez Menoyo, Julio Ruiz Pitaluga, and I, had decided to go ahead with the hunger strike anyway, and so did Evelio Hernández Ramírez, Ramón Méndez Pimentel, and Sergio Montes de Oca Gil. After more than a whole year of quiet waiting for the Deputy Minister of the Interior, General Enio Leyva, to fulfill his promise we would be moved to Combinado del Este Prison in Havana, now in order to vigorously protest that vile deception and delay, we six opted to continue the fast.

At the beginning, but without any commitment, besides the six of us, we were joined by some of the other 17 who had made it to the end of our strike, which had already lasted almost two months. But they did not make a firm commitment to continue with the fast because they might not have been sufficiently prepared mentally to do so or because, after so many days without eating any food (only water), their (our) deplorable physical condition would not allow them to continue on for much longer. Others certainly expressed to us their dissatisfaction from the first moment about our prolongation of the strike and made every effort to deter what they considered a "crazy" decision with unpredictable consequences. Both Eloy and Pitaluga were especially reluctant to have *me* continue, given how extremely frail I was from my bleeding and violent vomiting crisis. I was also concerned about injury to my stomach, but I was willing to take the risk and my irrevocable decision was to continue with the strike, as Eloy and I had agreed to do ever since we were first locked up in Pavilion 4B.

Almost as soon as the jailers had removed the bolts, Ramón Mendez Pimentel appeared at our cell #12 to tell us that Onofre Pérez Hernández, his cellmate in #26, had decided to continue the strike with us. This news did not surprise us. No one who knew Onofre Pérez would have expected anything else. As much as we would have welcomed such a brave comrade with us, because of his extreme physical deterioration, we could not accept his offer to join us. Just a few hours earlier, Onofre had been brought back from the medical unit on a stretcher after several days in critical condition.

Eloy was just writing him an explanatory note, explaining why we could not accept him for the continuation of the fast at this time, when he suddenly appeared like a ghost at the entrance to our cell. He was very upset by our radical position. Then, accepting the bitter reality, he bit his lip to hold back a sob, as if his soul were breaking while two tears streamed down his sunken cheeks.

Eloy reached out his hand through the small opening of the bars onto Onofre's head in a gesture of affection. "Come on! What kind of silliness is this?" he asked him, roughing up his hair. That same night, Onofre went to live in cell #27 with Rolando García.

Evelio Hernández and Sergio Montes de Oca, who had been

admitted to the prison infirmary when our colleagues had concluded the hunger strike, sent me a note confirming that both remained firm in what we had agreed upon. As their physical deterioration had not gone beyond the inevitable dehydration, we were glad to know that they could continue the strike with us.

Although we had planned to remain in 4B for the maximum possible time, at noon on December 14, higher authorities transferred us to the infirmary at about 2 p.m. There we all were, Eloy, Pitaluga, Pimentel, and I, together with Evelio and Sergio. All the beds were occupied, so with the help of Cusa, we were set up provisionally in the small lobby opposite the two baths, where Manuel Hernández Cruz had spent about three weeks during the hunger strike.

# CHAPTER 37

# An Urgent Poem

Shortly before dusk, at the door of the infirmary lobby where we had been placed, Rodolfo Suárez Cruz appeared. He was accompanied by Lieutenant Suárez, head of Pavilion #1. Rodolfo had abandoned the strike while I was being treated for stomach problems, agreeing to return to the "rehabilitation plan," something I tremendously regretted at that inopportune moment. If he had not been pressed by the aggressiveness of the jailers and our uncertain future in the grim bowels of those walled black holes in a fleeting moment of emotional upset, Rodolfo would have kept the faith. He had more than enough physical strength to resist and the necessary spirit of sacrifice as well. Proof of this was that in May 1979, he had voluntarily joined the hunger strike that a *plantado* group had started at Combinado del Este, frustrated about his chances to be pardoned. It was unlikely, given the characteristics of the crime for which Rodolfo was being punished: a political asylum attempt at the Venezuelan Embassy.

Moreover, on the same day of our arrival at Boniato, he had endured with magnificent fortitude his solitary confinement in one of those terrible dark enclosures in pavilion 4A, some of the most cruel and inhumane of this prison, before accompanying us again, until the very last instant, on an exacting hunger strike that lasted almost two months. That is, Rodolfo did not lack the courage to confront a siege of prison violence. If he had committed the error of abandoning our strike at such a critical juncture, I am sure, without fear of contradiction, that the shattering of his spirit of resistance was the result of inexperience and haste, and not because of a lack of confidence in himself or in his ability to resist the hard challenges imposed by our insane, vengeful, and cowardly keepers – the enemies of freedom.

That afternoon, of December 14, Rodolfo had a visit from his parents. When he came back, he had faced a rigorous search. Rodolfo had risked secretly passing on to me 16 batteries for our tiny radio and several letters my sister-in-law had squeezed into a little ball. To get the head of pavilion 1A to agree to let him see me to give me the letters and batteries, Rodolfo invented the pretext of delivering a message from my relatives for me to abandon the strike.

If he had appealed to the higher authorities, he surely would not have been granted permission. But Lieutenant Suárez, at the time not among the most extreme, made the serious mistake of deciding by himself, and, after a few minutes, he appeared with Rodolfo at the door. It was not difficult to get him to allow Rodolfo in to sit on my bed to talk with me about "the matter" in private.

"Good, but be quick. I cannot give you more than five minutes," Lieutenant Suárez told Rodolfo.

Even with only five minutes, we still had plenty of time for Rodolfo to pass me the package of small batteries and correspondence without Lieutenant Suárez noticing. But thanks to his careless, my good friend's visit lasted three times as long. As he was leaving, Rodolfo gave me a warm hug. He seemed to be holding back tears. Rodolfo, despite being a pampered only son, as he himself admitted, expressed extraordinarily noble feelings. He was a strong, healthy boy who regarded me as a brother he had never had.

Among what we discussed was a verbal message from my sister-in-law, Berta, transmitted via Rodolfo's parents. I had been able previously to clandestinely get a message to my sister-in-law, who was in Santiago at the time, trying to find out about our situation. As a result, she was able to make an urgent phone call to my parents in Miami and to talk with my son Danny, now age 12 —whom I had last kissed on the forehead when he was just 6 months old—to assure him that his father was not dead, loved him very much, and wanted to see him.

"All three boys love you," my sister-in-law had insisted. "David and Ernestico also call me from time to time, worried about your situation and they are driving Aly (their grandmother) crazy, asking about you. But for Danny, it's an obsession. Your mother says that he's always talking about Pipo this and Pipo, that" (referring to his nickname for me).

Already my brother had told me years ago that even in his childhood fantasies, Danny had invented scenes of me taking him to the beach and us playing together in the sand, and how I had taught him to swim and dive, and many other musings that would without question have been memories had I not been behind bars. I was there for his freedom.

Now, Danny's message, transmitted to me via Rodolfo in the Boniato clinic on that bleak December afternoon, stirred in me a feeling of longing and subtle reproach. My young son had lamented that I had never dedicated any verses to him, and had asked me to write a poem in his name to send it to him via his aunt Berta, already by tomorrow.

But writing a poem after 35 days of fasting was something like trying to thread a needle with my eyes closed. Yet it was the only request that my young son had made of me during his whole life. And I just couldn't do it! There is nothing worse than feeling helpless. Anguish gripped me. Any human being would understand how I felt.

Just as there are men who are beasts, there are also, in happy contrast, those who are beacons, and the poet Ángel Cuadra was one of them. So, I appealed to him and his fraternal response was this beautiful poem that, after a night of luminous insomnia, he put into my hands, reflecting his strong and sincere emotion:

REMITTANCE

*(For Danny, son of Ernesto, for whom he has requested my song)*

Probably I will not reach out to you
for the embrace that I have been entrusted to give you;
I probably cannot send out from my eyelids
that look of tender fire which I have been asked
to take and shine on you;
probably I will not be able to bring to you with my words
the message of love that lacks more than just language
and, finally, it is very likely
that even this poem won't reach you,
which was to be sent to you by those hands that had
made you
from earth's mud and a dream.
In vain I want to be the messenger,
the translator of an ineffable music,
in vain, this twilight can express the dawn.
But I do try,
try to even love you
—son and flower and hope and stone and wing—
with this borrowed heart,
with this friend's soul that I am now using
(so familiar and so different, mine and other),
that I am assuming now and that I care for
as if loving a bit of the homeland.
I want these to be words of water,
of glass, of palpable transparency,
simple as the flowers of the orange tree,
as revealing as the bird songs that you hear
and beyond, there in your heart mirroring the beats
and the song.

One day, your father said some words,
and those words tumbled on in the voices of the wind,
and they made songs
—fun... and serious—

and among the circle of children turning round and
round
(you were all those children, all with different faces):
they put on musical wheels and wings,
and all got on a carousel going
from cloud to cloud sailing along.

Small inhabitants of a distant kingdom, souls of new
wheat
which is made into bread, the food of life,
coming along on the journey of this round of music,
of song and dance.
Here they talked without lips
the flowers and trees;
and the animals
in your language
and wearing their typical costumes,
they will tell stories, tales and trances
only telling them to you…

A beautiful newness,
fresh and vibrant,
was left behind
by the carousel
everywhere.
And the world is amazed at
how your father offered you
so much tenderness from his prison.

Now, probably you're growing up fast
and leaving behind toys.
And perhaps an ineffable sadness
sometimes knots in your throat;
something that comes with music
that is not cheery, probably not,

and changes your outlook.
Danny, if you can smile, smile,
immerse yourself in the afternoon's free air:
twilight is only an omen of the stars,
grapes in time give forth good wine,
the furrow will give up shoots
and man will bring light and will make roads
where you will go, probably.
That if there is a man here struggling "upwind"
with those same hands
that created you from a daydream and mud,
with a fierce tenderness, that makes the song and the
struggle
fruitful as the good mud of your life.

Now, too, steep yourself in the afternoon:
Look out into the free air of morning
a carousel of love,
probably.

Ángel Cuadra, December 14, 1980 (Boniato)

It would be hard to find a phrase capable of transmitting with sufficient sincerity the extraordinary joy gifted to me in these heart-felt verses from my symbolic father-poet, my immense gratitude to my friend. Today, it gives me immense satisfaction that the poetic work of Ángel Cuadra Landrove has won its deserved recognition beyond national borders. Fifteen years of ruthless enclosure in Castro's dungeons was the price paid with dignity by this man of burnished glass, this man, defending the freedom of his homeland and showing bravery before the implacable enemy: "I don't put my poetry on its knees."

A while after Rodolfo had left, Lieutenant Milhet appeared, and after a fruitless effort to convince me to abandon the strike, gave an order to immediately begin an IV for all six of us. In addition to us, still on hunger strike was Luis Arroyo Ramos, who had started on October

23. On the following day, December 15, Arroyo decided to give up his fast. That same afternoon, he was moved to one of the cubicles where in September 1979, a group of twenty of us had been admitted during that previous hunger strike. The same happened with Antonio López Muñoz, in an effort to isolate the strikers from the rest of hospitalized patients. Thus, Julio Ruiz Pitaluga, Eloy Gutiérrez Menoyo, and Méndez Pimentel occupied beds in the first cubicle, while Evelio Hernández, Sergio Montes de Oca, and I were installed, with the help of Cusa and Marcos Campos, at the other end, separated by the vestibule and the two small bathrooms.

As I had taken my tiny radio with me to try to get proper information, my companions gave me a bed strategically located to allow me to look out through the bars into the lobby, guaranteeing that I would not be caught "red-handed" if some soldier decided to enter our cubicle while I was listening to the news.

# CHAPTER 38

# Dr. Font

From December 15-30, we hunger strikers were attended by Dr. Font. Unlike Dr. Stanley, Font was a very dynamic and emotive doctor. He expressed an apparent sincere concern about our physical wellbeing and did his best for us within the limitations imposed by prison authorities, which, according to him, were not in accord with professional ethics, so he was trying to get transferred to a civilian hospital. He made no effort to hide his astonishment at the prolonged period we had gone without eating any food, saying he had never known before that Cuban political prisoners engaged in hunger strikes. Dr. Font also recognized and criticized, in front of us, some errors of the Revolution with the same naturalness with which he praised what he considered its positive attributes. This soft-spoken young man who was just 27 was openly sympathetic to the Stalinist socialism grafted onto Cuba by our "Libertador" Fidel Castro (don't forget, he assured us, that Castro himself does not lie... when he says that our Caribbean island is the "first free territory of America"). Once asked if he was a Communist, Dr. Font smiled slightly before announcing: "I am a revolutionary."

This simple response may or may not define a behavior, a political attitude, an ideal. It all depends on the intention behind it or the genuine feeling with which it is being said. Who knows if for this young man, the titles *Communist* and *Revolutionary* meant the same thing? Who knows if he is one of many young people in this country who have learned to mask their real opinions to escape prison or banishment, or for sheer survival, in hopes of that inexorable hour when all the bitter roots will have been ripped away from our tortured land?

After the 1,000 cc of 5% dextrose prescribed for us by Lieutenant Milhet, Dr. Font prescribed two additional doses. On the 16th, we got rid of the annoying arm immobilization, after the doctor decided that instead of intravenous administrations we could take the serum orally, interspersed with small doses of black tea. From that moment on, our morning "breakfast" was a prick in the buttocks – or at least what remained there (mostly just skin) – to inject us with a vitamin cocktail which burned like a wasp sting. I did everything to sabotage the syringe, and was frequently able to avoid it despite the persistent insistence of Pucho who, in a friendly gesture, agreed to inject us before reporting for duty in the X-ray room. We were still unable to banish the terror of the vision of Dolores, standing over our beds, syringe in hand. In retrospect, I am a little ashamed of how roughly we responded to her blunders.

December 24 was a black day for me. My vomiting reappeared before dawn and at the hour of our symbolic dinner, the 5% dextrose solution, I felt as if a bulldozer had rolled over me. It was also a day of nostalgia. I thought sadly of my empty chair at the family table, where I had always sat on Christmas Eve, and on at least thirteen other holidays and celebrations that year. I thought of the Christmas tree topped with a star, of the shattered hopes of my people. I kept thinking and thinking, inevitably, of the salty tears flowing from my mother's eyes, of the thorns in the hands of my children, so tender, yet so distant that their profiles merged and I could not distinguish each of their faces in my mind's eye.

At mid-afternoon, the serum began flowing into my vein. Lacking any other distraction, I spent a while contemplating the droplets, always identical, entering at a rate of 40 per minute. Evelio and Montes de Oca had concocted no fabulous projects like the day before. They remained silent. No doubt, they too were influenced by the date: December 24.

"Tell me something" —I asked them when it was already growing dark— "about anything but prison, or about shipwrecks or wars."

But neither replied as both continued staring at the ceiling. Lost in thought, it's likely neither heard me. Or who knows if I actually said nothing at all? Yes, that could have happened.

The following week passed without major setbacks in our health. Already, since Christmas Day, the doctor had been able to halt my vomiting. Pitaluga and Montes de Oca were suffering from more advanced dehydration and Dr. Font had to give them several IVs between the 27th and the 28th of December.

The New Year arrived with music. The people of Santiago celebrated by dancing at the overlook at the Port of Boniato, and drifting softly over the mountains, melodic chords came down into the hollow of our prison and its small hospital.

I was no less nostalgic than I had been on December 24, spending several hours plunged into a melancholy lethargy, pained by the inevitable evocation of my loved ones, so far away, and my feelings of distress, not only at my own prolonged absence from home, but also by the uncertainty of our fast which had already exceeded reasonable limits, with a big risk to our lives.

If there was anything that tore at my mother's heartstrings, it was hearing the Cuban national anthem being played on Miami radio stations at the stroke of midnight. During my years of exile, except in 1964, I had always been at her side for the transition from the old to the New Year. For me, it is impossible to fail to mention that it was my mother who showed the strongest family spirit. She suffered our penalties, but sometimes considered them insignificant compared with those which many other families were forced to suffer, and those of whole peoples obliged to wander throughout the world or being subjected in their own land to asphyxiating deprivation and cruel torments of all kinds: physical, spiritual, and moral. She was a humble woman of very limited education who had arrived at these conclusions by pure intuition, without ever having been informed of the appalling tragedy that Hitler's Nazism caused during World War II to the Jewish people dispersed all over Europe, including the approximately six million victims who perished in the gas chambers of Auschwitz, Belsen, Dachau, Buchenwald, and other fields of mass extermination. Or more recently still, the unfortunate exodus of the Palestinian people, the fratricidal war in Lebanon, pitting brothers against brothers during years and years because of religious, social, and political differences, plunging that country into painful and bloody destruction.

Nicaragua, El Salvador, Afghanistan, Vietnam, Laos, Cambodia, Angola, South Africa (racist South Africa), for my mother, these were no more than geographical points, nations where something bad has happened or is happening. And it hurt her human sensitivities no matter what side was involved. She was hurt, and I am not exaggerating here, even on behalf of our adversary who has shed my own blood and has prevented us during so many years from enjoying our own sublime family embrace each New Year's Eve, right on the stroke of midnight.

My love as a son, so very grateful for all her small but great things, yes, for my mother, so sobering and influential in the formation of my character, she has been for me, together with my father and my country, always my greatest pride, as she was for me that New Year's Eve at the Boniato infirmary; where she was still at the very center of my interior universe.

For you to understand her, and her strength, you have to know her words to me. In a smuggled letter from her, she wrote to me that she had been told I was destined to die from my hunger strike. If I was to die for what I believe in, she wrote, I should be at peace with it. She would accept my honorable death if that was inevitable, but could never accept it if I lived instead by surrendered to our enemy's tyranny. She was as committed to our ideals as the *plantados*.

Thinking of her, I fell asleep.

It was a short and restless slumber. Anyone who has ever been on a hunger strike knows from experience that it is impossible sleep more than two or three hours without interruption. I imagine that same uneasiness in sleeping is experienced by Haitian children, and the children of northeastern Brazil and of Bangladesh, and the children of many other corners of the world, mainly in Africa, Asia, and Latin

America, when famine assaults them. According to recent official UNICEF figures, each day, 40,000 children around the world die from lack of medical assistance and hunger. And the most alarming aspect of this gloomy scenario is that in that same 24-hour period, worldwide arms expenditures amount to more than 900 billion dollars. Someday humankind will have to eliminate the forces causing this rampant arms race and arrive at a greater understanding, a new order of justice, more humane and equitable. Otherwise, there will be no future; we cannot allow 100 million malnourished children. Nor will there be peace and respect among men. And there will come a moment when, in just punishment, our astonished eyes will witness ashes and massive deaths. Humanity is in grave danger. Hopefully our children will become aware of this and will become more thoughtful than we have been, and more worthy.

January swept in enigmatically with a rare cold that almost froze our bones. The strike continued squeezing our bodies without reprieve, but we hardly realized our progressive physical deterioration. After two months of fasting, the cadaveric appearance of the striker impresses himself least of all, assuming he has had adequate mental preparation. His weight will fall even further if he goes several days without being hooked up to an IV to prevent total dehydration. But the change is so gradual that it may pass unnoticed.

Without much to break the monotony of those long hours, always the same, always gray, I came up with the idea of further exploring the fascinating world of poetry. Wouldn't that be a novel experience for me under these conditions? During the previous hunger strike, I had written the first poems for my book *Upwind*. Now I decided to poetically explore the captivating world of children, but with something, different, not simply *Carousel,* something more serious in its conception, though still trying to maintain the transparency and rhythm required by the genre of children's poetry. *Bell of the Dawn* would be the title of this new book of poems. The task was not easy, to say the least. My son Danny had motivated me with his innocent request, asking me to dedicate some verses to him without realizing my precarious state of health at that moment. Danny, and all the world's children, populated my imagination. It was well worth a try, if I could still manage to coordinate my ideas successfully by pushing away all distressing emotions, so bitter and sharp, into a captive dark corner of my chest. Days before, Ángel Cuadra's beautiful poem devoted with so much love to my son had produced in me an exquisite sense of spiritual peace, so that shortly after being immersed in reading it, I wrote the following little poem:

TWO SIPS OF HOPE

Danny, my young one,
yesterday from your name
my sunken veins drank
two sips of hope.
Then, as the music
of the dawn arises,
the most sublime waves
of the soul washed over me.
And I was setting verses
to the strings of a harp
so you could
sing one morning
to those snails
left out on my beach
when night swept over
the fields of my homeland.

Could this poem
be two drops of water...,
or the broken wings
of a white dove.
But no, Danny: rather a spur,
a whip that explodes
as the waves burst
against the angry rock!

Thus, the youngster's yearnings were twice fulfilled. My verses might not equal the masterful poem by Ángel, but were, finally, verses that his own father had written expressly for him, something Danny would recognize as a grateful son, with no small pride.

# CHAPTER 39

# Colonel Clevert Martí Orders More Repressive Measures

Our hunger strike had gone on for 78 days when we got a visit from a government delegation led by Colonel Clevert Martí Lamber, from the Interior Ministry in Santiago de Cuba province. The group was composed of some seven or eight high military officials. Also with them was the warden, First Lieutenant Rufino Machado, and Boniato's medical director, Dr. Nelson Stanley, who had returned to the prison after his year-end holiday.

I witnessed their arrival from my hospital bed. Colonel Clevert Martí came dressed in civilian clothes. Even without knowing who he was, it was easy to guess his identity as he headed up the procession, while all the others swirled around him like drones circling the queen bee.

They went first directly to the cubicle housing Julio Ruiz Pitaluga, Ramón Méndez Pimentel, and Eloy Gutiérrez Menoyo, where each side acknowledged the other, but in a cold, hollow, and ironic manner.

"This one? What does he have?" asked Colonel Martí, pointing to Julio with his index finger.

Even though I couldn't see the entire scene, I could see and hear enough to identify the speaker and the subject.

Days before, Pitaluga had begun experiencing breathing difficulties.

The next morning, when his shortness of breath persisted, the doctor referred him for X-rays. They showed an infection in Julio's left lung, as Stanley explained.

"And the others?" Martí pressed on.

"Well, I would say they are all in critical condition," the doctor said. And to our surprise, he added, "and, by the way, quite neglected."

No doubt this simple recognition by Boniato's medical director was a positive gesture. And for those familiar with Stanley's extreme timidity, it improved our opinion of him, at least for the moment. I considered changing my mind about him, although several days after his return from his holiday he had displayed such a cowardly attitude of subordination toward the repressive apparatus of the dictatorship that six of us had begun rejecting his medical services. This, of course, left us the main losers, since the prison administration adamantly insisted that Stanley, and no other doctor, would attend to us. Because of the hostile atmosphere, despite his pulmonary condition, Pitaluga had refused to accept the antibiotic IV solution that Dr. Stanley had prescribed. And he would have even refused the X-rays except that we had insisted, concerned that he might actually have something more serious than acute bronchitis.

Following his interrogation, the ministry delegate cynically asked whether that critical condition was due to any specific disease.

"Well, not exactly a disease," said the doctor. "It's from the fast."

"And what are you giving them?" asked Clevert Martí.

Stanley replied that during only the last few weeks, three cups of tea per day and an intramuscular vitamin complex every morning. No intravenous solution.

The delegate spoke again, this time to say that he was thin as well and was not taking any tea or injected vitamins. And he ordered Stanley to suspend both immediately.

Eloy intervened to ask to the colonel, with marked irony, if he were a doctor.

"No, I am not a doctor," he replied, "but I'm the boss around here."

Clevert Martí then asked Stanley, "Are they ambulatory?"

The doctor's response was negative.

"But they are able to move their legs, right?"

"Yes, move their legs," Stanley said, and added, "with difficulty."

The colonel then gave the order to render medical assistance only to Ruiz Pitaluga, since the hospital was meant exclusively for cases of illness, not for strikers.

Once more, Eloy replied vehemently and precisely, leaving not the slightest doubt that we would continue with the strike, regardless of the repressive measures the government might take against us to force us to give it up.

After a fast of 78 days, with only a few IVs and some cups of black tea, already our physical state was truly alarming, especially Ruiz Pitaluga's and mine. However, although we were on the brink of death, we tried to belittle the possibility. From the very beginning, we had made a firm commitment to deal with the situation to its ultimate consequences and had so informed the interior minister in an official document signed by the six of us which we had sent on December 21.

Knowing well the arrogance of dictator Fidel Castro, whom Ramiro Valdés would have informed immediately, it was not surprising that the official response was new repressive measures, more brutal perhaps than even before. The attitude was worthy of a regime of force and terror that was holding the full reins of power in its hands, emboldened to exact severe punishment, even so severe as to result in physical elimination. We were not ignorant of this. While none of the six of us wished to be assassinated, we could not have allowed our letter to the interior minister, backed by an iron-clad hunger strike, to be timid in its expression, making our letter a very dangerous potential boomerang against us. Knowing the arrogance of Castro, and his no less arrogant interior minister, we would have anticipated a hysterical reaction at first, but, after that initial response, we had hoped they might consider our fair demands before embarking on a horrendous crime, even if it were only one more in the long list of murders perpetrated against defenseless Cuban political prisoners.

Before leaving, the entourage then entered our cubicle. Neither Evelio nor Montes de Oca exchanged a single word with them, nor did I. Not that I could have, even if I had wanted to, because at the precise instant that the group appeared at our door, I underwent another spate of bloody vomiting.

Stanley pointed out the blood and, gesturing at me, said, "This case has me very concerned. In my opinion, his is the most serious of all." And he described my stomach perforation.

Clevert Martí wanted to know what type of medical attention I was receiving and if I had had recent X-rays.

"His situation is the same as the others," was all Stanley said.

"And have you not taken X-rays?" the Ministry official insisted.

"No, but we should," Stanley agreed, adding – "those lesions are very dangerous."

The doctor's words were followed by a brief silence. There was an exchange of glances between some of the delegation and the Minister's representative.

"Well," the province's MININT Chief answered, "we have been giving them the required medical attention."

Then, as they were leaving, he commented aloud for all to hear, "They are just killing themselves because they feel like it. It's no solution. We won't respond to blackmail."

Shortly after midday, Stanley appeared with a rubber tube and various other implements, among them two syringes with a liter of gluco-physiological serum and a jar of aluminum hydroxide. He was accompanied by the nurse Elia.

"I know," Dr. Stanley warned me, "that in your present condition, this is a torture, but you need to do your part and endure. I need to drain all that contaminated blood and excess acid out of your stomach."

At that moment, I felt very ill, so I had no choice. Already the doctor had said that, and had also said the word "torture."

Torture? That simple word does not cover the extent of the torment to which I was subjected without any perceptible result. Stanley nonetheless insisted on inserting the line, which for my throat and swollen esophagus felt like a firetruck hose, then, after giving up doing it via the mouth, he opted instead for pushing it through my nose.

For quite a while, Stanley repeated the operation of injecting a mixture of whey and aluminum hydroxide through the tubing, then suctioning it out via the same syringe. Then the guard corps called out urgently for him to attend to a common prisoner, as Pucho told me, a prisoner who had arrived at the clinic nearly suffocated by a very violent asthma attack. Stanley instructed the nurse to finish my drainage and departed hurriedly.

But Elia apparently was also in a hurry: "It's done," she decided after completing the operation one more time. And without thinking, she hastily pulled out the hose, causing me a pain so intense that I almost cried out. I made a supreme effort not to vomit at that moment.

The physician soon returned. He asked smiling how it had gone with Elia and if I now felt better.

I moved my hand to indicate "so-so."

"Try now to see if you can get some sleep," he advised, and said goodbye to all three of us.

Stanley had already started to leave when he looked back at me with a serious face.

"Tell me something," he said. "Did she remove the probe slowly?"

"Oh, yes… slowly, slowly," I answered sarcastically, spreading out the words.

He shook his head, indicating his dismay.

Days before the visit from the Interior Ministry of Santiago province, the voice of the United States of America had transmitted the news that six Boniato prisoners had started a hunger strike on November 9, and were still fasting and in serious condition. A woman had explained our situation, but was not identified, so we didn't know who she was. In naming the six, they omitted Juan Evelio Hernández Ramírez and included, in error, the name of Onofre Pérez Hernández. On the following night, the same station transmitted an interview with former Commander Húber Matos about the Boniato hunger strike. Matos read a document that he had prepared to send to Amnesty International denouncing the violence unleashed by Cuban authorities against political prisoners. Although the campaign against the violation of human rights in Communist Cuba's prisons, mainly in Boniato, was gaining force abroad, motivated by the brutal beatings of our comrades Zúñiga Rey, Servando Infante, and Roger Reyes Hernández, and by our long-running hunger strike, is very likely that the repeated transmissions by the Voice of America had irritated the tyrant Fidel Castro and his interior minister, forcing them to defend their pride by taking even harsher action, very typical of their cowardly approach.

That same afternoon, on January 26, 1981, on orders from Colonel Clevert Martí, Dr. Nelson Stanley released about 5 or 6 prisoners from our pavilion from the Boniato infirmary, after their recovery from health conditions suffered as a result of the 33 days of total fasting that they had endured between November 9 and December 12. Even though during the last visit of the delegate of the Interior Ministry, Eloy had affirmed both to him and to Dr. Stanley that we were being hospitalized against our will, and would be quite willing to be sent back immediately to the walled cells of 4B, that day none of the six of us still on the strike was released.

Beginning two weeks before (on January 13), Pavilion 4B prisoners had again been confined in the walled cells by "orders from above," despite an agreement with the assistant warden reaffirming, once again, that for the Communists, keeping their word has as much value as for a flea.

By January 27, medical care was ordered suspended by Colonel Clevert Martí. No longer did the nurse arrive at dawn to inject us as usual. I rejoiced. Actually, our attitude was one of absolute indifference.

Around 8:00 that morning, Stanley appeared to communicate officially that given our critical condition, Pitaluga and I would continue to be provided medical assistance, but not to the other four, since they had no other complications except those caused by prolonged fasting.

I said that in that case, I would not accept assistance either.

Dr. Nelson Stanley insisted on an X-ray to determine if I still had the stomach lesion. The doctor, apparently, knew I had spent the whole morning vomiting. But my decision was irrevocable, which I made clear so he would leave me alone.

By mid-afternoon, Noaldo Pérez appeared with orders to relocate Evelio Hernández and Sergio Montes de Oca to the other side of the clinic, where we had been admitted during the previous strike.

Cusa doubted that a stretcher was needed. First, he carried Montes de Oca, then Evelio. They also took out Pimentel Méndez and Julio Ruiz Pitaluga, and immediately pulled the walled planks down over the cubicles where Eloy and I were staying, isolating us from the rest of the group and from each other. In this dispiriting isolation, I spent some very difficult moments. My vomiting went from bad to worse and my stomach ached terribly. At dark, I felt as exhausted as on that first night when we had entered the infirmary, some 44 days earlier. I even stopped listening to the BBC and the Voice of America, the international stations that came through most clearly on my small Sanyo, despite the surrounding mountains.

The next morning, I remembered that it was the birthday of José Martí, the apostle of Cuban independence, and, making a superhuman effort, I wrote a few short lines paying tribute to our national hero, hoping that a friendly hand would appear to get the message to my fellows in Pavilion 4B. I was able to achieve this thanks to a timely clandestine visit from nurse Marcos Campo.

Even better, I later learned that Alejandro Novo Álvarez had given a reading, in a very loud voice, reaching all the 40 enclosed cells of Pavilion 4B, of my own simple message honoring that greatest, most brilliant of Cubans.

A perhaps significant detail is that, in the absence of paper, it had occurred to me write it down on the back of the label of the last serum that I had been given. I remember that it read on the other side: "5% dextrose. Date: December 24, 1980."

"I don't know how I was able to finish reading it. Just when I started reading, I got a huge lump in my throat," Alejandro Novo confessed to me a few months later when we got back together again.

The morning of January 29 went quite badly. As I had asked Dr. Stanley to leave me alone, ever since the 27th, he had not returned to my cubicle —I imagine not to the others either— which was fine. At noon, Eloy cried out to me, asking how I was. I told him that I was all right, not to worry.

During the rest of the afternoon, the walled door never opened up. My loneliness seeped in through my pores and my soul shrank.

It was already getting dark when I made the supreme effort to take a few steps to keep my legs mobile. Contrary to what Dr. Stanley had predicted, 80 days into the strike, we could not only move our legs, but all six of us managed to stand up and take some steps by sheer force of will. I know about cases of others who, only two weeks into a hunger strike, already could not stand, and others who, after 30 or 40 days, became paralyzed for quite a while, sometimes even for years.

Shortly after dusk, Marcos Campo handed me through the window a clandestine letter that Ángel Cuadra had squeezed into a tiny ball. In it, my dear friend confessed his anguish about our situation and delicately inquired whether it might not be possible for us to end our fast so as to avoid a terrible and untimely death. He thought an 80-day hunger strike had already been sufficiently risky, and that if we were still were among the living, it was by the pure will of God. Then Ángel made a series of counter-arguments. But we were simply determined, whatever the price to pay. While our body seemed to have arrived at the conceivable limit of deterioration, our spiritual fortitude remained tremendous, allowing us to squeeze out an extra margin from our bodies, unless something unforeseen should occur.

After a close analysis of Ángel's letter, I wrote him a few lines, expressing gratitude for his concern and letting him know about our firm determination to continue on with the strike. I don't recall in detail what I told my friend on that night of January 29, 1981, mainly due to my deplorable condition, but I do remember the basics and that I had to interrupt my writing at times because of intense fatigue. Marcos was commissioned on the following day to get my letter to Ángel.

January 30 turned out to be quite stressful. At mid-morning, Eloy was taken out on a stretcher and also Montes de Oca, Evelio, Pimentel, and Pitaluga. I heard about it that afternoon, thanks to Marcos who appeared at my window to let me know that my companions had been taken to building 4C (a punishment pavilion). Marcos was very upset, telling me that each striker had been confined alone, leaving an empty cell between each to prevent any sort of communication and the doors were all enclosed by steel plates as in Pavilion 4B.

During the rest of the day, I waited for them to come for me as well. At about ten at night, since I had not been taken to the punishment pavilion, I made a few taps on the door with a large nickel-plated vessel that Cusa had provided that same afternoon for vomiting or urinating. I failed to stand up properly and in the process, the vessel rolled over on the floor, spilling its contents on my feet. I slipped and hit my forehead on the corner of the mental table causing a slight skin tear and a huge bump. I don't like to remember my rage at the foul viscosity clinging to me. I gave a few knocks against the steel plank before I collapsed on the floor, where the nurse Luis found me, almost unconscious, a few minutes later.

With great difficulty, Luisito helped to lay me down on the bed. It had been hard for me to even stand up in that gelatinous puddle. Since I was in a kind of convulsive shock by then, Luisito took my blood pressure, which, according to him had soared alarmingly, so he left and returned immediately with a syringe in hand. But I flatly refused to allow him to inject me. If there was no medical care for my comrades, I could not justify it for myself. Nothing and no one was going to make me change my mind.

Next, I don't remember ever having felt such intense cold. After lamenting my decision, and the decision of the High Command to suspend all medical assistance to my companions and to send them to the punishment dungeons after 82 days of fasting, the nurse covered my body with three thick blankets while I was shaken by violent seizures.

I had already forgotten what had impelled me to get up to tap at the door. I didn't care whether or not I was taken to those black holes myself. I was going to die that very night anyway. "Perhaps in less than an hour, I will be leaving this violent, cruel world, this world of injustices not made for my tender conscience," I dared to think. My fellows would die later, probably with a subtle hand covering their nose and mouth to accelerate their transit toward nothingness. It did not matter when or where. To die at any moment, it is enough if one has lived with love and has left good seed behind. However, at that final moment, I didn't want to be alone in the dark. I didn't understand why, but for the first time, the darkness was causing me some anxiety —or fear—making much more intense the loneliness of my isolation between those four walls. Although lights were usually turned out at 10 p.m., the nurse agreed to let me keep a light on during the rest of the night. Perhaps he thought that that was just my final request, so he decided to allow it.

I slept fitfully, stealing a few minutes of sleep during the night, while death haunted me like a starving wolf.

When day began to dawn, I had the absolute certainty that I still had many more days to live. The vomiting continued, but I no longer had that feeling of a vacuum dragging me toward the infinite precipice. Once more, the power of the spirit had won. On that strange dawn, I was cheered by bird songs. I heard the mockingbird chirping above from the security wires. But my joy was brief.

Very early in the morning, from the other side of the metal plank, came the unexpected news of that one of my five companions transferred to the punishment pavilion had been found dead in his dungeon. At first, I thought this was a false report from the military made to upset me. I knew very well the lack of scruples of our adversaries. But the reality soon became apparent.

"Put the corpse there in the lobby until mortician arrives," a voice ordered amid a hum and some footsteps. And although I couldn't tell for sure, I thought the speaker was the Chief of Internal Order. Then I felt the noise of doors and bolts unlocking. Next, I heard the wheeled stretcher moving towards the interior of the small lobby, and again the bolt and lock noises.

From the other side of the door, someone joked to the deceased: "Don't move from there, stay still," at the same time celebrating his evil actions by releasing a stupid laugh. Oh God! How can some beasts in human form be allowed to walk this earth?

"Who could it have been? Pitaluga, I thought with bitterness. Or maybe Eloy... Yes, Eloy; they must have killed him... or maybe Montes de Oca? The day before we were separated, Montes de Oca had been complaining of chest pain. And Evelio? No, I don't think that it was Evelio, nor Pimentel. They were the two strongest."

All these ideas assaulted me in a rapid succession of painful images, plunging me into a terrible anguish.

As soon as it grew quiet, I got out of bed, and like a tightrope walker, with uncertain steps, I advanced, reeling, until I could lean up against the wall plank. Then I imagined that the voice giving orders, the noise of the padlock and the bolt, the miserable taunts, the stupid laugh, and all the rest were simply products of my tormented imagination and mental exhaustion, and a ray of hope lifted my battered spirit.

But it was no more than a fleeting hope. Lifting up the small porthole, used at other times to pass food into the sick, the corpse appeared there before my eyes. It was placed on a wheeled stretcher and covered with a white sheet. No doubt, the first of the strikers had died. And what else could be expected? A fast of 83 days was too much for any human being to endure.

My efforts to guess which of my five colleagues had been the victim were useless. Looking at the shape under sheet, the shape of the body and of the head, I guessed one or another, as the flies swarmed around.

As much as I wanted to stay there until they came for the corpse, after a few brief moments, my legs started giving out and I was forced to return to bed. The rest of the morning plunged me into a sadness that tore into my soul and clouded my mind, still fully aware that before the reality of death, there was no another remedy than to accept with resignation that the person has left us for a journey into eternity.

The corpse was not removed until mid-afternoon. From my bed, I heard the same voices and same cynical jokes. As I had been vomiting just minutes before, I didn't have the strength to get up to look through the porthole, or perhaps I lacked the will (the bravery) to witness the departure of a beloved friend.

During the rest of the day, the lobby door did not open again. Not even Marcos looked through the window.

I slept badly, even though my vomiting had diminished.

The next morning, I received a visit from Colonel Juan Berenguer, also a medical doctor. He explained that given my critical condition, he had wanted to talk with me in person. But I insisted that I would not allow any type of medical assistance unless my fellow strikers were offered the same. I did not want to ask him which of my five colleagues had died the previous day. If the jailers had left the corpse inside in the lobby less than three meters from my bed, that obviously had been done to torture me. I was not about to ask a single word in that respect.

The dead one was already dead, and even though I had suffered a deep, personal loss, I was unwilling to reveal it. I had decided that simply showing any interest in knowing his identity could be interpreted as anxiety on my part. Before such a perverse enemy, it was best to display complete indifference and absolute ignorance of the tragedy that had occurred the day before. "No, I will not stimulate them by showing them my sore soul," I told myself.

Apparently, the High Command had already been convinced of the futility of the most recent repressive measures. The punishment dungeons could not bend us as they had hoped. So, then they took a step back by ordering us into the same cubicles where we had been when Colonel Clevert Martí had visited on January 26. Only after Col./Dr. Berenguer had guaranteed medical assistance to the rest of the group and had received the order from the minister for us to be together again immediately did I agree to a checkup. Since he had already told me about my urgent need for an IV, I agreed to allow it until noon. If around 12:00, the others had still not returned, I would pull out the needle. In end, if the chief of medical services for the Interior Ministry for Santiago was lying, he would not have fooled me for very long.

The first thing that Dr. Berenguer did was to check my blood pressure. According to him, it was very low at that moment. But, he said, given my many days of fasting, it was normal that it just came to 80 over 50, less dangerous than the extremely high reading found by nurse Luisito two nights before. Without a doubt, Colonel Berenguer was well informed about the health of each one of us.

After he had taken my blood pressure and a careful listening to my chest, he wanted to examine my legs to check for muscle deterioration from the effects of polyneuritis.

I was taken aback. Anticipating a sudden search, when not listening to the tiny radio, I kept it hidden inside the double lining of the crotch of some athletic underpants, which I had camouflaged by wearing more standard underpants on top. When Berenguer put his hand under my right thigh and had me lift my leg to check my reflexes by hitting my kneecap with the edge of his stethoscope, he almost touched the radio with his forearm. My own arm hairs stood on end. I hastened to assure him that I could still easily move both legs.

Before leaving, he insisted that we accept treatment from Stanley. I told Berenguer that I would discuss the matter with my five colleagues. When I said "my five colleagues," I fixed on his eyes, but the doctor appeared serene, expressionless. Despite my subtle hint, he said nothing about the identity of the deceased of the previous day.

Fifteen minutes after the colonel/doctor had left, Cusa appeared carrying a bucket of hot water.

"Get up, I'll give you a bath, which you could really use," he told me warmly.

The guard who had brought him in left right away, leaving the cubicle door open. Immediately, I asked Cusa the question that I had been burning to know for the last 24 hours. I am ashamed of the joy that I felt when he reported that the corpse of the day before was that of a young, common prisoner, last name of Marrero, who had hanged himself in a punishment cell. It was not necessary for me to confirm the intentions of prison authorities in leaving the body next to my door almost for the whole day of January 31. In addition to torturing me mentally, they might have been trying to convince me of the uselessness of our strike and to abandon it before it was too late.

This time, Cusa refused to allow me to walk to the bathroom while leaning on his shoulder. Instead, he lifted me himself from the bed and set me down on a metal chair next to an immense metal caldron of hot water. He soaped me twice from head to toe, scrubbing my skin until it shone like a chalice. After rinsing, he dried me and dressed me in clean pajamas before putting me back into bed. Then he placed a jug of ice water at the head of my bed. But I only dared to take a few sips for fear of vomiting. After the bath, I felt a new surge of strength and did not want to jeopardize it. It was not the first time that I was aware that the mind exerts a big influence on the physical body and that deterioration is not always progressive in a straight line.

# CHAPTER 40

# Return from the Punishment Pavilion

It was about 10:30 a.m. when Dolores appeared with a serum to insert into my vein. She seemed bouncy and happy to be taking care of me again. Dolores, although she was usually rather undemonstrative, was also noble and sensitive.

"I like taking care of him," she once confessed to Evelio, referring to me. And when Evelio wanted to know why, Dolores replied with tremendous candor, "Ernesto is so simple!"

This alleged preference of hers was due to my lighthearted efforts at not wounding her feelings and trying to boost her confidence. "I'm faithful to you," I told her, "not like those others who wait for Pucho to hook up their IVs."

And on an earlier occasion, I said, "Don't worry about all the punctures. Think of this arm as yours. And if you cannot find any veins, you may have the other one also."

Did my nerve falter? Not at all. But when I offered her my sacrificial arm, my heart was in my throat. And the worst of it was that she took me at my word and achieved a new record of punctures back then: eleven, in all—then twelve, before I appealed to "Lefty" for a half-hour timeout.

Dolores then reappeared after that timeout, very determined... inspired that time, announcing as she came through the door, "Get ready, as my wrist is on fire!"

I heard her from under my quilt, not daring to show my face. But imagine her disappointment at seeing that I had emptied the entire liter of dextrose on the floor, thus cowardly violating our established covenant. From that moment on, I swore off the needle to such an extent that for more than a month, nobody dared ask me to extend an arm, not even Pucho or Luisito, true experts. My irreverence at spilling the dextrose that she was about to give me wounded the sensitivities of that noble nurse back then. And from that moment on, for Dolores, I was no longer "simple" Ernesto who deserved special consideration.

So, given my offense, I now took the opportunity to start over with her. I again presented myself to the sacrifice. After all, a pinprick more or less is nothing of great importance, provided it does not exceed eleven. Fortunately for me, it was Dolores' lucky day and it took her only five attempts.

It was not until mid-afternoon that Pitaluga, Méndez Pimentel, and Evelio Hernández returned. We were happy and excited to see each other again. Although they arrived later than the ultimatum that I had given to Dr. Berenguer, I had chosen to wait quietly until dark, since Cusa had assured me that they would be returning to the infirmary. He told me that he had seen the guard corps preparing several IVs. Furthermore, he had been given orders to mop the floors of their cubicles and make up the beds with clean sheets, erasing any doubts I might have had about my friends' return. Additionally, the steel planks enclosing both sections had been left open since morning.

After they had arrived, Cusa also bathed the three of them and gave them clean pajamas.

Montes de Oca returned amid some uncertainty, about 9:00 p.m., and Eloy not until after 1 a.m. Since Montes de Oca was lying in Eloy's bed, impatient to talk with Evelio and with me, and angry by about how long it was taking the jailers to remove Eloy from the punishment pavilion, he first opened up the flow of serum that Elia had given him, then, when 400 cc of dextrose still remained, he pulled out the needle and threw the rest into the nickel-plated urine bucket. Then he crossed the lobby, stumbling, and had to lie down completely exhausted after the effort of those 10 or 12 steps, weakened as he was by his prolonged fast. That was between 11:00 and 11:30 p.m. After midnight, despite our protests, fearing that he might faint or fall down again, he went back across the lobby once more to discuss with Pitaluga and Pimentel what attitude to assume if Eloy did not show up in two or three hours.

For the tranquility of all concerned, approximately an hour later, the orderlies arrived with Gutiérrez Menoyo, guarded by Sergeant Noaldo and two officials. By then, Montes de Oca lacked the strength to take another step, so Cusa took charge and carried him back into our cubicle.

That night, the head of Internal Order assured us that us we would not be taken back to the punishment dungeons. When we let him know that we had no confidence in his word, he argued that it was a decision of the High Command, thereby giving it greater credibility. In this respect, Noaldo Pérez was telling us something of the truth. We already knew by then that even the warden could not take measures regarding us on his own. And not only that, he would perhaps not even dare to suggest doing so.

By the next morning, I learned from Eloy that on the very afternoon of January 30, William Rivas Porta, Jorge Valls, and Dr. Alberto Fibla had visited him in his cell in the punishment pavilion, trying to convince Eloy to put end to his strike. It bothered Eloy a lot, he told me, when they raised the issue, and his immediate reaction was to reject their advice. The ties of friendship that linked us to those three companions were too solid and sincere to break simply because they had taken the initiative to intervene directly on the issue of our fast, trying to persuade us that by living, we would be more useful to the cause of Cuba's freedom than by being dead. At that moment, they were thinking objectively, while we, with admitted quixotic romanticism and more than a little stubbornness, had also made a cold calculation. We knew well the moral damage that we were causing the Cuban government with our prolonged hunger strike, because overseas international news agencies had echoed our just protest. The more we could extend the strike, the longer the campaign would be against the Communist regime in Havana, showing the world with concrete evidence that the violation of human rights in Castro's Cuba was a resounding reality.

The conversation of Fibla, Rivas, and Valls with Eloy had lasted an hour. When the dungeon door had closed behind them after their visit, the three of them were convinced that as long as we still had an atom of strength left to resist, there was no way that we would give up our strike, no matter what violence was unleashed against us, even if our lives were at stake. That same afternoon, Fibla had requested that the Interior Order Chief authorize the prison to provide us medical assistance. But the higher authorities had refused to grant that permission at the time.

The first days of February passed in relative calm. The situation with Stanley had been resolved favorably after I reported to my companions about my private conversation with him the day before their release from the punishment cells. The two liters of serum infused into our veins had given us new vigor. But in my case, it would not be a lasting recovery. On February 4, I woke up feeling as if a mountain had fallen on top of me. A little later, when Pucho entered the cubicle to inject me, he was surprised to see my pale face.

"Are you feeling tired?" he asked.

I reported that I had been vomiting frequently all morning and was feeling quite ill.

Pucho checked my blood pressure.

"No wonder you feel ill; it's plummeted to the floor!" he said, going out hastily in search of Dr. Stanley, who had arrived at the hospital earlier than usual. Stanley, after checking my blood pressure again, immediately ordered an IV. Pucho himself hooked me up. Stanley, who was still there, regulated the flow to make sure it entered slowly.

I didn't vomit again after midday. By evening, I was already feeling somewhat better. However, Stanley indicated that I should keep on receiving another dose as soon as one liter was empty.

After the last news report on Voice of America, I fell into an intermittent sleep. Evelio and Montes de Oca spent a quiet night. Pitaluga, on the contrary, was awake most of the time, struggling to breathe, although receiving antibiotics for his lung problem. The reflection of light from the lobby shown dimly on his bed, where I saw him tossing and turning. Eloy and Pimentel slept until dawn.

I woke up when the nurse was changing my IV. It was the fifth or sixth liter emptied in less than 24 hours. Through the window bars,

I could see the outer security cordon. The guard on duty was dozing peacefully. A hundred meters beyond, under a mango tree, an emaciated cow was devouring a piece of cardboard. "That poor beast is doing as badly as we are," I thought. The drought was awful. I didn't see a single blade of grass or a green leaf. The cow's hunger was involuntary and out of options. While the consequences of physical hunger are serious, the psychological aspect is worse. A castaway can die of starvation after 10 days even if he has enough water. Yet a hunger striker can survive without food beyond conceivable limits if his spirit is strong. I know of a comrade who spent more than 15 days not only on a total fast, but taking only tiny sips of water. And this was not by choice, but was his jailers' imposition. According to medical statistics, a human adult could not live beyond 9 or 10 days under such conditions. But this fellow had an exceptional spirit and survived that horrendous involuntary torture. His name is Osvaldo Baró Miranda, a name deservedly remembered as a symbol of will and bravery. Osvaldo Baró, after his odyssey, managed to get the following letter into our prison infirmary:

"March 20, 1983

To all the brothers of 2A and 2C, Boniatico [a smaller interior enclosure for political prisoners within the main prison]:

Briefly, I'd like to share with you the most important aspects of my own strike since my arrival here on January 20, after embarking on my strike on the 10th of this month.

I was locked into the cubicle beside the room for mental inmates. There is no sink or toilet there, just a bed and a small table. The door is a hermetically sealed with a plank and the window is blocked by a mesh that prevents almost all air flow.

I heard them bringing Ismael [another *plantado* prisoner] into a neighboring cubicle where at least the window was open.

The warden came in on January 23, warning me to cease my attitude, giving me a deadline until the next day to see if I officially persisted in being on strike with all the consequences. He authorized giving me water. We discussed my strike, the situation of Boniatico, our rights, etc. He left and on Tuesday, on the morning of the 25th, Zamora came in representing the warden, saying that because of my negative response, he had been commanded to remove the water.

In the afternoon, Cobas himself arrived and commanded removal of all my personal property (eyeglasses, toothbrush, toothpaste, etc.).

As the days went on, thirst tormented me, although I felt in good spirits. On Monday, the 31st, Captain Matos arrived and we talked, reaching an agreement about books and other property, although he told me that he could not guarantee monthly correspondence. He left, saying the doctor would come the next day.

Stanley came on the next day and recognized me. I thought he came to give me medical care, because he was even accompanied by Zamora. They went out and, after a while, Captain Matos arrived with a change of clothes —dark blue [the uniform of rehabilitation plan prisoners] —and told me quietly that my agreements and requests would have validity if I accepted that clothing and, at the same time, accepted the rehabilitation plan, as per an order of the national minister regarding those declared to be on strike. Instead of dying, I had to accept the plan.

I told him to go fry some asparagus and he left, not returning for days. Zamora and Sergeant Despaigne then came in several times a day trying to get the blue uniform on me. At first, I argued with them but then I began feeling so ill that I ignored them. They left the clothes on the bedside table. I threw them down. The duty guard would look in on me every so often to see how I was.

My thirst was terrible; it's something you have to experience to appreciate. Stanley, Caballero, and an inmate physician named Hugo, always very proper, saw me on a daily basis.

On Friday, February 4 (the anniversary of Estebita's death), Berenguer came to see me and promised to come back, but never did. The next day, a provincial doctor came to see my condition. From then on, I was in critical condition. I had several crises, dislodging a corner of the bed, trying to open up the wall to get to a water pipe, but I was very weak and made little progress. I tried to dislodge the window covering, and started to remove it, but found not a drop of water. They removed my bed and left me the mattress, although most of the time, I lay on the floor as it was cooler. I lost consciousness several times. I was told that I had banged my head against the door plank. When I came to, I only thought about water flowing through familiar rivers and streams, pitchers of lemonade, and glasses of cold water, etc. Anyone who has gone through a similar experience will understand. But I also thought of all of you, of those years of struggle and incarceration and the high price demanded of me.

So, I fell into a coma, as I was told later. Picked up off the floor, I was bathed on a stretcher, dressed in the blue outfit, and given medical assistance. I was given 13 consecutive IVs, the first four flowing open. My blood pressure was 80/60. Pucho gave me an electrocardiogram and took my pressure several times a day. According to Stanley and Despaigne, they began treating me on Tuesday, February 8, when I had already gone 13 days without drinking water. On Feb. 11 or 12, I woke up (I was given water by mouth and also cold tea, first via a syringe and then with a tube). I saw I was wearing the blue outfit, which I took off and threw away. They brought it back later. Then, as I became a little more responsive, I ripped it up so as to leave no doubt about my attitude. The pieces were removed and no more of those clothes arrived.

On Monday, the 14th, a tall, skinny black guy arrived, saying he was a psychologist. He began explaining the advantages of the [rehabilitation] plan and, above all, that many inmates of Boniatico were hoping to use my death as a flag of combat, of propaganda, etc. Of course, I rejected him. He came back again in the afternoon, but after getting nothing from me, he left.

On Tuesday, the 15th, I took a sitting bath, helped by Cusa, and I was given some purée to eat, as I had already sipped some broth and done well. Soon warden Cobas appeared with Despaigne and Zamora, and I was given a note from Casasus, whose handwriting I recognized immediately, and another from Wilfredo, inquiring about my situation and bearing the names of several more brothers. Then Cobas asked me to write back to them, telling them the truth, i.e., that I was receiving medical attention and food. I did it to reassure them, since Cobas said that the group been rejecting food to support me (which turned out to be part of a trap).

That night, Captain Matos insisted on the clothes and the plan. He said they wanted to help me, asking questions about my family, my sentence. I answered as much as I had to and he said my attitude was regressive. Soon, the head of Internal Order arrived, whispered to the guard and they opened part of the half-welded entry door so they could look inside without opening the door. I suspect something was wrong with all of this, and indeed, the next morning, Wednesday, February 16, Despaigne came early to tell me that the prison was withdrawing food and medical assistance. They took the tea, cold water and my things that had been returned. They left me only with the bed and shoes without laces. I replied that I was glad because already I had thought of dying the first time and they had not let me.

The next day, he returned and suggested I write a letter to the minister renouncing the strike. I told him that Cobas had deceived me, that if he wanted a letter for the minister, he should send another to Reagan to install attack missiles at the Guantánamo base. Zamora was gone. The only one seeing me daily was Stanley, who was surprised at my little apparent deterioration although I was very thin, but my pulse remained normal or even accelerated. Despaigne began to appear again with the same time.

On Thursday, the 24th, there arrived Moré or Morell, the captain of security whom we all know, along with two others, one dressed in civilian clothes, the other, military. He said that my case was in the hands of State Security by order of the minister, and to recall the cases of Boitel, Cuadra, Cuevas, and the rest, whom nobody remembered any more as the instigators of those strikes, some right here in Boniatico. I said that my case was different. He suggested that I get dressed and go to Building #5 where Tejera Milián and several others were. He returned the next day and, getting nothing from me, he said was going to Havana and would return on Tuesday or Wednesday of the next week.

I felt bad. As before, I thought about water, but decided to demonstrate the greatest stoicism possible to uphold the image of political prisoners.

After several days, I was not in crisis nor had I lost my mind, though physically I was skin and bones. I talked to Stanley and asked him to leave me alone, that already I no longer belonged to this world because I was resigned to dying on behalf of my political ideals. He seemed distressed, excusing himself for not being able to do anything unless so ordered by the warden.

Then on the morning of Wednesday, March 2, while I was lying on the floor, Captain Matos came in and asked if I recognized him. I told him that I did, to which he replied that headquarters had decided to reevaluate me and to take me to Havana to carry out the operation I needed in a proper place. Then he left.

Soon after, intra-venous hydration began, the cold water, tea, etc. although with less urgency than the first time, because my condition was less serious despite lasting 14 days this time, February 16 to March 2. Stanley scratched his head and confessed that as a doctor, he didn't understand how I had been able to survive. He showed me my clinical file, where he had documented everything, day by day, in detail from the very beginning.

On Thursday, the 3rd, Colonel Raúl García, second in command of MININT for the province, arrived with Matos. He was very friendly. He asked me how I felt and that he came in the name of the command to tell me that my problem was solved. As soon as I had recovered, I would be moved to Havana to a good hospital to operate on me, that he knew that the first surgery had failed and that it might take several stages to fix it, but it didn't matter because I would be there for as long as necessary, that it was a firm decision of Central Command. He added that Old-Man Ruiz would also be taken to Havana for his eye surgery. He said we would travel by ambulance wearing hospital pajamas, then be returned to Boniatico, our current proper location. Then he talked about nursing, saying he had been a nurse in his younger days.

On Saturday, the 5th, Director Cobas appeared. He told me what García had said and not to undergo another strike as it would damage my health —that the Revolution had decided to be generous with me and to give me a chance, because it would not gain anything from my death.

My medical attention has been good both times, from all the doctors and nurses, and the food as well. I think that altogether, including pitchers of tea, cold water, and juice, I have drunk 55 gallons at least. They inject me daily with B vitamins and give me Belladonna citrus three times a day. If I am alive today, it is thanks to

God to whom I have turned many times, to the prayers of all of you, and to the help of all our brothers who, at risk to themselves, supported me during such difficult hours. I reiterate my thanks to all. The experience has been amazing. But I would not wish it even on my enemies. Now, I'm waiting to be transferred. I don't know if I will go to Combinado, though I doubt it, nor how long I will be there, nor to what hospital I will be sent, although I presume from what García said that it will be the military hospital or the new one in central Havana at the old charity hospital. We shall see.

I am trying to get shorn there in Boniatico to see and talk with you before my departure, but am having some difficulty. That is why I'm sending this report. Already, I've found out that some of you have been released.

A warm embrace for you all until we meet again, God willing.

Baró

P.S. Naturally, there are certain facts and circumstances that I cannot entrust to paper. They will have to wait to until I can tell you personally.

Regarding Ismael, he stopped the IV and stopped eating until I convinced him to continue. He said he would eat in Havana. Colonel García told him that if he stopped eating, he would not have the strength to travel. Matos and Cobas urged him likewise and asked Ismael if he wanted them to search for his brother to deliver food to him at the Havana hospital, but that he should eat beforehand anyway. On February 17 or 18, they took him to 'Jagua.' Santiago's psychiatric clinic, where he told the warden: "Mr. Warden, you are crazier than I am." He was only there a day and a half. When he came back, he was given several IVs, but still refused to eat.

At noon on Friday, March 18, Matos demanded that Ismael be bathed. So, he was, and then he was told he was being sent to the Santiago provincial hospital. He answered that he was not going to eat there, that he would wait until he got to Havana. They took him and today, on Monday 21, he has not been brought back. You know how he is. May God resolve his conundrum. That's all."

# CHAPTER 41

# Back Again to the Punishment Dungeons

It would have been approximately 9:30 a.m. when Dr. Nelson Stanley quietly entered the cubicle of the three of us: Sergio Montes de Oca, Evelio Hernández Ramírez, and I.

"Let's hurry up with what remains of this IV and start a new one," he told me, and opened up the liquid to flow freely.

I wondered about this sudden haste and nervousness on the doctor's part. Actually, I was feeling pretty well compared to the previous day and had not even vomited.

In less than half hour, 600 cc of dextrose had gone into my vein. During those 20 or 25 minutes, I didn't know what Stanley was up to. But I didn't want to show my concern. After all he was the doctor, not I.

Stanley had just installed a new liter when the Internal Order Chief entered the front cubicle accompanied by two officials and notified Gutiérrez Menoyo to prepare to leave.

"Where is he going?" Stanley asked. Apparently very upset, he leaned over my shoulder, saying a low and broken voice: "It's the same damn thing as the other day. They are taking them back again to 4C."

Stanley only confirmed what we all already had imagined when we saw the military come swaggering in. Also, the return to the black holes of punishment was always a real possibility, a common repressive measure used to suppress hunger strikers. If days earlier, my five colleagues had been returned to the clinic after having been held in the punishment pavilion, the decision to rescind the crackdown had been due to the unwavering attitude of solidarity adopted by the near totality of the men of 4B, our courageous brothers in misfortune. Outraged, they had opted to declare a hunger strike until the five strikers were returned to the infirmary and given medical assistance. Three days after that massive fast had begun, fear of major complications if some should die had caused the higher authorities to step back, giving in to the demands of our colleagues. It had been a short but sobering protest. Even those who had not participated directly had provided moral support.

This time, more than an hour and a half passed after Sergeant Noaldo and the two officers took Eloy away on a stretcher before they returned to take the next striker to the punishment pavilion. This time, Pimentel said goodbye to us. After some 30 minutes, they came back for Montes de Oca and Evelio. Then the commander told us that because of our serious health conditions they had decided that Julio Ruiz Pitaluga and I should stay in the clinic receiving medical care.

This willful measure made me so furious that after an exchange of rough words with the officers I violently pulled the IV out of my arm. Accidentally, the liter of dextrose fell onto the floor, shattering into a thousand pieces. From the needle, still strongly secured with tape, blood trickled down. I started to remove the tape when nurse Dolores entered very alarmed.

"Calm down!" she screamed, "Let me do it!"

"Never mind," I arrogantly replied. And actually, I no longer needed her help. However, Dolores cleaned off my blood with cotton soaked in alcohol, which I allowed reluctantly.

"Do me a favor," I asked her after calming down. "Go tell Stanley that I want to see him right away."

For a few minutes, I was alone in the cubicle.

"What are you going to do?" Pitaluga asked me.

"I'm going to ask Stanley to release me and send me to the punishment dungeons too."

"No, don't do that. Let them do it; make them take responsibility."

"I'm not staying here, Pita. I have to join them right away."

Pitaluga thought for a few seconds, looking worried.

"Listen to me, Ernesto. Remember your vomiting problem? We've been left here because we're already screwed. In any case, we can continue the strike here if that is what you are interested in. Also, don't forget that those bastards are testing our fortitude and what's more, within a few days, the four of them will be brought back here again."

"Possibly, but these people are a phenomenon."

"Forget it; this time the door has been slammed on their ass. They've lost. Already, they don't know what to do next," Pitaluga opined. Then, in a burst of optimism, he declared, "They have to take us to Havana, like it or not, even though it busts their guts!"

"You may be right, but I'm still going to ask them to take me to be with the others."

"Are you going to leave me alone here then?" protested Pitaluga.

"That doesn't matter. I already did it and now it's your turn. Stay here quietly at least until the end of your antibiotics. Then you can join us if we are still there."

Pitaluga was pretty upset because that morning, Marcos, instead of giving him dextrose with antibiotics as Stanley had ordered, gave him a saline solution instead. He began thinking that Marcos had exchanged vials intentionally to eliminate him physically, since relations between them were very strained. Pitaluga was not persuaded that when the error was pointed out, Marcos immediately corrected it. In the mind of Julio Ruiz, the nightmare of attempted murder persisted.

"That guy is a viper," he said. "He has no scruples. He would sell his soul to the devil."

Stanley came in to talk with me, appearing nervous and worried. He said he had no decision-making authority over us; the High Command decided everything. When I pointed out his responsibility as a doctor, he said he had to follow orders or otherwise he would go to prison himself. "And I'm afraid of prison," he confessed. "I've seen so many things here."

Stanley often spoke of his obsession with avoiding prison. In vain, he tried to convince me to give up my effort to be transferred immediately to the special punishment unit.

"I have to certify to the High Command that this is your request, under your entire responsibility," he said finally, seeing that my decision was irrevocable.

"For the moment, yes," I clarified. "Someday others will need to respond to theirs."

Fifteen minutes later, the stretcher arrived to deposit me at black hole #19 in the punishment pavilion.

"Leave him here," the official in charge ordered outside the entrance.

One of the orderlies grabbed my arms while the other took my feet, together throwing me like a bag of straw on the concrete slab that served as a bed, which fortunately, unlike in the punishment cells at Combinado, had a mat, a sheet, and the further luxury of a small pillow as well.

I had the little radio with me. As long as I didn't risk losing it, I could tune in for a while to the main news of world events.

After the loud slam of the shutting steel plank, I was left alone, beginning a new cycle of isolation and torture. It was February 5, 1981. We had already been on hunger strike for 88 days and the authorities had not only *not* yielded to our just demands, but had increased their cowardly repressive measures, showing tremendous insensitivity to our suffering and our prolonged fast, undertaken by us simply to defend our right as human beings to be returned to our province of origin so as to be able to receive visits from our family. The hunger strike was the only weapon we had, since the regime would not want news of wholesale deaths from a hunger strike to get out into the wider world.

The abrupt change in environment addled my brain, plunging me into a painful lethargy. It was not very pleasant just to be looking at those four walls. Loneliness is a poor companion, even more so under such difficult medical circumstances. Now I had plunged into greater uncertainty, surrounded by untimely death, and, worse still, stalked and harassed by those regime hyenas who spied constantly through the tiny opening between the steel door and the wall.

My forearm felt sore. When I had abruptly pulled out the needle, a little vein had torn and a huge bruise covered almost my entire arm, from wrist to elbow. The wound, although small, continued bleeding and I had to press it for 10 minutes to make it stop.

That afternoon, I called out on two or three occasions to my companions, trying to make contact. I wanted to know where in that black hole every one of them was situated. But the hullabaloo of common prisoners also being punished there drowned out my voice and prevented me from listening clearly.

"Taking care" of us was a special guard unit composed of four officials, lieutenants Julio, Eusebio, Tomás, and Calderín. The first three were invariably hostile and, in the cases of Julio and Tomás, sometimes excessively so. Lieutenant Calderín, in contrast, while not failing to fulfill his painful mission, was always friendly and respectful.

The guard rotation was carried out every eight hours. Access to the punishment pavilion was strictly forbidden, both for common prisoners who used to do cleanup, as well as for military, unless so required by their duties and always accompanied by one of the four officers entrusted with our custody. The main objective was to keep each of the strikers in total isolation.

Already on that first evening, around 11:00 p.m., I managed to establish contact by shouting out to my fellow *plantados*. I soon discerned the location of each: Eloy was at the end of the corridor in dungeon #39; Ramón Méndez Pimentel in #35; Evelio Hernández in #31; Sergio Montes de Oca in #27; and I was in black hole #19, so I assumed that #23 had been reserved for Julio Ruiz Pitaluga. The others were left empty in between to prevent us from inventing some sort of communication.

Other political prisoners were being held as well in solitary punishment cells: Adolfo Vinent Bonis, Alfredo Mustelier Nuevo, and Samuel Tejera Milián. And common prisoners were in the rest. Cells #2 to #24 were occupied entirely by common prisoners with the exception of Diego Roche Periche, a political prisoner sentenced to death for leading a group of young men conspiring to conduct sabotage against regime industries. Periche was an outstanding boy, courageous in the extreme, and with a very firm ideology. Months before we had started our strike, I had had the opportunity to talk with him about our national problems.

At that time, although he had not yet been sentenced to death, he was sure that he would be shot and accepted it with tremendous aplomb. Weeks after he was transferred to the punishment unit, in the midst of our long fast, his premonition was fulfilled, leaving us with the pain of his physical absence and the imperishable example of his gallantry. At the time of his execution he was only 20 years old. His life was very brief, but rich in dignity and patriotism.

Two days after I was remanded to the punishment pavilion, Julio Ruiz Pitaluga was carried in on a stretcher, and, indeed, was put in dungeon #23. He told us later that the chief of Internal Order had appeared and commanded the removal of his IV.

"Get up," he had grumbled. "You're going to the punishment dungeons!"

He still had trouble breathing, Pitaluga had explained, and his back pain persisted. Moreover, his deteriorating physical condition could not be more alarming, as it was for all of us. If we kept ourselves alive, it was purely by the will of God and by the strength of our own spirit.

That night I decided to listen to the news, despite the risk. It was uncomfortable to always be carrying around the radio between my legs, hidden between two pairs of underwear. When I took it out, I had about 30 seconds whenever I heard a guard open the corridor door to reinsert the radio and cover myself up with the sheet and pretend to be sleeping quietly —30 seconds for this complicated operation before the flashlight beam fell on me through the small opening.

The radio yielded little important information that night —a plane crash in the Pacific where several high-level Soviet officials had been killed, among them the chief of Pacific naval operations.

Several days later, the Voice of America conveyed the news that a group of Cubans had taken over the Ecuadoran Embassy in Havana, demanding to be allowed to leave the country. I was upset when the reporter, Evelio Otero, referred to those Cubans as "unruly." I objected to the use of that adjective which ignored the despair of a people who had suffered for a quarter century the martyrdom of the most alienating tyranny that has existed on our continent. He probably meant no harm. Evelio Otero, I am sure, loves freedom as much as those unfortunates who invaded Ecuador's diplomatic headquarters to escape a Communist hell. His erroneous expression was due to carelessness, but I want to honestly express here my bitterness at his inappropriate description of them as "troublemakers" and "unruly." Much harsher words could be used to describe Castro's political police, who, days later, wielding automatic rifles, assaulted the diplomatic mission to arrest those sorry victims who had believed, perhaps, that they had finally reached their longed-for freedom.

Since our transfer to the punishment cells, the warden had visited us almost daily. Usually he was accompanied by the chief of Internal Order and another official. Their conversation with us was brief, inquiring about our health and trying to convince us of the futility of our sacrifice.

"Your request may be just," they admitted, "but the government cannot yield to pressure."

Our alleged illegal pressure was a constant echo throughout our hunger strike.

Lieutenant Rufino Machado, as a good Communist, was dogmatic and insensitive, also awkward. As director of Cuba's most repressive prison he carried out his profession of executioner well. So, I paid attention when on February 12 he told me that he was very concerned about Eloy's condition that morning.

"He's dying," he assured me, "with only a few hours left."

"All six of us are going to die," I answered, "no matter who is first."

The director left, a little bewildered at not having impressed me.

A while later, Col./Dr. Berenguer appeared. He said that an IV had been inserted into Eloy by force and the same would be done with Montes de Oca, even if he had to be tied up, as he was in very serious condition.

I replied that that situation had been created by those of the High Command who had suspended medical assistance in retaliation for our strike, making them uniquely responsible for our fast by closing all the doors to understanding and mocking us despite the consequences. I reminded him, among other things, of the trickery of the authorities during our previous strike.

Dr. Berenguer acknowledged their errors and offered "as an Interior

Ministry colonel and a doctor" to try to arrange for our transfer to Havana as soon as we stopped the strike, something I ignored, of course, knowing its true and only purpose.

As for medical assistance, Berenguer assured me that an IV solution would be given to us all as necessary. I sent a note that was given to Montes de Oca advising him to accept the IV because all six of us were to be included.

Montes de Oca understood my note. An hour later, nurse Carmona, in the presence of Lieutenant Carderín, gave each of the strikers an IV. That meant for us a new injection of life and the possibility of prolonging the strike several more days, helping us to further denounce the inhumane prisons of Castro's tyranny.

"The damage that you have done to us with this hunger strike is irreparable," Colonel Berenguer confessed to me.

His words indicated the achievement of our main objective, even if we had experienced no immediate benefits. Dr. Juan Berenguer also ordered that vitamins be added to our intravenous solution. And he said to replace each liter with another as soon as it ran out to avoid having to insert another needle. But when the nurse was late in doing so, I tried to change the bottle myself, but felt dizzy and fell onto my bunk. My efforts led to some bleeding and I began to feel terrible, so I took the needle out entirely. It was very cold that night and I was also plagued by mosquitos.

It would have been about 4:00 a.m. when Polito, a common prisoner being held in #15, belted out a folk song with all his strength while tapping with a stick to accompany himself.

"Tun-tun-tun... Tun-Tun; tun-tun-tun... "The tune was always the same; he only varied the improvisations, maliciously targeting other prisoners like himself, also being held in punishment cells.

Occasionally one of those allegedly targeted lifted his voice, irritated, to reprimand him: "Listen, Nagüe, change your tune!"

And as Polito persisted: "Hey, lady, stop singing so early in the morning to your husband."

And so, the "music" continued with infrequent interruptions until after daybreak.

In fact, that morning I had wished that Polito would be hit by a bolt of lightning. How could anyone be so inconsiderate when everyone in Boniato prison knew that six men were suffering on a hunger strike? I had to accept that since his childhood Polito had known only assaults, rape, drugs, and knife fights. Yes, the dagger was his only friend to help him survive in the alienated world of the stifling prison system.

Polito, locked up for 13 years since age 21, then further condemned for various bloody actions and a murder in prison, was no longer a normal person who thinks and reasons, so his irrational attitude could be understood and forgiven.

Carmona appeared around 8:00 in the morning to give me the second liter of serum. I complained about having felt a reaction from some substance in there the night before.

"That's impossible," he said, "All I added to the dextrose was vitamins B1 and B2. Probably you imagined it."

"That's not true, I had a reaction. I vomited. I'm not lying to you."

Carmona soon discovered the reason for my reaction, while trying to downplay its importance. Instead of giving me the serum intended for me, he had left in my cell by mistake one of the two liters destined for Gutiérrez Menoyo, to which had been added a drug to calm him down. These errors occurred often at Boniato. It wasn't just this case and Pitaluga's days earlier. Medicinal errors had also occurred with Sergio Montes de Oca, Marcos, and Pucho.

# CHAPTER 42

# Clandestine Correspondence

On February 13, 1981, I received a clandestine letter from my mother and two beautiful Christmas cards sent by a very dear friend, Amalia Hernández Cano of Tijuana, Mexico. I knew Amalia only by correspondence. Our friendship had started in a casual way. It began at the end of 1974, shortly after my sentencing to 25 years, together with Eloy Gutiérrez Menoyo, Félix Rafael Vázquez Robles, and Amaranto Cabrera Álvarez, when all of us had been accused of conspiring in prison to overthrow by force the "Revolutionary government of Cuba" and the "dictatorship of the proletariat." Amalia is one of those exceptional people who offered her noble soul in sincere friendship. She had already been writing to Amaranto Cabrera. In one of those coincidences of destiny, I happened to see a letter Cabrera had written to her, where he described the political and social situation of our country. To my astonishment, Amaranto presented himself not actually as a victim of Castro's totalitarianism, a political prisoner, but as a university student, a member of the Union of Young Communists, very proud and happy about the freedom enjoyed in Cuba and the progress of the Revolution.

His strange and cowardly attitude may have resulted from experiences with the military court that had judged us... and as reprehensible as his statements seemed, I decided not reprimand him, giving him some latitude because of the mental confusion inflicted on him by our prolonged interrogations by State Security. But I decided to intervene to let the young woman know who, and where, Amaranto Cabrera actually was.

Our friendship started there. I am sorry about its painful beginning. As already indicated, Amalia was an exceptional young woman of exquisite sensibilities. I cherish our friendship, which had already lasted more than ten years, as well as her efforts to salvage a considerable portion of my poetic work, including *Carousel, Bell of the Dawn*, and *Upwind.* Due to her extraordinary efforts, two books of verses by the poet Jorge Valls *(Keep* and *Flight of the Evening Dove)* were also saved, as well as a book of poems by William Casasús, and also one by William Rivas, all of which managed to reach foreign shores and today are already published or on their way to publication.

The two beautiful Christmas cards and my mother's letter arrived into my hands in my dark, sealed punishment cell thanks to the ingenuity of young Manuel Moinedo (El Pinto), taking advantage of a guard's neglect, at great risk of inevitable retaliation should he be discovered. It was a rapid maneuver, involving a plastic bag lowered outside my mesh window on a string taken from a mattress, after he and I had communicated by prison sign language. My mother's message gave me new courage to withstand my difficult challenges.

On the morning of February 15 something happened that initially caused me a lot of concern. Between 4:30 and 5:00 a.m., a group of soldiers passed outside my cell. I saw them through the opening at the edge of the door. They stopped at the end of the hall. Some minutes later I heard a common prisoner yell out that they were taking photos inside cell #39. Usually that happened only when an inmate had been murdered or had committed suicide inside his cell. At Boniato, both murders and suicides occurred frequently among those convicted of common crimes. In the case of the prisoner in #39, Eloy, those two forms of violent of death could be discarded, but not the possibility that he had died because of the hunger strike. A fast of 98 days, despite sporadic IVs and sips of tea, was more than long enough for any human being to cease to exist. But when the same voice announced that photos were being taken inside #35, and then #31, I then felt that it was simply a measure being applied to all six of us who were on strike, probably to satisfy the curiosity of Fidel Castro and his interior minister.

When Lieutenant Carlos arrived at my cell, he roughly pulled off my sheet, perhaps to impress me. Each of us had six photos taken, some of our whole body lying on the concrete bed.

After that, the days continued to pass slowly, enigmatically. The dungeon's loneliness became more oppressive over time. Sometimes I killed an hour by writing a poem, but only in secret, always aware that a moment of surprise surveillance could mean not only the loss of my work, but of my pen and paper as well. Even worse, it might result in a more rigorous search and the confiscation of my little radio, cutting me off completely from the outside world. So, I was always on constant alert, even during my fitful sleep. My radio news had already become quite limited as the batteries were fading.

Three days after we were photographed, Dr. Berenguer returned to order that each of us receive two vials of 1000 cc of dextrose at 5%. On the following morning, when I had taken in a little less than the half of the second liter, the prison's deputy warden appeared at my cell, accompanied by the head of Internal Order, to again insist that I start eating. In light of my negative response, Lieutenant Milhet then told me that the command had determined that if we did not immediately end our fast, all medical assistance would be suspended.

I replied that it was up to them, to do whatever they wanted, but we would not quit the strike until the government had formally agreed to meet our just demands. I reminded them that we had accepted medical assistance only at their insistence. And when we had advised them that such assistance did not interest us, they had responded that it would be given to us by force, because the government was unwilling to commit the same errors as a few years earlier, and therefore would not allow us or any other prisoner to die on a hunger strike, since that was against "the humanitarian policy of the Revolution."

"So, you well know," I concluded, "that what you now call 'adequate medical assistance,' is being done according to your will or interests, not because we've asked for it."

"The policy can change," Milhet argued. "Today we may decide one thing and tomorrow adopt something else, according to our interests at the time, as you just said."

Then, after a brief pause, he added, "Think it over now, while there's still time."

"Forget it, Milhet," I interjected. "There is nothing to think about. We already decided a long time ago. Don't waste your time. You can remove my IV right now."

"No, no. There's no hurry. We can wait until this liter is empty."

"Why wait?" I insisted, "Let's get it over with."

And as he saw me already beginning to peel off the tape holding the syringe on my arm, he told me, "Stop it; be careful!"

But I kept on pulling off the tape and removed the needle from my vein.

Lieutenant Milhet and Sergeant Noaldo, after exchanging a quick look of confusion, left the cell in silence. After that, I heard the clanging open of the door to Julio Ruiz Pitaluga's cell, and after that, in quick succession, those of Sergio Montes de Oca, Evelio Hernández, Méndez Pimentel, and Eloy Gutiérrez Menoyo.

Then we all underwent a rigorous search. Not only did the jailers take away all our belongings, in my case, underpants, a handkerchief, a notebook, and a pen, but also, all the medicines that the Dr. Berenguer had prescribed, even our water cups.

When I tried to find out the why this absurd measure was being undertaken, Lieutenant Calderín, apparently a little distressed, responded: "Think about it, Ernesto... Orders are orders, and although sometimes one does not agree, they must be obeyed."

"Even if they are unfair?" I retorted.

"Even if they are unfair," he affirmed. And after a pause: "Unfortunately, that's just how it is."

I could have argued with him, but it wasn't worth it. Lieutenant Calderín might have been a diehard Communist or simply one of those many unhappy souls unable to understand that human dignity cannot be fostered by giving himself over to the dirty service of a repressive body. And the proof was that he was there directly imposing criminal cruelty against us, against our small group of prisoners of conscience, peacefully defending our rights.

While the search of us all came by surprise, I managed to save, in addition to the radio, four ten peso notes, and some important documents squeezed into a "balita," a tiny ball of papers, all carried inside my athletic underpants, and several sheets of paper and a pencil nub so tiny that it almost got lost between my fingers.

We spent the rest of the day without any water. Since our consensus strategy was to resist all untoward winds and tides without showing any anxiety, however drastic, we were resigned to stoically endure our thirst.

That night, I could barely sleep. I felt my dry mouth and throat, asking myself how the others were doing and wondering how long our weakened bodies could survive without ingesting water. A week? Only three days, perhaps? "Death is sometimes a solution to great suffering, to irreparable human tragedy," I told myself. I imagined my colleagues were raising identical questions before reaching the same conclusion.

And I felt that death was pressing me from inside as I underwent another bout of bloody vomiting during the night until I was completely exhausted.

By morning, my condition was so serious that I began experiencing a kind of madness. It seemed that the cell walls were closing in on me, reducing the very air that I was breathing. I had never before experienced such desperate anguish. With great difficulty I stood up, and because the cell was so small, I braced myself by extending my arms out to the walls on either side to prevent them from pressing in on me.

I don't know where I derived the strength to stay upright, even if only for a very short time. I felt like shouting to escape the alienating loneliness that was consuming the last gasps of my spirit. I wanted to walk, walk, walk in those few inches of space, to make sure life remained in my legs, so that in my future, if ever I escaped from this diabolical trap, that I would not be confined to a wheelchair. But just as I took the first step, I collapsed and hit my head, losing consciousness.

I don't know how long I lay on the floor. When I came to, I saw the guard peering in at me and heard the padlock hitting against the steel plank. I instinctively moved my hand to the tiny radio. Still a little stunned, but with superhuman effort, I managed to get up again and fall down on the bed.

"What happened to you?" asked the guard.

"I don't know," I responded breathlessly.

"Did you fall out of bed?" the official asked.

"Yes, it seems while I was asleep."

"Were you injured?"

"No."

Nothing would have been gained by telling him the truth.

"Do you need help?"

"No, I'm fine. What time is it?"

"It's early."

"Thanks," I said, while thinking it was both a stupid question and a stupid answer.

"Are you thirsty?"

No comment. Considering the mockery of his question, I turned toward the wall, giving him my back as a response. I heard him close the flap over the small opening. A very strange sensation of spiritual peace then flooded over me. From the mountainside, there drifted in the voices of children playing. I thought of my sons, little Danny, David, and Ernie, all so far and yet so near. I told myself, "My passage through this life has not been in vain."

I was deep into these meditations when I discerned the jingling of keys on the other side of the steel plan and, then I heard the click of the padlock opening. An official entered carrying an aluminum cup and a half-full liter of dextrose, the same one removed from me the prior afternoon.

"Take this," he said, extending the cup filled with dextrose. "The doctor has ordered that you drink this three times a day."

"If so, okay," I said. (The authorities, apparently alarmed by my fall, did not want me or any of us to actually die.)

I took two or three sips and put the cup on the floor.

"No, no, you have to drink it all right now," the officer admonished. "Our orders are not leave any vessel in the cell."

"That's a stupid order," I retorted angrily.

"That's the order," the official affirmed, unmoved by my outburst.

I was going to say something else when I remembered that our motto was to resist to all torture and all vileness without complaint. We must not show any sign of weakness or concern.

I raised the jug to my lips and drank it all down, but inside I was raging.

Judging by the shadows, it must have been about 8:30 a.m.

To add to our martyrdom, this new provision prohibited us from being allowed to drink water, only dextrose until we ended our strike. The faint sweetness of the dextrose would increase our thirst, augmenting our agony and only delaying our dehydration and death.

This new measure left us little room to maneuver. We had three choices: first, since our protest involved a total fast for an indefinite period, regardless of consequences, inasmuch as the thirst strike had been imposed by force, we could then decide to end the fast. Second, since the authorities had denied us water against our will, we could reject the dextrose. This would put us in a coma in less than a week if we were still alive. We had made an sacrosanct commitment, that if any of us died during the protest those remaining would be forced to continue the strike until they died, unless the authorities fully met our demands. Since the main objective of the hunger strike was political, to stimulate a campaign from the outside world against the violation of human rights in Cuba, thereby impacting (directly or indirectly) favorably the Cuban political prisoner, it was best to extend our fast as long as possible. So, we then decided to observe the new "rules of the game" that our enemy had imposed.

# CHAPTER 43

# A Poem for the Children

A dog began barking incessantly out towards the palm grove by the mountain. I heard the moan of a cow, then the joyful voices of youngsters playing. At that instant, the bitter reality of our strike, with all its attendant miseries, aroused in me an irresistible wish to depict a more beautiful world of song for those purest and most important of God's creation: our children.

It was then that I took a piece of paper and my pencil stub, inspired by those tender creatures who had rescued me from the dark abyss, and wrote all at once a poem that has had the greatest spiritual significance for my life: "Children of all peoples."

## CHILDREN OF ALL PEOPLES

Children of all peoples,
come play with me.
In this forest of prison bars
we will make four paths.
One of very white soil,
white, white like the nest
of the white butterfly,
and the lily and the edge

of the silver froth
in my cup of wine.
Another blue, like the seas
where the old sailors
sing early in the morning
while the waves curl,
falling leeward
meek as the gentle noise
of the bells of Easter,
meek, meek as wheat
and sheep and the seagull
and the circus elephant,
meek as the pigeon,
meek as the sky itself.
Children of all peoples,
come to play with me.
In this forest of prison bars
we will make four paths:
One of honey and smiles,
of surprises and sighs...
and we will create windows
always open to the spray,
to the eye of the rainbow,
to the star and to the trill
of the canary and the mockingbird,
and to the music of the cricket.
Another green, pale green
clear as the air I breathe,
green as the hope
of the queen and the beggar,
green always, always green
like the five senses,
green as the throat of the lemon and the pine,
green-green, pure green
as the hands of a child.

If I have let these verses so dear to me fly away in a symbolic gesture, it has been thanks to the great love that children inspire in me and in gratitude to those little ones who have returned my peace of mind with their sweet voices, giving me the strength to continue to endure courageously the hot coals of our enemies.

Our days continued on with their usual monotony; the desolate and cold nights seemed to last an eternity. Our lips began to crack. Small bitter particles, like sand, rolled off our tongue. Thirst gave us no truce. It had become the blackest agony, the most oppressive torture imaginable.

One morning, around 2:30 am, we heard Julio Ruiz Pitaluga's desperate pleas for a sip of water. Pitaluga had not managed to recover psychologically from an incident involving a serum error and, as if this were not enough for his confused mind, it had occurred hours before they had carried him on a stretcher to the punishment dungeon, right after Julio had asked Marco to please correct the needle's position in the vein, since the dextrose had overflowed as if from an obstruction. According to what Pitaluga later told me, apparently, the blood was coagulating and stopping the flow. This contributed to his psychological imbalance, verging on madness. We were unaware of this, of course. If we had known about his critical situation, we would have demanded that he withdraw from the strike. Julio Ruiz Pitaluga had won our affection because of his extraordinary moral sense, self-denial, and spirit of sacrifice, and his dedication to the cause of the freedom of our homeland. And he was revered not just among us, but also among the vast majority of his comrades in misfortune. The men of Cuba's political prison are a great spiritual family. Our prolonged years of harmonious coexistence have created a strong sincere brotherhood established in the midst of the worst vicissitudes, of the most distressing torments. We have united in unequal combat against a bloodthirsty and cruel enemy, fighting an ideology of hate and rancor, overcoming personal discrepancies and differences, creating a real and basic democracy, not relying on censored lips, chains, or shackles, learning in the blare of combat and in the pain of jail to respect and love each other like brothers.

"Water, water. I have the right to drink water," Pitaluga begged the watch officer who opened the walled plank and entered his cell.

"What's the matter, Pitaluga?" the official asked. "Did you have a nightmare? Were you dreaming?"

The questions could not have been crueler.

"No, no. My thirst is burning me up inside..." Pitaluga paused, then added: "Do me a favor, Tomás, bring me a little water."

"I can't," he immediately answered him. "Water is not prescribed by the doctor and I have to follow that."

Pitaluga protested angrily: "But, since when is water only to be taken on prescription? That's absurd."

Lieutenant Tomás put forth an argument both rhetorical and grotesque. Among other things, he said: "If you refuse to eat, we have the right to take measures we deem relevant."

And he repeated the usual refrain: "The hunger strike is a pressure tactic and you must face the consequences."

At the end of that speech, Lieutenant Tomás slammed the metal plank shut and continued his rounds from cell to cell, banging loudly on each steel surface and rattling the padlocks before sitting down in the small lobby, unconcerned about a man agonized by thirst. After all, Julio Ruiz Pitaluga was an "enemy of the Revolution" and, as a good Communist, the officer might have coolly thought that enemies of the Revolution must be dealt with mercilessly — "crushed like filthy rats."

Several weeks earlier, Dr. Stanley had stopped visiting us. The last time he had entered my cell was a few days before the thirst strike had been imposed on us. He had expressed being torn between his medical vocation and his duty to his superiors and seemed to have been sincerely hurt by our suffering despite his own cowardly complicity. But every man has a moment when his conscience shakes him.

I remember Stanley being concerned about the mosquitoes that had attacked my forehead, leaving an eruption that felt like sandpaper. Another matter was the intense morning sunlight falling directly on my dehydrated body. The prison director and Dr. Berenguer knew, everyone knew, but nothing was done about it.

So, when Stanley had asked if the sun bothered me, I replied with irony that I enjoyed it because it reminded me of my days at the beach.

Before leaving, Dr. Stanley, in a moment when we were alone while he was taking my blood pressure, told me in a low, confidential voice, that the High Command had given orders that none of us would be returned to the infirmary unless we abandoned the strike, and he expressed his disagreement over the inhuman measures being applied against us.

"I'm going to try to get away from here," he said finally, "away from Berenguer and these people. I don't need this responsibility."

Many times, I've wondered whether Dr. Nelson Stanley could absolve himself of guilt? I don't think so. But my right does not extend to deciding on his future in a free Cuba. My right only involves pointing out honestly his behavior in this, my own historical account.

We did not see him again for the rest of the time we remained on strike. I don't know whether Stanley was able to achieve a transfer. I don't honestly know whether Berenguer, being an agent of greater reliability and less scrupulous, had been tasked with continuing to carry out the biological experiment to determine to what extent a human being was able to resist such brutal physical and mental conditions.

Days after that last visit of Dr. Stanley, we were visited by the National Chief of Jails and Prisons, Colonel Arsenio Franco Villanueva, later Brigadier General, who had recently taken over for Colonel Medardo Lemus Otaño.

Franco, following the tradition of the hierarchs of the regime, arrived accompanied by a select entourage, including Clevert Martí, Colonel of Counter-intelligence Manuel Blanco, and ten other high-ranking officers, including the Chief of Jails and Prisons, the Chief of Prison Security for Santiago province, and First Lieutenant Gerardo Carrazana.

From my bed, with my back leaning against the wall, I caught a glimpse of them as they descended the central corridor between buildings 3 and 4. A few minutes before we had been alerted by a loud whistle to look out the window, as Pinto had informed us via sign language that the chief of prisons was in the facility, accompanied by a numerous retinue. Then we heard multiple footsteps on metal stairs leading to Hall 4C and, soon, lying on my mat, through the vertical slit, I saw them passing my cell going toward the end of the hallway.

They entered the cell of Gutiérrez Menoyo.

I was glad they went directly to talk with Eloy, because from the beginning we had designated him to discuss with the authorities all issues concerning the strike.

According to what Eloy told us when we met again in the clinic after the fast had ended, the new chief of jails and prisons was interested in knowing how the authorities had managed the earlier strike, and especially about the promises made to us in the name of General Enio Leyva by Lieutenant Carrazana, which Eloy explained in detail in the presence of the latter, attacking him harshly for his deception.

"You're a liar who doesn't even respect himself, Carrazana," Eloy told him, "or else Enio Leyva is lying. Remember what you promised, including going with us personally, to ensure our physical recovery at the Combinado del Este prison hospital? If we had known that was a hoax, we would not have stopped that strike (referring to when we had stopped a previous hunger strike after false promises from the authorities) and we would have avoided all that conflict. Already, you can see what has happened now because of your irresponsibility."

Eloy told us that Carrazana, without flinching, silently accepted the recriminations.

The conversation between Gutiérrez Menoyo and the chief of jails and prisons was wide-ranging. For 30 minutes, they discussed the most salient points: Eloy, defending our rights, Colonel Franco, trying to justify the inhuman regime imposed by the Communist government on political prisoners according to the tyrant's capricious will. Making a timely comparison rooted in historical reality, Gutiérrez Menoyo pointed out the abysmal difference between the treatment of political prisoners under Fulgencio Batista, including their very own Colonel Arsenio Franco, Fidel Castro, Interior Minister Ramiro Valdés Menéndez, and the rest of the Moncada assailants, and that received by those sanctioned for combating Castro's tyranny. "We would feel grateful," Gutiérrez Menoyo assured him, "if you would grant us only a 30% of the rights enjoyed by political prisoners in Cuba under the Batista dictatorship."

No agreement was possible. The stubbornness and arrogance of the new masters of our Caribbean island did not allow them sensible reflection. No one doubted that reason was on our side; not even those of the High Command dared deny the correctness of our approach. But force has its own logic and our jailers were in power, backed up by tanks and cannons, which they could call on at will, no matter how arbitrary their actions might be, always wielding the sledgehammer and skewering the rights of their victims on the tips of their bayonets "Made in the USSR."

Before this official intransigence, there was no alternative but to continue on with the strike, even when our bodies, converted already into human offal, would refuse to resist for many more days the hunger and thirst continuing to assail us. We had only our spirit to spur us on. We had only one concern now regarding our brother Sergio Montes de Oca Gil, who had only a little more than a month to go on his 20-year sentence. Eloy asked Colonel Arsenio Franco whether it might be possible to convince Montes de Oca to abandon the strike to allow him to recover his health, to the extent possible, by the date of his release.

From Eloy's dungeon, Franco Villanueva and his companions went on to that of Ramón Méndez Pimentel, next to that of Juan Evelio Hernández, and then briefly to Hernández Ramírez. In the cell of Julio Ruiz Pitaluga, they stayed about five minutes. Finally, they came to #19, where the chief of jails and prisons, after summarizing the discussion with the rest of my comrades, reported that as the official representative of the minister of the interior, he needed to let me know that the response to our letter of December 21 letter was negative.

"We've looked at it carefully," Colonel Franco told me, indicating that it had apparently irritated the Lord Minister. Anyone familiar with the excessive arrogance of Ramiro Valdés, a faithful imitator of the tyrant Fidel Castro, could imagine the angry reaction our energetic letter might have produced. We knew that before sending it, but our dignity, our pride, wouldn't allow us to beg for a right. We claimed our rights as required by the historical moment or, otherwise, we would have to resign ourselves to renouncing them idly before a powerful enemy who kept us with our hands tied. Either variant was reasonable; we chose the least easy, given that we had already embarked on the strike.

I did not want to discuss the letter with Colonel Arsenio Franco. I just listened to him and only when he had finished, did I tell him, without arrogance, but firmly, that my attitude would remain unchanged as long as there was no favorable response to our proposal.

Soon after the departure of the retinue, Pinto was brought into the punishment pavilion. He was locked up in #14, not far from me. As soon as the lieutenant had left the lobby, he began shouting for me to peek out through the slit by my door.

I had not stood up for days and wasn't sure my legs would hold me. However, at Pinto's insistence, I decided to try, despite my previous fall when I had hit my head. It has been said that the only animal that stumbles twice on the same stone is man. Making a supreme effort, I took two lurching steps to reach the door. When I peered outside, Pinto smiled at me from his porthole. It turned out that many prisoners, including El Pinto, managed to loop a boot lace through the opening to keep it open.

After greeting him, I told him to hurry because my legs were already trembling.

"Go lie down, lie down. I just wanted to see you. Are you okay?' he said.

And without giving me time to answer, he added, "I'll tell you later."

"What happened?" I wondered and went back to lie down on the mat. My heart was throbbing rapidly as though I had just finished racing from Los Angeles to New York. El Pinto seemed in a very good mood even though he faced 21 days in the black hole. From my bed, I listened to his shouted-out story of how he had surprised Lieutenant Bandera, responsible for the punishment pavilion, when he had reported to Evelio about the pending visit of the chief of jails and prisons, in what he called "a live report."

Three days after the visit of Colonel Arsenio Franco Villanueva, the head of the prison's Internal Order, accompanied by lieutenants

Escalona, Julio, and Eusebio, entered my cell in mid-afternoon for a surprise search.

Lieutenant Escalona was one of the most repressive prison officials. Soon after our arrival at Boniato he was named Chief of Internal Order, making his mark with his excessive abuses, mainly against common prisoners, whom he attacked with tremendous ferocity, using sticks and thick rods of corrugated steel. Lieutenant Julio and Noaldo Pérez were no less criminal. Those three goons had mastered the art of torture and massacre. Regarding Lieutenant Eusebio, we didn't know what to expect, as he had not been seen before at Boniato until being appointed to guard us in the punishment pavilion during our hunger strike. Given his hostile attitude toward us and his harsh despotism, it was not difficult to deduce that he was a hyena from the same litter.

When I saw them enter my cell, my first thought was a question. Would my little radio survive? So many times, I had managed to save it from the clutches of the jailers, but due to my deplorable physical state, I wasn't sure this time.

Noaldo spoke first. He asked if I could stand up so they could search the mat and the pillow.

"Don't forget I've been on hunger strike 110 days," I reminded him, in case he had forgotten. And after a brief pause, I added, "Does that seem short to you?"

Noaldo turned toward the Lieutenant Escalona, "110 days," he said, "what do you think?

"Incredible!" he exclaimed. "This must be seen to be believed."

"These darn bugs have nine lives just like cats," commented Lieutenant Julio, "and I only wish they would die so we'd get rid of them."

The four of them smiled in amusement. Julio's words neither amused nor displeased me. I was used to hearing their crap; I knew that, like a crab, inside his head was a ton of shit.

Then, Sergeant Noaldo leaned over and looked like he was about to lift me down onto the floor.

"No, no, not like that," I said as it looked like his arms would go under my thighs.

If it had not been for the radio, I would have accepted.

Instead, I sat up on the bed with my feet flat on the floor, then Noaldo and Lieutenant Escalona grabbed me under the armpits and dragged me to a corner of the cell.

Although the new mat had been given to me 22 days before, when we had been sent to the punishment pavilion, Lieutenant Eusebio ordered to have it replaced by a new one, the same with the pillow. I immediately understood that they wanted to tear them apart to search them thoroughly. In Cuba's prisons, and perhaps in those of the whole world, only an inexperienced prisoner or a fool would risk hiding something prohibited —and something he did not want to lose— inside a pillow or a mattress, as jailers often tried to surprise us with these searches. This usually occurs only with political prisoners, as common prisoners usually sleep on a piece of canvas stretched out over a metal frame about as comfortable as a sparrow's nest. A mat and pillow are exceptional luxuries only enjoyed sporadically by prisoners of conscience.

As I lay down on the brand-new mat, Noaldo felt inside the pockets of the pants that I was wearing to protect me from the intense cold.

"Okay," he said, having finished the search and finding only a button, something that I don't know why I'd saved.

Eusebio was the first to leave. Noaldo and Escalona had already left when Lieutenant Julio, unhappy to leave empty-handed, intervened: "What about his underpants?" he said, without waiting for the others to respond, ordering me: "Remove your pants."

"Let me alone, Julio," I protested. "Don't bother me, you've already done enough."

Noaldo and Escalona stared at me undecided. But since Lieutenant Julio insisted, the former, just to please him, asked me half-heartedly: "Do me a favor, Ernesto, take off your pants."

"No, no! That's quite enough!" I told Julio, using an authoritative tone.

"This fucker is going to find my radio with his Sherlock Holmes psychosis," I said to myself, "Let's see if I can escape from this."

Slowly, I started unbuttoning, then I looked at Julio who had planted himself at the foot of the bed, "I don't think I can get out of the pants alone; I'm already getting tired."

The chief of Internal Order was leaning against the wall with his arms crossed. Lieutenant Escalona was standing next to him. Neither showed any interest in participating directly in the new search. But neither stopped observing me.

Julio grabbed the pants from below and began to pull them down laboriously, because I was keeping my legs together to reduce visibility, hoping the briefs were not too loose now because of my skeletal thighs.

Once he had the pants in his hands, he inspected them fold by fold, seam by seam.

Apparently, he was already about to give up when he fixated on my athletic underwear with its jock strap.

"Let's see, let's see what you have down there?" he said, dropping my pants on the floor.

His eyes sparkled like a snake that has just discovered a wounded dove.

"That's a support given me by the doctor for Peyronie's Syndrome," a disorder I invented on the spot, trying to confuse them.

But Julio did not swallow the bait.

"Pull down your underpants," he ordered, distrustful.

"Still I have a possibility of circumventing this... one possibility among thousand," I figured. And with a quick movement, I pulled both pairs down together to mid-thigh.

"If you want to see my balls, enjoy the view," I said just to freak him out.

But Lieutenant Julio showed himself to be a man freed of all complexes. He didn't even smile. He had renounced all shame when he had joined the side of the victors on January 1, 1959.

"Let's see what you've got there in your underpants," he insisted.

I realized that my last trick had failed. That meant a costly defeat for me, since I would lose all access to information. But even more than the loss of the radio, I was bothered the fact that it was precisely Lieutenant Julio who had scored that victory.

Ever since I'd started unbuttoning my pants, I had been sitting on the mat which partly hampered the visibility of Lieutenant Escalona and Sergeant Noaldo. Aware that there was nothing left to do, I dropped back on the bed like someone giving up their king in a game of chess.

"Let me know when you get tired of searching," was the only thing I could think of to say.

Lieutenant Julio pulled down both underpants at the same time. At that moment, I had turned and slightly opened my legs so the radio rested on the mattress between my knees. At the same time that Julio was starting to reach, I pretended to cough twice, taking advantage of the movement to squeeze my thighs onto the radio.

He may have become convinced that in reality I didn't have anything hidden, or perhaps because the athletic underwear was too grimy since I had gone one or two months without washing it, after separating one pair of underpants from the other, the officer limited himself to feeling around the waist.

Even seeing with my own eyes and hear it straight from his lips, it seemed incredible when he extending to me the two pairs of underpants and told me: "Go ahead, put them back on."

"That's enough. Leave them there on the bed as I'm so tired," I argued, without daring to move my legs. I knew that if I tried to put on the underpants in the presence of the jailers, the tiny radio would be revealed, spoiling everything. The only salvation possible was to pull the sheet over me and wait until they had left, claiming fatigue, so I did.

Still I dared to tell Lieutenant Julio, already sure that the danger had passed: "Didn't I warn you, that I did have anything?"

He gave me a stupid, sickly smile before leaving.

As soon I was alone, without taking off the sheet, I put on the two pairs underwear, then the pants. I started then to tremble from head to toe from emotional stress. My nerves had endured a tremendous challenge. Now I felt depleted. Certainly, this was not the first time that I'd endured an apparent absurdity.

One by one, the rest of my colleagues suffered a similar search that afternoon and all, like me, escaped serious trouble.

After the visit of the chief of jails and prisons, we were plunged into total stagnation. The interior minister had emphatically refused our demands, claiming that the government could not yield to pressure. We, for our part, kept strictly to the fast, in support of our just and indispensable right. Realistically, we could not harbor the slightest hope of a friendly solution after having been officially informed of the government's decision by Ramiro Valdés, no doubt at the behest of Fidel Castro himself. However, considering the political and moral damage to the regime that our very prolonged fast was causing, recognized days before by Lieutenant Colonel Juan Berenguer, we were unanimous in our resistance, which boosted our mental energy.

The latter precisely began to falter for our brother Sergio Montes de Oca at the beginning of March, and for me as well.

There is nothing more overwhelming than solitude, than total isolation under such terrible conditions. One feels a tremendous vacuum that dulls the senses, chipping away at the spirit, and weighing down the soul. And if this occurs when the sufferer has lost all hope of reaching the desired goal, the sacrifice may seem useless. Therefore, from a practical, objective perspective, it was perfectly understandable that some days later, Montes de Oca would abandon the hunger strike. Without exception, the rest of our colleagues who had kept the fast —and even those not participating— understood his decision.

"Don't look for a silly justification for me," he told us outright. "My freedom had nothing to do with my decision, absolutely nothing. I left the strike because I was convinced that these people were never going solve anything, nor show any balls, and I was tired of just lying around on my bed staring up at the ceiling."

The honesty of that endearing friend touched me, so that I wished more than ever that our brotherhood would remain eternal, constant, and indestructible.

# CHAPTER 44

# Incommunicado

Political prisoners at Boniato were due for a family visit on March 11. It was our only opportunity to let them know about our continued hunger strike, undertaken in part to make their visits more convenient for both us and them. As my sister-in-law was coming to visit Miguel Ángel Álvarez, whom she had married in June of the previous year, one or two days later, my brother and my parents in Miami would receive her call, informing them directly about our situation. This communication link was a great support for us, along with that provided by the relatives of other members of our group in Boniato prison. It was a way to get our message out to the world. And proof of this was, among other significant and valuable steps, the document that Commander Húber Matos was able to send to Amnesty International.

Most prisoners waited anxiously for the visit and the opportunity to share precious hours with their loved ones, but visits also served as channels for clandestine communication, both incoming and outgoing.

A few days before our inspection in the punishment pavilion, taking advantage of a pen and some sheets of onion paper, I had written a last report on the strike, directed to the Secretary General of Alpha 66. Although El Pinto was unable to evade surveillance to get into the patio outside our compound, he coordinated with a friend, a common prisoner working on the clean-up crew, to pick up the matchbox that

I threw out between the window railings. I was not comfortable with involving a third person, and I knew a fair number of common prisoners were confidants of the jailers, which made me wary. But since El Pinto insisted there would be no problem, I threw the matchbox out at an opportune moment.

The prisoner immediately swept it up into the dustpan. After making sure that nobody had noticed, he tossed the item to El Pinto, who caught it from his window. After some fifteen minutes, I saw on a point on the wall of building 3C a flash of sunlight reflected from a mirror. That was the password I had given to Miguel Ángel Álvarez to report that it was in his possession.

But all my efforts to reach out to the exile community with such necessary information were wasted. On March 10, just 24 hours before our long-awaited family visit, the prison's higher authorities decreed once again on a change of clothing for *plantado* political prisoners (something of great symbolic importance for us), namely that we would be forced to wear the blue uniform of common prisoners. Those not complying would be deprived of all rights, including medical assistance and family visits.

By mid-morning of the following day there were some 30 *plantados* returned to Pavilion 4D who had chosen not to participate in the massive hunger strike that began on November 12. The authorities' retaliation against them for refusing to accept the common prisoners' black uniforms was identical to that against the 70-something men who had maintained the strike for 32 days, including those in walled punishment cells. Days before, the doors of 4D also had been covered with thick metal plates, even for those prisoners of advanced age.

I found out about the interior minister's new decree a couple of days later. The prison's deputy director transmitted that unfortunate news to the five of us still on the hunger strike. He was accompanied by the head of Internal Order. Lieutenant Milhet knew there was no way that we would accept their capricious order. He told me: "I know that you guys are not interested, but I am obliged to let you know, just as we have done with the rest of the *plantados*."

I did not need the deputy warden to tell me about the reaction of the hundred or so rebellious comrades who remained in Boniato prison. I knew well their attitude toward an imposition of this nature. But Milhet affirmed it: "Only one accepted the new uniform: Jesús Sánchez Arango. For now, we are going to keep him in the infirmary. We are looking into his case to see if he will be authorized his family visit."

And indeed, Jesús Sánchez Arango was the only *plantado* prisoner at Boniato to accept the measure. I imagine that for him it was a very painful decision, due to his usual implacable attitude sustained during years and years, ever since 1967, when the government first tried to force *plantados* to wear common prisoners' uniforms, leading often to our wearing only underpants.

But Sánchez had every right to act freely, to change his strategy according to his personal circumstances, whether or not these coincided with our collective interests. Moreover, his 20-year sentence was about to expire. But Jesús was not released. Using one or another trivial pretext, after keeping him in the prison infirmary for three months, they decided to send him to solitary confinement to a walled cell of pavilion 4C. Then he was informed that he would be relocated to one of the pavilions for common prisoners. Furthermore, the same measure would be applied to all political prisoners in the so-called re-education plan. This sparked an angry rebellion among youth in building 1A, a dozen of whom, among them Rodolfo Suárez Cruz, were sent to the punishment dungeons.

If the Communists thought they could crush Jesús Sánchez Arango, taking advantage of the circumstances that led him to change his mind by accepting the uniform that he had rejected so energetically years before —after suffering the cruelest reprisals during the decades that he had remained in his underwear—they were sadly mistaken. Expressing a healthy pride, Sánchez flatly refused to live in humiliated among common prisoners. Days later, he and Félix Vázquez Robles, who by then had also accepted the same uniform, were both confined in the punishment pavilion. Both of them then stripped off the black clothing to the satisfaction of all their friends.

For two more years, Sánchez Arango was forced to remain naked behind bars, without medical care, not allowed to go outside or to have family visits, forced to endure two more years of arbitrary deprivation of freedom without undergoing any sort of judicial procedure, after having already served his excessive 20-year sentence.

While this and other flagrant violations of human rights occurred at Boniato and at other prisons all over the island, "President" Fidel Castro, at the 68th Summit of the Inter-parliamentary World Union, held in Havana in the summer of 1981, shamefully dared to denounce, the "intransigence" of British Prime Minister Margaret Thatcher for her reaction to the demands of the Maze strikers, clamoring for recognition as political prisoners. The immorality of the tyrant of Cuba in appointing himself as redeemer-judge of the Maze martyrs, when he was committing in his own country the very same abuses, the same crime against prisoners of conscience who had served more than 20 years, requires no further comment. The facts, the true history, are laid out for all to see. Honest people can draw their own conclusions.

The month of March was advancing amid greater uncertainty. The days stretched out longer, evenings seemed endless despite the alienating commotion of common prisoners extending well past midnight. And between 4:00 and 5:00 a.m., we continued receiving almost invariably Polito's "entertainment" of tapping with a stick on his window bars, or sometimes, for even more "fun," against the steel plate covering the dungeon entrance. Only when I was able ingest a respectable amount of Benzedrine could I resist his ballpark cries.

At noon, around the 15th of the same month, I committed my most serious flub during the entire strike. Lieutenant Julio had assumed guard duty and had entered my dungeon to give me one of the three drinks of dextrose we were supposed to consume every 24 hours. As was his custom, he stood right next to my bed without taking his eyes off me, while I sipped the required liquid very slowly, not only to hide my desperate thirst, but to stretch it out as long as possible. I cannot explain the stupidity of lifting my right leg in Julio's presence. Perhaps I did it unconsciously to ease the intense pain I was feeling at that moment due to the polyneuritis that had assaulted me many days before. After stretching out my foot, my leg landed directly down on the tiny radio with a loud "crack" that froze my blood. The expression on Julio's face made me fear that this time, the radio was indeed lost.

I guess that I must have paled, despite my effort to appear unflappable.

"Raise it, raise your leg again," the astonished official demanded.

At this point, I had completely forgotten my thirst, but following a mechanical impulse, I drank down all the dextrose still left in the jug.

"Stop that! Do you think that I'm just a monkey entertaining you?" I cut in, "My leg is really hurting."

July shook his head, telling me: "You're going to end up crippled by your stubbornness."

"It doesn't matter. Already the minister has ruled that we need to die," I reminded him, "and the dead don't have to worry about becoming crippled."

If he had not been so cowardly, he would have forced me to undress. Julio is of those beasts who like to display their fangs, but never dare to bite while by themselves. Attacking is simple if he is backed up by the herd, whether of hyenas or piranhas, as was his nature. No one could doubt his cunning. If he had any virtue, it was his mastery of the ingenuity of evil. I did not doubt his capacity to cause harm to his victims. As soon as he had left, I focused on escaping the storm that certainly would assault me in just a few minutes.

While it pondered where and how to hide the radio from the impending inspection, I heard Julio's footsteps, the squeak of his new boots going out toward the lobby. Then there was the noise of him lifting the phone handle. "He's already alerting the warden," I told myself. "I need to hurry."

Days before, anticipating the eventual possibility of the moment when I might be stripped of the radio, or perhaps due to my deteriorating physical condition, I had inspected the bowl of our Turkish toilet, essentially a hole in the floor that we had to squat over to do our necessities. To hide any object in its interior required an extremely thin arm and hand, which I now possessed, thanks to our prolonged fast, allowing me to insert my arm up to the elbow. The hiding place was good, but due to its excessive dampness, the radio could only remain there a very brief time without becoming ruined. Also, the wire antenna, wound around it, made it too wide to fit fully into the toilet opening.

I tried to pull out the wire, first with my teeth, then by pressing it against the edge of the concrete bed. Unfortunately, I lacked the strength to crush a flea. Since the political prisoner is an animal not easily resigned to defeat, and slightly by instinct and a little by faith, I returned to test the toilet hollow to see if it would open miraculously, as happened to Moses with the Red Sea opening to the people of Israel escaping from Egypt, according to the Biblical account.

And the miracle actually happened! My efforts to unscrew the base of the tiny cable had gained enough space to allow the radio to pass though the narrowest part of the toilet opening. Having overcome that obstacle, with one of my socks, I collected stagnant urine in the duct three or four times, which I threw outside the window, and with the other sock, I wiped my hands. I had thrown out as much as I could toward the section occupied by common prisoners.

I had just hidden the radio inside the toilet when Lieutenant Julio arrived at my doorway. I had not heard his footsteps because of the shouts of a common prisoner asking for more food. But there I was, lying on my mat, looking unconcerned.

"Hey, I'm glad that you've come," I said. "Come inside for a moment, as I want to ask you something."

Intrigued, Julio turned the key in the lock and entered the black hole.

"What is it?" he inquired curiously.

I was reclining against the back wall on the courtyard side of the cell.

"Look, the problem is that I have gone more than two months wearing this same sweater and jock strap underwear and already they are so funky that no nose will resist... Well, I guess you noticed it the other day when I was being searched. Just looking at it makes you want to vomit."

"Don't think that I'm going to wash it!" Julio said. "Unless you've gone crazy."

"No, don't panic. I know you are fastidious," I joked.

"I'm not fastidious," he replied with annoyance. "I'm just not a stupid SOB."

"Look, let me finish explaining; what I need is just some help in removing my clothes and taking them to Rolando García or to Negro Cardentey so they can give them a scrubbing —to them or to any of my colleagues.

By the expression on Julio's face, I saw that he was getting excited. "No problem compadre," he answered instantly. "Let's do it right now."

Sitting on the bunk, I leaned forward to strip off the sweater, then I lay face up on the mat to unbutton the pants. While officially, I was not authorized to still be using the yellow uniform, the prison authorities had not come by to collect mine, so I continued wearing the yellow pants to stave off the cold and because they had helped me hide the little radio in my underpants.

At the end I was, with Julio's "generous" assistance, as naked as when my mother had brought me into the world, and so the official could confirm that I had nothing on me other than a fair amount of dirt, but he scrutinized me anyway, speechless and with his eyes dilated. Then he looked carefully all around the cell, examining it inside out, centimeter by centimeter, involuntarily shrugging his shoulders.

"To Negro Cardentey or to Rolando García," I reminded him, acting nonchalant, despite my skeletal nudity.

Julio took the sweater and the athletic briefs, but I put on the underpants and yellow trousers again. I do not deny my secret amusement at my efforts to convince Lieutenant Julio that the sound he had heard before when I sat down was just a trick of his imagination. But, indeed, the staff of Boniato soon entered my cell to undertake a more thorough new search, this time a lieutenant colonel, a very rude and arrogant guy, a perfect henchman, accompanied by the warden, the chief of Internal Order, and, of course, Lieutenant Julio himself.

I was struck by seeing a lieutenant colonel personally searching a cell in a prison which had more than 150 recruits and officers to carry out this difficult task. This indicated a clear distrust by the hierarchs of their subordinates, at the same time, as in this case, making them look ridiculous.

Lieutenant Machado showed somewhat better composure. He limited himself to turning on the faucet to make sure no water came out because of the order to deprive us of water and a routine look at the toilet where the radio remained out of sight. None of their hands, even that of Julio, the slenderest of the group, would have fit through that opening. Nonetheless, my heart beat faster.

Sergeant Noaldo and the lieutenant colonel examined centimeter by centimeter the mat and the pillow, then the four of them left my cell. However, dissatisfied and somewhat frustrated, the lieutenant colonel, without even closing the door, asked Julio to explain in detail about helping me undress. From my bed, I could see the lieutenant colonel's back. I tried to hear what Julio was saying, but he spoke in a very low voice. Machado twice interrupted him, first to ask what happened to the athletic briefs, second, to make sure he understood exactly what Julio had been saying. I was unable to discern Julio's replies, but I did clearly perceive what the lieutenant colonel then said, "It doesn't matter, anyway since we are going to move him to another cell."

I trembled from head to toe! Nothing could be worse for me. It was like drowning in a pond where the water only reached to my ankles after having swum across the English Channel. "I have to play the last card, the only one that I have left," I told myself, "even if they surprise me and all pile on top of me in their fury."

And without further ado, I jumped up to retrieve the radio from the toilet hollow. But even by pulling and pulling, perhaps because of the angle or my extreme weakness, I was unable to extract it. After my failed attempts, I lay down on the mat, defeated. The personal bravery of every man has a limit. Many times I have felt fear in my life, but only supermen are capable of maintaining calm in the face of serious threats.

Outside the lieutenant colonel had begun talking again, or at least I thought I heard his voice, but I couldn't understand what he was saying. At that moment, I began trying again, determined to rescue the radio at any price. And, once again, a miracle happened!

Without losing a second, I returned to lie down on the bed. I had just placed the little radio in my crotch beneath my underpants when Lieutenant Julio entered.

"We're going to move you to a more comfortable cell," he informed me. His argument made no sense, but that's what it had occurred to him to say. For my part, I tried to display the most absolute indifference. I only moved my lips to indicate that two of them should grab me under the armpits and drag me, aware that was the only way to keep the radio pressed between my thighs, which, without the extra security of the athletic underpants, ran the risk of falling to the floor. If, on the contrary, Julio decided to carry me by himself, the odds of the radio not being discovered when he put his arm under my thighs were reduced almost to zero. But the officials decided on another variant which I had not thought of, transporting me between two men while I remained still lying on the mat. A common prisoner called Dog, a confidant of the jailers, who worked cleaning up and distributing food to the punishment pavilion, helped take me to #27, vacated by Sergio Montes de Oca when he had moved to the clinic after ending his fast.

When I was alone again, I marveled at my incredible luck in once more keeping the radio from my jailers' clutches. Then, through the small opening, Lieutenant Julio threw in the athletic briefs and the sweater. "Here they are, take them," he grumbled.

They were still impregnated with stench and filth. He didn't even give me time to ask why he had returned them without being washed. "Well, after all, today, he has not behaved so badly," I whispered in satisfaction. And I began whistling a funny ditty my mother had taught me while I was nursing at her breast, ... still at age four!

Even though during March, due to our progressive deterioration, we were being given an additional dose of dextrose about 11:00 p.m., our thirst continued unabated. The rain also, in an irony of fate, tortured us as it was the cold season and, when the north wind blew, we spent the whole night shivering.

After multiple pleas, our jailers condescended to tie a piece of jute sack over the window to help protect us from wind and downpours. In any case, we stoically withstood rain and cold. They were part of the contingencies forced upon us, testing our tactic of resisting without expressing a complaint, that is, with dignity and fortitude. Several of our companions who had ended the strike commiserated with us later. One, Rolando Molina Contreras, who had shared with me other days of hunger and appalling miseries in the 1970's, confessed: "Whenever a downpour occurred in the middle of morning, I thought of you. It seemed impossible that those frail bodies could withstand the damp and cold... Sometimes the anxiety kept me awake at night."

And Rolando Molina confessed also that he had been tempted to petition the authorities to force-feed us. When I asked him half-joking how that might be done, he said: "How? By tying you up and inserting a hose into your mouth or your nose or ... Well, enough said. In any case, I wasn't about to let you die."

Molina said he foresaw our logical hostile reaction to such a proposal, but since he considered us his brothers, he was motivated by his conscience without caring about "criticism or alleged historical responsibility," according to his own words. Even though such an action would not have met with our approval, I want to honestly record my personal thanks for his concern here. And my thanks go as well to Ignacio Leal Denis, who also wanted us to put an end to our extended fast and managed to hold a long, fruitless discussion with the higher authorities. Jorge Valls Arango, Guillermo Rivas Porta, Alberto Fibla González, Rolando García Fuentes, Miguel Ángel Álvarez Cardentey, Ángel Cuadra Landrove... these, and many other colleagues whom I omit to prevent this from becoming an endless list, all tried, in one way or another, to rescue us from untimely death.

CHAPTER 45

# Julio Ruiz Pitaluga on the Verge of Death

March was almost over when one night, shortly after dark, Julio Ruiz Pitaluga called out to Gutiérrez Menoyo, saying that he could not survive many more days. In a few words, he explained that his lung condition had worsened since being sent to the punishment dungeons, barely allowing him to breathe and, for more than three weeks, he had lost all mobility and sensitivity in his legs.

"Pita, we are all in the same condition," I spoke up, sure I was not wrong. I knew it from my own experience because, for several days, I had been experiencing serious breathing difficulties, my legs had not responded, and I had blood in my urine.

Then I reminded my colleague about a very significant event that would certainly take place in the United States in less than a week. As many know, on the initiative of our compatriots in exile, every year in Florida, on April 5, a tribute is held, the "day of the Cuban political prisoner." Since we were so close to that date, it would be for us a spiritual triumph —and a moral one also, of course— if we still managed to hold out on our hunger strike when the City of Miami was evoking our memory, as was traditional on that date, with thousands

308

and thousands of Cuban exiles putting on an impressive display of solidarity and affection.

I imagine, by logical deduction, that April 5 had been chosen because that was the date –in 1869– when José Martí, the apostle of our independence, still practically only a child, had entered Cuba's political prison, initiating his very moving "Via Crucis" in the stone quarry prison yard of San Lázaro in Havana.

Then Eloy re-affirmed the criteria for continuing on with the strike. However, Pitaluga suggested that we think it over some more to see if we could find a solution, that is, if we could arrive at a consensus to end it.

Gutiérrez Menoyo gave him a vague response, but the tone of his voice indicated that the idea of simply abandoning the fast right now had him pretty upset. At that point, he harbored a subtle hope—as Eloy confided to me days later— that if we were about to fall into a coma, the High Command might then take a step back to at least partly meet our demands. But it was not possible to convey this approach aloud for the enemy to hear. So, beginning with that night, we mostly kept silent. I had already entered a stage of almost total physical collapse, obliging me to remain always lying face up, the only position that permitted me to breathe.

On the night of April 1, Julio Ruiz again called out to Eloy to see if he had reconsidered his proposal, and when he got the same negative response, he said, more or less, that persisting with the strike was useless because already it was safe to assume that the authorities were not going to yield on the question of our transfer. Pitaluga's idea, as he explained it, was to abandon the strike and recover so as to be able to embark on a future showdown.

Menoyo interrupted him, saying this was not a matter to be discussed out loud, so both stopped talking. Again, Eloy had sounded annoyed. Evelio then weighed in. He said he considered it better to postpone that conversation for a more appropriate time, as now our jailers could hear us. I was inclined to be more sympathetic, worried about Julio Ruiz's alarming physical state, as well about his psychological imbalance, evident already two months before. Only with a will of steel can a man withstand the mental and physical pressures in conditions so terrible and prolonged. From this viewpoint, analyzing the matter objectively, his sacrifice had much more merit than my own, since, with exception of the unfortunate incident on day 102 of the fast, when my brain had suffered an instant of eclipse, I was fortunate to have been able to keep my mind reasonably clear.

By mid-afternoon on April 2, after a violent crisis of bloody vomiting and acute abdominal pain, Ramón Méndez Pimentel was forced to abandon the fast, communicating this to Dr. Berenguer as soon as he had entered the punishment pavilion. Ever since the thirst strike had been imposed on us, all medical assistance had been suspended, but Berenguer continued to visit the strikers once or twice a week, among other things, I imagine, to directly observe the evolution of the biological experiment.

While Méndez Pimentel had asked Berenguer to convey immediately to Julio Ruiz Pitaluga that he had stopped the strike, the latter did not find out until the next morning, just before they had taken Pimentel to the prison clinic. The official on duty transmitted the message to Julio Ruiz, because, apparently, Dr. Berenguer dared not do so without the prior consent of the higher authorities.

A while later, Pitaluga called out to us that Pimentel had put an end to the strike. The news surprised me, but was perfectly understandable. From a human perspective, wasn't a man who had been able to endure, stoically, 146 days of fasting despite having his health broken by years of brutal imprisonment, worthy of admiration? And, as further proof, he had spent the last 44 days without drinking even a single drop of water. The three or four daily drinks of 5% dextrose, as is known, may have helped the body survive without drinking water, but they provided only a bare minimum of calories, and far from satisfying our thirst, only made it more acute.

Pitaluga once again expressed his concern, insisting on seeking a solution together to maintain the cohesion of the group. His voice was weak, very weak, despite the effort to make himself heard. No doubt his physical and mental strength had reached its limit. His urgent message spoke for itself. But when asked about his health, Pitaluga reiterated that it was very serious.

"Hey, Pita," I told him then, "Don't worry just because Pime has stopped the strike. That's not important. Moreover, I believe that in the condition in which you find yourself, the best thing you can do is to go with him to the infirmary."

Believing that already that there was not the remotest possibility of the dragons of the High Command agreeing to our demands, now what interested me was to rescue our courageous friend from the clutches of death, or, perhaps, even worse, the irreversible loss of his mental faculties. That was most urgent right now. Then those of us who had stayed behind would decide on the right time end the strike.

Despite his alarming condition, Pitaluga decided to make one more effort.

"No, Ernesto," was his response, "I appreciate your gesture, but I'm going to carry on."

It was not until the following morning, after another suggestion from me and after long reflection, that Pitaluga opted to end his strike. However, he did not want to go to the clinic, preferring to stay with us in the punishment pavilion. I told him that was not advisable because of the inevitable risks arising during initial recovery from a long fast. We knew about that danger from personal experience, having suffered serious digestive disorders ourselves previously. Comrades had even died in prior years because of adverse reactions to the first food consumed after a prolonged hunger strike. Furthermore, Pitaluga needed IV hydration right away from having been held in a cell infested with rats, cockroaches, mosquitos, and flies.

And there was still another reason, although of lesser importance. If Pitaluga remained in our pavilion, he would set a precedent that the same conditions would be imposed on the rest of us when we concluded the fast. He said he would think about it.

By the next day, Pitaluga had decided to give up his idea of staying in the punishment pavilion. When he told us that he would ask to be taken the prison infirmary, we were glad to hear it. That same night, I gave Evelio and Gutiérrez Menoyo my own opinion that it was useless to keep clinging to the fast. I was concerned, and told them with all sincerity, that the rest of our prison partners might see us conveying a false image of stubbornness or immaturity, as if this final stage of the strike had become a strange macho competition to see who could resist longest. The other reason, analyzing the situation realistically, was that our circumstances were completely adverse. On the one hand, our isolation was total and we were being held incommunicado without any family visits. That was the only way we had to send out information about our situation. We had already reaped a propaganda victory abroad by our efforts, undertaken to an extent to promote the freedom of our homeland.

Our enemy was so dishonest, so vile, and so petty, that in end, that it would not hesitate to eliminate us physically with no scruples. I am not saying that we were unwilling to face the worst possible consequences. Not just with words, but by risking our very lives, we had shown that we accepted without hesitation the challenges of destiny. On more than one occasion, the flavor of death had crossed my lips, and some of my companions had had similar experiences; some nights, for example, when we were certain that if we fell asleep, we would not wake up again. It happened to Evelio Hernández, and to me on at least two occasions. Each of us sat upright on our bunk with our back against the wall, engaging in deep mental concentration to revitalize the body through the psyche. The results obtained with this experiment could not be better. I confess that I am unable to describe what happened and how it felt with precise clarity. But we were able to stay awake and alert all night.

Although mentally Menoyo, Evelio, and I maintained our high spirits and kept our minds in excellent condition, at least so it seemed to us, our physical condition was so critical that we only had a week or two left, maybe three at most. I consulted with Eloy and Evelio to see if they were in agreement that all three of us should leave the strike at the five-month point, four days later. "All three!" I emphasized. "Otherwise, as long as one remains, I won't forsake the strike."

Evelio agreed. Eloy did not object, but also said, "Let's see when the time comes."

Pitaluga, who had not yet been transferred to the clinic (he was taken there the next morning), shouted out his congratulations to me for the way in which I had framed the issue. After his transfer, he later reported, "At noon, they brought me milk, mashed potatoes, and fried chicken. But what my body was craving was just cold tea."

The eve of the date we had set, April 9, soon arrived.

As agreed by the six of us who had continued on with the hunger strike after the mass fast had concluded on December 12, Eloy would be our spokesman with the authorities. Around 9:30 p.m. the evening before our scheduled end date, I called out to him to give us the final word.

"What's your rush, Ernesto?" he asked me.

We had been on strike for five months, but apparently, Eloy had lost track of time.

"No rush," I protested, "I just thought that the other day we had all agreed. But don't worry, forget it, let's keep on going. You decide, okay?"

In all honesty, one of my major concerns was about Eloy himself, because the last time we had talked, he'd told us told that for several days, he had been experiencing bleeding from an ear. But I vowed to say nothing more about the fast. "If Eloy wants self-immolation, then we all three will die, that's all," I told myself. He would tell us to end the strike whenever he decided.

But Eloy had misinterpreted my statement, shouting out from his cell: "All right then, let's put a stop to this, but I'm doing so under protest!"

"Then under protest, agreed," I replied sounding lighthearted, seeing that he had finally decided.

Evelio joked also, in the same vein.

"Good, how are we going to let the authorities know?" I asked Eloy.

"I'll take care of that," he said, already sounding a little more resigned.

Actually, for none of the three of us was it easy to take this step. But the time had come to make a final decision.

That same evening, when Lieutenant Tómas entered his cell to give him his last dose of dextrose, Eloy asked him to convey to the warden that we had called an end to the strike. But it not was until the next day that we were moved to the prison infirmary.

The first one to be taken out at around the 11:30 am was to Gutiérrez Menoyo. Some 40 minutes later, the orderlies came for me, guarded by Lieutenant Félix Zamora. When I met Eloy in the lobby, lying on a stretcher, he immediately told me in an aggrieved tone: "They did not release Montes de Oca."

That was quite regrettable. Sergio Montes de Oca had completed his 20-year sentence the day before and we were hopeful that he had been freed.

Cusa had just given Menoyo a tremendous bath. Seeing him looking so lustrous, the first thing that came to my mind was the radio and the "balita" with the rolled-up documents and money inside which, despite all my troubles in the punishment dungeon, I still carried on my person. If Cusa undressed me without any military present, there would be no problem. But if Lieutenant Zamora distrustfully stripped me of pants and underpants at the same time, at least the little radio would be lost, so I nervously pondered how to pass it on to Eloy. Then, luckily, Marcos came to greet me, pretending to be looking up something in the clinical records. And while the official was looking the other way, I put the radio into Marcos' hands, wrapped up in the sweater, and asked him to give it to Montes de Oca. Marcos, when he felt the little radio, whispered to me, amazed: "And you kept it with you all that time in the punishment pavilion? You're crazy–crazy as hell."

"Go on, hurry up," I urged. "Let's not lose it now at this late date."

Marcos left in haste for the cubicle where Sergio Montes de Oca had been admitted alongside Luis Zúñiga Rey, who days before had entered with a violent nephritic colic, and also Jesús Sánchez Arango.

Five minutes later, I was in the bathroom myself on the same metal stretcher as before, where Cusa soaped me all over and rinsed me off with a hose. As always, his attentions could not have been better.

With my crust of filth removed and wearing brand new pajamas, I was taken to another room where Dr. Berenguer took an electrocardiogram. He then applied the stethoscope to my chest and back.

"You're healthier than I am," he remarked with irony. He then gave me a plate of fried chicken and plenty of mashed potatoes, and a glass of cold milk.

"Go ahead," he ordered. "Eat that! I imagine you have a good appetite."

"How? Mashed potatoes and fried chicken all at once, after five months without eating any food?" I protested alarmed. "Can you imagine the condition of this stomach?"

"Don't worry, I know what I'm doing," the doctor argued. "That's what modern medicine recommends."

That seemed crazy. Recklessness! Who knew if it might be a trap to physically eliminate us? But hunger is a bad advisor and so I was persuaded to eat, but only half of what was served, and to drink the glass of milk.

Eloy, who only drank half of the glass of milk, ate nothing. When I told him what I had eaten, he advised, "No, not you, with all your experience, knowing well that it can cost you your life."

I didn't even try to apologize, because I was too angry with myself for letting my fierce hunger corrode my judgment. How many times had I advised others not to gorge after a strike? So stupid!

Evelio Hernández had been placed in the front cubicle, along with Méndez Pimentel and Pitaluga. Even after several days in bed, the latter remained in extremely delicate health, and was also suffering from very worrisome mental distress. Despite his extreme condition, he had not been given any serum or any treatment at all. Nor had Pimentel, Eloy, Evelio, or me, as Dr. Berenguer was giving orders to Dr. Stanley, who had reappeared among us. Berenguer had decided that none of the strikers after five months of fasting was dehydrated, and consequently needed no medical care except for bed rest.

That same afternoon after our arrival at the infirmary, shortly before dusk, we were served cabbage soup, mashed potatoes, two fried eggs, and bread. Since our earlier lunch had not caused me any digestive problems, I ate again. I was doing well until the following afternoon, when I was suddenly overcome with fatigue and felt I was dying. It was after 4:00 p.m., when no medical staff was on duty at Boniato. The duty guard let Dr. Velasco Santa Cruz (a fellow *plantado*), assigned to the same cubicle as Montes de Oca, examine me.

Velasco arrived hurriedly. I had begun vomiting, but was already feeling better. The fatigue was also ebbing. Luckily, Velasco explained, it was nothing more than a simple rejection of food due to the condition of our bodies, without major consequences. Although he was characteristically discreet in his comments, Velasco disagreed with giving us so much food at the initial stage of recovery after such a long strike.

"I imagine that each doctor has a personal method of applying knowledge," he said respectfully, "but I would say that fried eggs are not indicated after such a violent fast."

He advised us to eat moderately, slowly, step by step. Although my fatigue had abated, I was very ill and in pain all night. The next morning, as soon as I saw Dr. Stanley, I demanded an IV. Stanley asked me to consume only liquids for the time being. "Ideally, orange juice," he said, "but yesterday I looked in the warehouse and there is not even one orange."

In response to the rebuke of what Dr. Berenguer had recommended after the fast, Stanley commented: "Berenguer may be a very good doctor, but he has no experience regarding hunger strikes and diet."

Stanley thoroughly examined Pitaluga, who kept on declining, making both Eloy and me concerned that he might be close to death. From my bed, I witnessed the distressing spectacle of his daily, minute by minute, apparent dying without remedy. Dr. Stanley recognized the extreme gravity of Pitaluga's condition and both Eloy and I urged immediate intervention if they did not want responsibility for his death on their shoulders. And, indeed, Stanley recognized the need to act promptly, and immediately ordered an infusion of blood plasma.

We had been in the clinic for three days when Eloy woke up with immensely swollen legs and feet, looking like elephants' feet. Some hours later, when his edema had extended to the testicles, Dr. Stanley decided to put him on an IV, the same with Pimentel and Evelio, who were suffering from an acute crisis of vomiting and diarrhea. After receiving two or three liters of dextrose in our veins, our bodies had begun to stabilize, allowing us to assimilate food without major setbacks. The progress of Julio Ruiz Pitaluga was slower, but a week later, already out of danger, he had started recovering both mentally and physically.

However, some of our health problems persisted for months, as we each weighed only about 90 pounds after our fast.

Our stay in the hospital was relatively brief and marked by frequent conflicts with the authorities. Dr. Nelson Stanley had been giving us relatively compassionate care, but he was soon replaced by Dr. Bernardo Veloz, who immediately suspended tests and treatment, considering them unnecessary. His attitude showed either marked hostility or simple indifference. Instead of examining us, he would often ask whether it had rained the night before or if the cows grazing outside the prison perimeter looked healthy to us. Then he would turn on his heel and depart.

# CHAPTER 46

# Complications at the Prison Clinic

As the days progressed, due to the repressive or dismissive attitude of Dr. Bernardo Veloz, we were forced to protest again by refusing food.

We had gone back on the fast for three days when Sergeant Noaldo Pérez reported that we were being released from the clinic. Ten minutes later, we were put on stretchers and taken to Pavilion 4B, condemning us to confinement again in walled cells, deprived of all medical assistance despite our deplorable physical condition, but at least not in solitary confinement. Three days before, the same measure had been taken with Sergio Montes de Oca. Although we would have been happy to be together with any of our comrades, Evelio Hernández and I had the luck of sharing cell #22 with Miguel Ángel Álvarez, one of our best friends. Eloy Gutiérrez Menoyo also had the good fortune to be sharing #12 with Sergio Montes de Oca, while Ramón Méndez Pimentel shared #29 with Alejandro Novo.

We were all still suffering from serious digestive disorders and extreme weakness in our legs, making it hard for us to squat over the hole in a corner of the cell which served as both toilet and shower drain (had water been available to us). Therefore, the head of Internal Order authorized our access to the pavilion hall during one or two hours a day. Negro Cardentey would carry us in his arms out to four rather damaged old toilets used by prisoners in past years. He also helped bathe us, sitting us on a wooden stool.

Julio Ruiz Pitaluga, unlike the rest of us, was permitted to stay at the clinic, as his health continued to be seriously impaired. Years before, Pitaluga had been submitted to urgent risky surgery as a result of a perforated ulcer, which had left him on the verge of death. Sometime later, due to another ulcer, he underwent a second operation which removed much of his stomach. Julio Ruiz, whenever he embarked on a long fast, also suffered from a rectal prolapse and acute bloody diarrhea. Added to that was his lung condition and mental imbalance, which required adequate treatment, but not at the hands of the indolent and rude Dr. Veloz. Yet his pitiful condition notwithstanding, only two days after us, Julio Ruiz Pitaluga was also sent back to Pavilion 4B.

Despite the limitations imposed by the locked walled cells, which hampered to a large extent our physical recovery, still, simply by sheer dint of will, we exercised every day and after two weeks had already managed, with some support, to take a few steps.

But then a new, unexpected complication arose. On June 1, the head of Internal Order told Novo and Argüelles that everyone in 4B would be transferred immediately to building 4D. Because part of that pavilion had already been occupied since March 11 by a rebellious group from the eastern provinces, plus about 10 more from Havana, the unwelcome transfer meant all *plantado* prisoners would have to be three to a cell no larger than 18 square feet. This overcrowding caused irritation and imposed even more suffocating conditions.

We had wanted to maintain the same cell mates in 4D as we had in 4B. But when their efforts failed, Menoyo and Montes de Oca announced that they preferred to return to their previous punishment cells, something I decided not to do, as I didn't think protesting the transfer was worth the effort. In the end, five of the six of us, with myself as the exception, decided to go back to the punishment cells. But then Montes de Oca appealed to me to join them so as not to break up our group cohesion. To avoid problems, I swallowed my annoyance and ended up in the punishment pavilion again in a cell with Evelio Hernández, fortunately not in solitary there this time.

The living conditions we had had in 4D were really the same as those in the punishment cells, since both were enclosed by "tolas" or steel plates. But there was a difference. Certainly, common prisoners were usually friendly toward political prisoners being held in both places. Yet, the excessive punishments imposed, such as a 20-year sentence for stealing a portable radio, had aroused in some of the common prisoners an understandable anger. And as might be expected, those assigned to the punishment pavilion might actually have been more aggressive or mentally disturbed, such as "The Moor," who had murdered an unfortunate teen after raping him. "Tuti" was also an inveterate rapist of minors who would stab his victims in surprise attacks, and there were other common inmates with insatiable criminal instincts. But for us, that was not the worst. What in truth made life more difficult for us there, or at least for me, was the constant hullabaloo among common prisoners, their exchanges of gross offenses and loud shouts all day and night. I was also tormented by the daily abuses committed by the jailers against weaker inmates. Still today, sometime after that actual bitter experience, I remain especially distressed by the memory of Pedritín, a skinny, sickly young teen whom Sergeant Noaldo Pérez kicked to the floor outside my cell, leaving him unconscious and lying in a pool of blood. That was in mid-June in 1981.

That unhappy soul had spent all morning crying because of a terrible molar pain that had started a week before. The following early morning, I heard him calling out to the officer in charge of the punishment section in a pleading tone, asking for the dentist, as he had awakened with a swollen face and was in unbearable pain.

"We'll see about that later," the sergeant replied callously, departing without further ado.

During the next four hours, Pedritín desperately called in vain for help from the soldiers who entered the pavilion. He rejected lunch, sobbing, "I need to get this tooth pulled." A common prisoner named "Dog," distributing sausages, mocked him and walked away. By mid-afternoon, now back in his cell, the boy began hitting and kicking the steel plank, asking for a dentist or at least some aspirin.

At this point, my cellmate Evelio took three steps forward, leaning up against the wall, and peered out the tiny opening in the steel plank. Using a piece of mirror, he looked over into the pavilion lobby. Then he turned back and lay down on his concrete bed.

"I think that Pedritín is going to get torched," he said. And when I said nothing: "He won't be left with an intact bone in his body."

And Evelio's words proved prophetic.

The unfortunate Pedritín had just emitted a 10-minute barrage of angry protests when suddenly a platoon of the Boniato gestapo burst into the punishment pavilion hall, wielding thick marabou sticks. The arrogant boss of Internal Order led a military assault. After pulling the boy out of his cell, the group began beating his fragile body. The first blow landed on his ribs. The other guards imitated the "brave" sergeant, striking with unbridled fury on the boy's head, back, and arms, then again on his back and on his head. From their cell openings, Alfredo Mustelier, Adolfo Vinent, Samuel Tejera Milián, Wilfredo Martínez Roque, and several common prisoners —mainly Cánova and Ricardo (both later executed by firing squad)— began shouting angry cries of "Lackeys! Murderers!" and any other verbal atrocity that an enraged mob of helpless prisoners could hurl at their tormentors. The six of us, of course, also raised our indignant voices to denounce that group of shameless torturers.

Already having knocked Pedritín down on the floor, the demonic Sergeant Noaldo repeatedly kicked him before carting off his bloody body to the infirmary, though I wasn't sure he would actually arrive there alive. So, it was a surprise when a half hour later, the boy returned, walking on his own two feet with his head wrapped up in gauze and tape. "They took out my tooth... they extracted my tooth!" he announcing loudly and proudly, not mentioning the countless stitches on his scalp or his many welts and bruises. "My tooth has been pulled!" he repeated over and over with childish glee. Despite the brutal beating, he seemed happy to finally have gotten rid of that accursed molar.

A few days after the Pedritín incident, Polito, who had been moved to Havana a month earlier to appear before the Supreme Court. The court was to decide the fate of that violent young man, Polito, who, at age 8, had been ripped from his mother's arms, never to return to the bosom of his humble home. After 13 years in prison, Polito ended up condemned to death for rape and murder of another prisoner. Thirteen years of infinite agony during which the child, Polito, whose full name was José Antonio Duruti Faure, had lost his homemade toys and his family's warmth, then himself was a victim of rape in prison. Later in prison, he had become addicted to marijuana. Thirteen years, in short, of dehumanization, depersonalization, and gradual physical disintegration, so that at age 21, he was toothless and malnourished, prematurely old. Then Boniato prison authorities proceeded to put an end to his young life by sending eight bullets into his chest in the name of revolutionary justice.

Our stay in Pavilion 4C was relatively short: four weeks to be exact. On June 29, Gutiérrez Menoyo decided, after an exchange of notes with each of us, to withdraw us from the punishment pavilion, and that same afternoon the six of us were moved back to building 4D. Again, I felt forced to act against my will. I considered it an inappropriate move at that time. The week before, on June 23, to be more precise, Sergeant Noaldo Pérez had informed us that all special diets had been suspended, including for ulcers and other chronic conditions. It does not require a medical degree, especially if you have had the privilege of spending 15 or 20 years in that great university known as a Cuban prison, to know that fresh cow's milk, besides being an excellent food, neutralizes stomach acid, and that someone prone to ulcers must not ingest excess fat or spices at the risk of a perforated ulcer, as had happened to Julio Ruiz Pitaluga on two occasions.

When Gutiérrez Menoyo asked if the order to end our special diets had come from the doctor, Noaldo said that those in charge were the military and the High Command, who did not have to answer to anyone about such decisions. So Evelio, Pimentel, Montes de Oca, Pitaluga, Eloy, and I agreed to accept no food until this arbitrary order was lifted with exception of breakfast and any fruit. After a week in this situation, the unwelcome idea of moving back to 4D had arisen. When Eloy, as our leader, had asked my opinion, my answer was clear and specific.

"We should have thought this out before asking to be brought back here," I wrote in my note to him, and I expressed my opinion that we should either undertake a new hunger strike or stay now in 4C, accepting only breakfast and fruit, until the conflict was resolved. Eloy let me know that he agreed, but not everyone was on board because of their own physical or psychological condition. "This has happened," he said finally, "because of doing things halfway."

So then, we moved back again to building 4D. I walked there on my own two feet supported on Novo's shoulder, happy to be sharing cell #13 with two exceptional friends, Roberto Azcuy Cruz (El Niño) and Luis M. Zúñiga Rey, who were glad to be with me as well. Eloy went to cell #10 with Ignacio Leal Denis, while Pimentel was installed in #19 with Alejandro Novo and Julio Flores Franqui, and Pitaluga was sent to #11 with Wilfredo Martínez and Samuel Tejera Milián. Montes de Oca went to #34 with Junco Benavides. Then, in addition to the suspension of special diets, our food ration was greatly reduced, and only disgusting, inedible food was offered. So, the food was often rejected, leaving us consuming only watery powdered milk and bread. There were weeks during which we ate just three or four meals in total. And it was no surprise to encounter a mouse, lizard, or cockroach inside our food. I could get along just with breakfast and urged my cellmates to make their own decision, although they insisted on *breakfast only* in line with my own choice. The prison directorate knew perfectly well, without any need to be told, that in each cell where one of us was placed, we were going to find the same human solidarity that I found with Zúñiga and Azcuy.

Our "rejection" of most meals was a symbolic act, to which the authorities reacted with apparent, if not actual, indifference. As a result, we spent more than two and half years, day after day, returning lunch and dinner uneaten. There was a point at which the disagreement was about to be resolved. That was near the end of 1981. The chief of Internal Order had said that our diets would be determined on a case-by-case basis by Dr. Stanley, each case separately, according to our health.

Days later, the administration decreed that access to the prison infirmary required wearing the same uniform as common prisoners. Instead, most of us had fashioned a type of Bermuda shorts, using sheet fabric to cover our nakedness, and we had been authorized to attend medical consultations wearing this and a white sweater. We agreed to remove the sweater while there, but not the "shorts," and that all together, we could have up to 10 appointments per week.

The day of the first consultation under this agreement, at Fibla's suggestion, we agreed to give priority to the neediest cases, at that time, the five of us who were refusing most food, as well as Ernesto Palomeque and Reinaldo López Lima. But it happened that when we entered the search room beforehand, Lieutenant Bandera, then in charge of pavilion 4D, demanded a strip search. After our refusal and a heated discussion, we were returned to 4D, losing that medical appointment. The measure was presumably not a whim of the lieutenant, but a premeditated provocation by the warden.

"I simply carry out orders," the officer said defensively when confronted by Novo and Argüelles for his breach of our prior agreement on searches.

It would be easy to deduce that the breach was deliberately designed to hinder the provision of medical assistance to us, since, according to Dr. Berenguer, we had caused the government "irreparable damage" with our prolonged hunger strike. Perhaps coming from anyone else, those words would not have had great importance. But when spoken by Lieutenant Colonel Juan Berenguer Pérez, chief of medical services for the province, rather than being a mere lamentation or reproach, his words implied a serious threat to us. The threat began transforming into direct retaliation as soon as we had ended our fast, or even before so, starting with the visit to the Boniato clinic during the middle of the strike on January 26 by the Interior Ministry delegate to Santiago province, Colonel Clever Martí Lambert.

The irritation of Boniato authorities could also have been aroused by a letter delivered by me days earlier to Dr. Stanley, during an inspection visit to building 4D, which went as follows:

Dr. Nelson Stanley, Medical Director, Boniato Prison

Dr. Stanley:

I hereby ask you to revoke the ulcer diagnosis that

was made several months ago by the authorities of this prison. I consider that after 151 days without eating food, my stomach might be found to be in perfect condition, and as you are prevented from checking it through a medical examination, given that the color of a uniform in my unhappy homeland is given greater importance than the health of a human being, I don't wish to erroneously be given an evaluation as ulcerative and provided medical assistance that I do not actually need.

Respectfully,

Ernesto Díaz Rodríguez, Boniato Prison, September 5, 1981

A week after our failed attempt to consult Dr. Stanley, ten other companions of pavilion 4D were at the clinic. On that occasion, the search was carried out without any difficulty, in line with our prior agreement, without the need to strip. This continued every week for months. But our five names were consistently omitted from the lists of patients to be examined.

Evelio Hernández had somewhat better luck. When he was at State Security being interrogated, he suddenly came down with appendicitis. Taken by ambulance to Santiago's military hospital, he had emergency surgery. After three days of post-operative recovery, he was moved to Boniato's infirmary for a little more than a week before returning to join us again in Pavilion 4D. From January 12, 1981, through the end of year, with few exceptions, our doors were not opened except when the jailers came into the cell to search our belongings. Food was passed to us through a small opening, normally covered by a metal plank, without opening the door.

The extremism and evil of Boniato authorities was manifested particularly in regard to papayas, abundant in the eastern provinces, which could be cut up and passed to us in pieces, or else the main door could be opened and a whole fruit passed inside. Instead, the military, without any scruples, took them (and whatever else they could) like true birds of prey, taking them home to their own families, who were surely also victims of scarcity and the dreadful miseries to which the new masters of Cuba had subjected the whole population.

To occupy my time in Pavilion 4D, I began re-reading and re-organizing the group of poems I had written during our long fast. I confess that what most impressed me, perhaps the only thing, was the introduction I had written for the book *The Bell of the Dawn,* my collection of poems dedicated to children. I think that is one of the few times in my rugged life as a "poet" that I've felt satisfied at having captured an idea, an emotion, a feeling, because often, attempts to render the whims of imagination on paper end up being distorted.

After selecting poems for the book *Upwind* and those destined for *The Bell of the Dawn,* I sent the latter to my dear friend, the poet Ángel Cuadra, accompanied by a letter inviting him to write a foreword so that one day, we might have the great satisfaction of emerging out into the world together as brothers in a work written under such difficult circumstances, expressing to all our blood bond.

Ángel Cuadra enthusiastically accepted the challenge of my request even though it might jeopardize his own release, since the end of his 15-year sentence was approaching. «My poetry,» he said, «is not something done on my knees.»

Indeed, those of us sharing a fraternal coexistence with Ángel behind bars for so many years have come to know his inner spirit and understand his poetry as a sacred thing, symbolized for him by that magnificent phrase, so lovely and so true that I have seen fit to highlight as an instructive example.

Before his beautiful gesture of human solidarity, I cannot do less than express my great admiration for my faithful friend and my gratitude for his efforts in writing that wonderful prologue in a dark corner of his cell to present to readers of *The Bell of the Dawn.*

Many and wise were Ángel's suggestions for my poems, giving them greater harmony and a more solid coherence within their subtle cohesion. And I say "subtle" because, fundamentally, the 36 verses that make up that book, each clad in different clothing, radiate the same light, and go hand in hand toward a same destination: children and adults together each displaying a clear and simple soul despite the bitterness of life.

Another special notation destined for that book was the following dedication: "To César Páez, to his memory and to all the martyrs who have been so terribly devoured by the jaws of the ants of barbarism." Those who have had the opportunity to read the allegorical introduction I wrote for *The Bell of the Dawn* will be able to easily unravel the symbolism of the barbarian ants' jaws.

And who was César Páez? Surely more than one reader has asked that when encountering this martyr's name in the dedication in that book of poems. Sometime, I will have to write César Paez's beautiful story; about his beautiful revolutionary trajectory. I have already mentioned in this book that in the insurrectional struggle against the dictatorship of Fulgencio Batista, for his intelligence and bravery, César received deserved recognition by being awarded the rebel army's highest military honor, a commander's star. He was a shrewd observer, so, after the overthrow of Batista, it did not take him long to detect penetration by Communists, who began to subtly crawl toward the pinnacle of power, and then on January 1, 1959, even had started to monopolize positions in the "Revolutionary government" with the complicity of Ernesto "Che" Guevara and under the sponsorship of Fidel Castro himself.

In vain did César, along with many other prominent figures, among them President Manuel Urrutia and several commanders of the Sierra Maestra and Escambray, try to close off their path, aware of the danger represented by that plague of rabid rats who threatened to devour the nation. For the immense majority of the Cuban people, intoxicated by the victory, Fidel Castro symbolized the hero of heroes —and the homeland, love, and prosperity. Those unfortunate souls remained blind, never suspecting that he was a man without scruples —ambitious, insane, a traitor. And facing the impossibility of rescuing by them by peaceful means from "the Revolution" that had betrayed them, Commander César Páez was one of thousands of honorable, idealistic men seeking freedom and independence for their nation, not the vile submission to a power foreign. In the summer of 1960, he took up a rifle once more against the new dictatorship, again in the legendary mountains of Escambray, where he wrote new pages of glory in an unequal fight against a well-armed and seasoned enemy outnumbering his guerrilla contingent one hundred to one, or even more.

After months of heroic resistance, César fell into the hands of Castro's forces. Sentenced to 30 years, after supporting with dignity and gallantry a prolonged process of torture, César suffered with admirable stoicism additional physical and moral attacks, first in the fields of forced labor on the Isle of Pines, and later in multiple prisons all over Cuba, where he was kept incommunicado from the rest of political prisoners during the last years of his life. His death, which occurred at approximately 10:00 p.m. on November 9, 1977, left us with an immense vacuum because César Páez was so well loved due to his extraordinary human sensitivity, his honesty, his nobility of soul, and his bravery under duress. With his physical disappearance, Cuba lost an exceptional son, and Alpha 66 lost one of our most capable and self-sacrificing leaders. Those of us who had the privilege of sharing with César Páez Sánchez the responsibility of trying to organize a coup against the Communist dictatorship of Cuba from the very bowels of the tyrant's dungeons, in coordination with dissident forces seeking to rescue the principles of freedom and justice for the democratic revolution for which we all had fought, have the absolute belief that he was vilely murdered, a conviction shared in one form or another, inside and outside the country, based on knowledge of the dark conditions that must have produced his death.

# CHAPTER 47

# Clandestine Electricity

We had gone several months without any light in those terrible, dark enclosed cells when Ernesto Palomeque thought of obtaining electricity clandestinely, from an outlet in the hallway, via the bronze strips embedded in the granite floor. He shared his idea with the somewhat similarity-named Enrique Palomino, who in those days helped Novo and Argüelles Garrido in the hall. Enrique and the very same Argüelles performed tests and explored how to camouflage the connection to the current. But with only a single line, it was not possible to plug in both cables, positive and negative, without creating a short circuit. This problem was resolved by using the metal tank supplying water to all the cells as a neutral conduit, providing us with a magnificent "ground." All we needed was a light bulb and a piece of cable to plug into the battery of the water tank and into the connection on the floor. Everyone got ahold of whatever they could, and, in a few days, almost everyone had what they needed. My efforts were facilitated by El Pinto, all in less than 24 hours. Our bulb was small, only 25 watts, easy to hide during searches. And El Pinto also provided 6 or 8 meters of phone cable, very fine but sufficient to support the bulb. It was also easy to roll up the cable to hide from the jailers. The socket was constructed from the base of a toothpaste tube. To avoid the risk of losing it all, in the evening we would light the bulb down in a corner near the floor, making sure that the light would not be perceived from outside the cell. For greater security, we improvised a cardboard lamp shade. Thanks to the initiative of Ernesto Palomeque, and to all who collaborated to provide that very useful hidden lighting, nights became less painful and sterile.

August was coming to a close when the Chief of Internal Order appeared, accompanied by several jailers from Pavilion 4B. Without giving us any explanation, we were all immediately ordered to go out to the patio. The first thing that came to mind was that they would be doing a thorough search. We had not been ordered to the patio since we had been confined to the walled cells. Since a few refused to go out, Lieutenant Bandera met with them in the lobby and told them that the warden wanted us all to be shaven and shorn out in the patio that same afternoon. When the order came down, with exception of that small group —some 7 or 8 guys in all— the rest of us were already stretching our legs out on the grass between buildings 3 and 4. The sun blinded us and we walked stiffly because of the many months spent cloistered in those enclosed dungeons where the space was so cramped that we spent virtually all the time lying on the rough canvas mats on our bunks.

I immediately took stock of the situation. Having several of us in the courtyard shaved with the same blade, the same system used with common prisoners, was quite humiliating and therefore unacceptable, and possibly dangerous or even fatal. We recalled the summer of 1980, when Boniato authorities were trying to impose the same regimen on us.

"There is no reason to make any distinction between you counter-revolutionaries and common prisoners. For us, you all are worth the same and nothing different," I had heard Lieutenant Milhet say.

Roberto Azcuy and I had once engaged in a strong argument with Milhet, refusing to be shaved for a file photo, though we each had by then a three-month beard.

As a matter of basic hygiene and habit, most political prisoners shaved whenever circumstances permitted. Many spontaneously tried to do it daily, holding onto a mirror fragment which might be removed in a search and using the single blade provided us each month. But in recent times, on a whim, the High Command came up with something called "parallel prison," in practice, considering prisoners of conscience the same as those punished for common crimes. We refused to abide by this arbitrary designation and, in retaliation we were no longer being supplied with blades, though some continued shaving with the old blades.

Out in the courtyard, Luis Zúñiga told me that he refused to be shaved or have his hair cut out there. I told him that I had arrived at the same decision, so we went to sit down on the grass to see how events would unfold. Anticipating that we might be involved in a conflict with the jailers, through sign language, I asked Montes de Oca in a cell above to lower a bag tied to a string to pull up the radio that was hidden on my person. The radio still had battery power, thanks to batteries from a sympathetic soldier who admired our determination.

Once the little radio was safe, I breathed easier. Silvino Rodríguez sat down next to Zúñiga and me. It was not necessary for us to inquire about his decision. Silvino was one of the most rebellious political prisoners, with an explosive temper and absolute intransigence.

Two hours later, besides Zúñiga, Silvino, and I, still in the courtyard were Carlos Pons Watler, Wilfredo Martínez, Servando Infante, and Miguel Ángel Álvarez.

Noaldo tried to persuade us all to comply with the orders of the prison's administration. But he soon realized that it was a lost cause, so he got angry and threatened us, trying to get us to obey. That was just about the worst thing that he possibly could do, like throwing fuel on the fire. After he had issued the challenge and we had accepted the confrontation, he had only two alternatives: look ridiculous by sending us back to our cells to avoid a conflict or call for backup and impose his will by force.

"While I am Chief of Internal Order around here, we are going to do what we consider suitable, and so we are going to barber and shave you all right now, for better or for worse," the angry sergeant declared, walking briskly toward the prison office.

We waited for half an hour for Noaldo to reappear. When he came back he was accompanied by three other officers. He sat down in a chair by the courtyard door and almost immediately called Alejandro

Novo over. Novo was the chief of our prisoner's section, so he might have been trying to work out a solution and avoid a confrontation. One by one, Noaldo called each of us over to talk. By his tone of voice and extreme courtesy, in contrast to his previous rabid threats, it was easy to deduce that he had received a counter-command from his superiors. Noaldo acted genuinely interested in our explanations for our attitude. After hearing us out, he said he was willing to let us have a razor to shave ourselves in our cells or "wherever you like." We had no objection —that was exactly what we had been asking for.

Although we were suspicious as usual, it seemed that the celebration in Havana of the 68th Summit of the World Inter-Parliamentary Union might offer us some substantial improvements. In the showy Conventions Palace (especially built for the event with the sweat of the Cuban people at a cost of several million pesos), the echo was not drowned out of the voices of visitors bravely challenging Castro for his immoral policies in the service of Russia and for the repressive nature of the Revolution. Meanwhile, in Boniato prison, political prisoners began to perceive favorable signs. A concession that more than surprised us was being allowed —for a limited time only —to buy certain items from the military dispensary, such as toothpaste, yogurt, fruit, candy, and cookies, all, of course, at exorbitant prices, using money that our families had deposited for us there, as we were not allowed to possess any money ourselves. But after so many months of famine, this seemed like a real privilege, a gift from heaven.

The first time this was allowed was on September 18, 1981, three days after the start of the 68th Summit. But three weeks later, our options had shrunk to just toothpaste, candy, and a few other items. Almost three years later, we were still waiting for the next purchase opportunity. Finally, thanks to the visit of the Rev. Jesse Jackson in 1984 to meet with "humanist" Fidel to coordinate opposition to the "dictatorship" of President Ronald Reagan in the U.S., every *plantado* political prisoner was allowed to buy two deodorant sticks.

# A Child Martyr

It is truly poignant to see a young child locked up for political reasons. Humanity should shrink back in horror at witnessing such an appalling crime. But the world today lives facing inward, with eyes distracted by too many concerns and too much entertainment to stop to think about what this really means.

So, when Santos Orlando Rodríguez Mirabal was imprisoned in Communist Cuba at the tender age of 12, many shrugged with majestic indifference. Only his family and neighborhood classmates shed a handful of tears and sought out the help of the village parish priest, but the latter explained that it was God's will and nothing could be done against his will. On that occasion, the disconcerted priest was not referring to the creator of woodland animals and wild flowers, of the seas and sea spray —the benevolent God of the universe, an immense and merciful deity —but rather to another sort of god with a poisonous beard and diabolical eyes... a god who imprisons children and murders ideas, a god of mud and salt who feeds on the blood of his people.

Not even the "judges" who sentenced the child Mirabal probably imagined that the young one with shaved head and restless eyes would become old in the Communist dungeons. An old child, you might say, because despite the shadows on his face, the many wrinkles on his soul, during the almost two decades when his childhood was held hostage, Santos Orlando continued floating inside a soap bubble as if in a fairy tale. Because "Santico," as he was called affectionately by his companions in misfortune, continued dreaming dreams and waiting for the world someday to symbolically open up its arms to rescue him from that hell. But he doesn't know that the world has too many concerns and too many distractions —as I've said— to stop to think that this man-child needs its support, needs its voice.

In July 1979, Santos Orlando Mirabal Rodríguez, along with a hundred other political prisoners, was transferred to the sadly infamous Boniato prison. It was then that he realized that he had been officially excluded from the pardons program, because that had been decided by the heralds of the hammer and sickle. There he found himself subjected to all type of reprisals and torture, even though he was temporarily paralyzed on at least two occasions due to repeated hunger strikes and malnutrition. His health was deplorable. As with his colleagues, each day moved him closer to an inevitable and premature death. From deep inside the bowels of his walled cell, he dreamt of his tormented mother, already just a blurred profile in his memory, because for 15 years, his captors had not allowed him to see her; he dreamt of the wife and child he would have liked to have; he dreamt like every man of goodwill, about the freedom of his homeland.

According to his initial sentence, Santos Orlando should have been released at the age of twenty-one. But abrogating its own laws, the all-powerful Interior Ministry ordered him kept in prison.

Seven years after the expiration of his sentence, Santos Orlando Mirabal sent a letter to "President" Osvaldo Dorticós Torrado, reporting that he still remained in the prison and that his stay there was illegal.

The authorities legalized the situation by imposing an additional penalty of 10 years on August 5, 1981. There was no trial, no defense lawyer, or even right to an appeal. His crime? "future dangerousness." So, already a hero, the child-martyr Santos Orlando Mirabal Rodríguez then remained in prison "legally."

Once more, Cuba's Communist government had achieved "justice!"

As additional information emerged, to the astonishment of the world, it was learned that Santico, at only the tender age of 12, had been subjected to an alienating process of interrogations that lasted two years, from April 24, 1966, the date of his arrest, until April 15, 1968. By way of comparison, for the assault on the Moncada barracks that cost many lives on both sides, leader Fidel Castro was kept in prison by Batista for 21 months and 15 days.

After almost 20 years, Santos, then in his 30's, was finally released and moved to the United States in 2003.

# CHAPTER 49

# Indefinite Detention

Of all the reprisals that *plantado* political prisoners had been suffering over the prior two years, mainly in Boniato and Combinado del Este prisons, the most cruel and outrageous, almost beyond belief, was a measure applied to those unfortunates at the end of their already excessive sentences; that is, instead of being released, they were forced to remain *indefinitely* in the dungeons of the regime with no end in sight. This arbitrary measure of vile hatred, contempt for human dignity, and abject cowardice enforced by a government ruling at gunpoint, for more than a quarter of a century, led a group of esteemed companions to decide upon a hunger strike as their only weapon to achieve their rightful release, expressing their willingness to immolate themselves if necessary in the interests of such a sacred right. The same prisoners whose sentences had been completed decided that only those who had fulfilled their full sanctions should participate initially, an idea that carried moral legitimacy coming directly from them. Because of a lack of communication during the prior one or two years, we had lost all contact with Combinado prison, so the hunger strike project materialized at Boniato among those agreeing to accept the sacrifice.

By the end of September 1982, those who had completed their convictions were the following, showing name, original sentence, and official (now expired) release date.

| | | |
|---|---|---|
| Santos Orlando Mirabal Rodríguez | to be released at age 21 | 01-24-1977 |
| José Oscar Rodríguez Terrero | 20 years | 02-15-1981 |
| Héctor Cabrera Torres | 20 years | 03-24-1981 |
| Eduardo Capote Rodríguez | 15 years | 03-28-1981 |
| Pedro Santana Camejo | 20 years | 04-8-1981 |
| Sergio Montes de Oca | 20 years | 04-8-1981 |
| Manuel Hernández Cruz | 20 years | 05-5-1981 |
| Raúl del Valle Vilardel | 20 years | 11-7-1981 |
| Ernesto Palomeque Bussier | 20 years | 11-11-1981 |
| Armando Martínez Yong | 20 years | 12-13-1981 |
| Servando Infante Jiménez | 17 years * | 12-24-1981 |
| José Manuel del Pino González | 20 years | 01-17-1982 |
| Jesús Sánchez Arango | 20 years | 01-19-1982 |
| Remberto Zamora Chirino | 20 years | 02-10-1982 |
| Alejandro Miguel Novo Álvarez | 20 years | 04-13-1982 |
| Julio Acosta Lozada | 20 years | 05-19-1982 |
| Nelson Eduardo Rodríguez Pérez | 18 years | 05-20-1982 |
| Pedro González Rodríguez | 20 years | 05-29-1982 |
| Julián Domínguez Lima | 20 years | 06-15-1982 |
| Roberto Alberto Azcuy Cruz | 9 years ** | 06-16-1982 |
| Pedro Miguel Montey Hernández | 18 years | 07-18-1982 |
| Ismael Hernández Luis | 20 years | 08-07-1982 |
| Ángel Francisco De Fana Serrano | 20 years | 09-10-1982 |
| Augusto Roque Fabelo | 20 years | 09-19-1982 |
| | | |

* He was originally given 12 years on December 24, 1976, but was arbitrarily sentenced again, in the summer of 1977, to an additional 5 years.

** Had previously served another 9-year sentence.

The date chosen to start the hunger strike was October 10, a date of great significance for the Cuban people, being a day in 1868 when our war of independence started. And for the solidarity among Cuban political prisoners, that date was also our expression of joy, of patriotic reaffirmation, of recommitting ourselves to continue the fight against the oppressive Communism that has plunged our people into a horrendous night of thickets and thorns. Because who does not feel stifled in today's Cuba where every movement, all acts of every man, woman, child, or senior are subject to the whims of a despot, a madman, who should be in an asylum bound by hands and feet? A madman, yes, a dangerous madman, as has so rightly been described by the representative of the United States at the United Nations, Jeane Kirkpatrick.

Following a tradition rooted in the Cuban political prison, even under the most adverse conditions, each year we used to pay tribute in a simple ceremony, full of gratitude and love for our homeland, to the heroes who made it possible for Cubans to have an anthem, a flag, a national identity as a free and independent country, but also in recognition of the glorious martyrs who risked their lives and sacrificed so much for such a noble ideal. As can be imagined, starting a hunger strike on October 10, 1982, the date of the 114th anniversary of the historical uprising against Spain initiated by Carlos Manuel de Céspedes at La Demajagua, a location in the Gulf of Guacanayabo in Manzanillo, aroused strong emotions among Boniato's political prisoners. This was not just a simple strike designed to create difficulties and hit back politically and morally against the enemy, but a very special, very different kind of strike led by a group of courageous comrades against an implacable enemy. They were willing to reconquer the freedom seized from them by force, or else to deliver up their precious lives in a magnificent sacrifice.

And in the midst of so many divergent and strong feelings, mindful of the anguish of our last hunger strike, I was aware of the hard test to which my companions would be subjected that would likely result in the death of more than one, if not of them all. It was my task to warn them all of such an outcome in my closing words about that historical act whereby, inevitably, the strike was scheduled to begin on that same day at 6:00 p.m., amid an atmosphere charged with extreme emotion.

Unable to evade the commitment entrusted to me by my brothers in captivity, I had no choice but to accept the task my brothers in agony had given me. And my lucky star on that memorable October 10th day blew the wind in my favor. Thankfully, despite the tremendous emotional pressure, I was able to control my nerves from beginning to end.

It was an unforgettable farewell discourse for me, where each word, if I may say so, twisted my very soul. When I had finished, my peers gave me vigorous applause. They then rushed toward me, encircling me so I couldn't take a step, and one after another, they embraced me. I had never before received so many signs of affection all at once, a warmth both spontaneous and fraternal. I was not surprised to see tears running down the cheeks of so many of these steely men. Alejandro Novo, Servando Infante, José Manuel del Pino, Isnaldo Fernández Guerra, the Hernández Padrón brothers, Guillermo Escalda Montalvo, and still countless others, men of steel, men of stone, ready to confront the cruel enemy that the adversities of life had imposed upon them, but expressing an exquisite sensitivity at a same time.

A strike by those who had already completed their sentences put the High Command in a very embarrassing position.

Even though from the beginning, the strikers requested that the prison authorities remove them from Pavilion 4D to spare their compatriots the anguish of witnessing the painful spectacle of their physical decline, the transfer of the group to the Boniato clinic was delayed for several days. When they finally came for them, I felt a little sad, and I am sure that all experienced that same sadness, because we all knew that our brothers in misfortune were bent on regaining their rightful freedom through such a risky enterprise as the hunger strike, anticipating very difficult days ahead. We had just witnessed the tragic death of Reinaldo Cordero Izquierdo, giving us more than enough reason to worry. We had seen the life taken from that magnificent young man, so horrendous a crime that even many years later, the simple evocation of this tragic fact tightens the throat and floods even the most noble eyes.

Experiences like this, even for the more optimistic, while recognizing the necessity of the strike being undertaken by those who had fulfilled their time, made us nonetheless feel a blow deep in our chests. Embraces. Handshakes. Last-minute tips. Around fifty prisoners had crowded next to the door of Pavilion 4D around those going forth to heroic sacrifice.

When the bolt clanged shut for the second time and we were separated by bars from the group of hunger strikers, a volley of thunderous applause followed them. Immediately, in one voice, we sang out our national anthem. It was a very warm and heartfelt farewell, a farewell which they roundly deserved and which we were glad to give them.

The following days were marked by great uncertainty. In the first contact we in Boniato established with the strikers around a week later, we were informed that Ismael Hernández Luis had joined the strike. This news could not have been more troubling. Ismael was a man with a tremendous zeal for sacrifice. But at the time, his health was seriously broken because of a series of strikes that had ended on the previous 20th of December, some of which had lasted more than 50 days. He had suffered psychologically as well, due to the lengthy process of torture inflicted on him. During his most recent strike, Ismael, in an act of desperation, had tried to commit suicide. He was found near death, lying in a pool of blood. However, despite this dangerous incident, the authorities kept him in solitary confinement. By sheer luck, Hernández Luis was able to partially recover, both physically and psychologically, after accepting food and consenting to allow several liters of serum to enter into his veins after the terrible odyssey of his repeated fasts.

But, and in this we all agreed, his body and mind had both suffered during the last few months, so he needed to be prevented from joining the current strike. Contact had been established for that purpose shortly before October 10, with favorable results, although no one could be sure, having fulfilled his punishment, that he should actually be excluded from participating in the strike. Because we knew very well the character of Ismael Hernández, his extraordinary courage and dynamism, we were not surprised by the news of his finally joining the strike.

And we were not surprised that around October 20, Juan Rodríguez Esquia, Justino González Ramos, Ángel Luis Argüelles Garrido, Wilfredo Martínez Roque, and Silvino Rodríguez Barrientos also joined, and, then, a few days later, Armando Martínez Echevarría, Fernando Villalón Moreira, and Antonio López Muñoz. Nor that later on, they were also joined by Orlando Molina Contreras, Juan Soto Guevara, Placido Díaz Millo, Luis Arrollo Ramos, and José René Martínez Carratalá. These were all supporters, not original strikers.

When the first support group was declared to be on hunger strike, then just 48 hours later, on orders from Major Israel Cobas Montes, who some five months earlier had assumed the position of warden all of us in 4D were confined to our cells. The ban prohibiting our access to the dining room and hallway was taken in retaliation for an incident that had occurred when, intending to provoke us, Boniato's prison administration had hired a small musical contingent to play and sing next to the punishment pavilion, a few meters away from the entrance to 4D. This was something unprecedented, miserable, and humiliating in terms of its location and timing, requiring an adequate response because of the indignation that this unwanted intrusion caused.

Silvino Rodríguez, Wilfredo Martínez, José Oscar, López Muñoz, Pastor Macurán, and several other comrades lifted their voices to denounce the attack on our striking brothers (among other measures, the hunger strikers' water had been withheld) and to ask the same musicians to disclose the crime upon their return to Santiago de Cuba.

The next morning, our cells were not opened for breakfast. From that day on, we were sentenced to permanent enclosure in our walled and covered cells. A new repressive escalation against us had begun.

By carefully analyzing what could have influenced the higher authorities to confine us full time again to the walled cells, I concluded that in addition to the incident with the musicians, the High Command must have been irritated by the appearance in Santiago of hundreds of proclamations denouncing that *plantado* political prisoners were being confined illegally after completing their sentences and publicizing, in particular, their hunger strike. Those proclamations, and this must have most enraged our adversaries, were made by ourselves and smuggled out of prison under the direction of Teodoro González Alvarado, from our own walled cells in Boniato's Pavilion 4D, despite the fierce isolation imposed on us for the last two years,. There were no more than 1,400 in total, because only a few of us were able to work on their preparation: Alvarado González, Ángel Pardo Mazorra, Barrientos Rodríguez Silvino, Luis M. Zúñiga Rey, Ángel De Fana Serrano, and myself, now writing these pages, hoping someday, if they manage to survive the multiple searches of our jailers, to let the world know exactly what occurs inside Cuba's prisons.

I have shared the most significant outlines of the happenings in Boniato's Pavilion 4D during this transcendental hunger strike. And what was the experience of the strikers in the prison infirmary? What was the fate of those glorious men?

The stoic sacrifice of that group of heroes who risked their lives and endured courageously Spartan torture, hunger, and thirst, had a happy ending. For the Cuban political prison, it was a significant moral triumph. The prisoners who had completed their sentences were to be allowed to return home according to a formal commitment made by the authorities on that unforgettable November 4, 1982.

The news of this well-deserved victory came to us soon after the agreement had been made between the strikers and the delegates of the Interior Ministry. Lieutenant Colonel David Beltrán, Chief of Operations for State Security for Santiago province, reported it directly to the rest of us in a brief meeting held in the dining room of Pavilion 4D. He said that the High Command had decided to release them all within a month.

That same afternoon, the first secondary strikers who had had started 16 days earlier in support of those seeking release after completing their sentences, were admitted to the prison infirmary. Although none were in serious condition, Dr. Juan Caballero, the new Boniato medical director, ordered IVs all around to speed up their recovery.

# CHAPTER 50

# "Boniatico": Special Experimentation and Torture Center

It was Nov. 6, 1982. Two days had elapsed since the end of the hunger strike. Two days of joyful abandon, despite our locked, walled cells and the dark forebodings of my good pal, José Oscar.

"I don't see the matter so clearly," he repeated 20 times, expressing dire suspicions. "I don't like the look in the toad eyes of that chubby guy."

The man José Oscar saw as having toad eyes was a very talkative, stubby, low-level official in the entourage that accompanied Lieutenant Colonel David Beltrán when he met in the dining hall of Pavilion 4D with a group of prisoners that completed their tenure, those who had not participated in the hunger strike, just to let them know that they too would be freed.

At about 6:30 a.m., José Oscar was still asleep, his legs stretched out. He was probably dreaming of being free. Or about a pack of cigarettes, because the night before, half an hour before falling asleep, he had smoked the last stub of an aromatic cigar carefully saved in a Russian meat tin, since prisoner tobacco purchases were limited.

"Political, political," a young common prisoner shouted out to Luis Zúñiga from building 3D, when Luis approached his barred window to watch the sunrise or else to see the rats scurrying around the patio scrounging up the last crumbs before entering their underground burrows.

From Zúñiga's gestures I realized that the boy was using sign language, but he was wasting his time because Zúñiga did not understand prison sign language. I had not the slightest desire to get up yet, so I turned over on my bunk and covered my head with the sheet to escape the buzzing flies already starting to invade our cell.

"They are going to take you to Boniatico!" the common prisoner screamed when he realized that Zúñiga had not understood his sign language. Boniatico, "little Boniato," was an even more isolated, secure, fully enclosed, and dark inner sanctum within the main prison, designed to keep political prisoners from escaping or having any contact whatsoever with other prisoners.

I jumped up beside Zúñiga, peering over his shoulder, but already the young man had disappeared, fearful of being seen by the sergeant who had just crossed the corridor between buildings 3 and 4, guarding the cart transporting drums of milk and loaves of bread for breakfast. Reaching out to another 3D prisoner brushing his teeth near the window, I sent out a call to Aramís, another young common prisoner closely identified with us, from whom many political prisoners had received signals of support and friendship.

After a short wait, we were informed that Aramís was still asleep. The others were reluctant to wake him, but finally did so at our insistence. When we talked with him, he had no bad news to pass along, so both Zúñiga and I were inclined to believe that the jailers, or even other prisoners, could be tossing out one of the many speculative rumors supposedly destined to arouse or confuse us political prisoners.

José Oscar, who had been awakened by the first cry from the prisoner brushing his teeth, became quite grumpy when Aramís emerged again, this time to ratify that by tomorrow, we *would* actually be transferred to Boniatico. I immediately took up the task of uncovering the niche where I had hidden 16 batteries, because although my little radio had been confiscated in a search while in the custody of someone I had lent it do, they would insure —at least for a while— a supply for López Lima, in case during the transfer inspection that everyone assumed would be violent, they captured his radio transformer. The first idea I had was to distribute the batteries among three or four men, but I had just finished removing the seal and repainting the niche cover when several officers entered the pavilion hall. No longer able to move from cell to cell myself and with no time left to pass the batteries through holes in the walls, the only alternatives were to resort to Zúñiga and José Oscar or take them all myself. I opted for the second choice, realizing that Zúñiga also needed to save some important items himself, including the headset, and that it was not worth taking the risk for José Oscar Rodríguez Terrero after the recent promise of his release, even less so due to the package of clandestine correspondence that had been found just three days before he fulfilled his sentence.

The move to Boniatico began the next morning under strict security. Contrary to what we had expected, we were not all taken out of 4D together, but in groups of four. When my turn came, around 10:30 a.m., I was grouped in the lobby with Eleno Oviedo, Eloy Gutiérrez Menoyo, and Pablo Prieto Castillo. Immediately, we were given the order to march. Escorted by a pair of officers and two or three guards, we crossed the central corridor between buildings 4 and 5. Between building 5 and the prison kitchen, there waiting for us was the paddy wagon which transported us along the narrow dirt lane encircling Boniato prison, parallel to the security cordon. The wagon's trajectory was just 150 meters.

We climbed out at the entrance to Boniatico, where a considerable number of officials waited, several of high rank. We were ordered to leave our belongings. I set down two cloth bags holding all my worldly goods, including my books, all of which were seized. Lieutenant Enrique Tomás directed me inside cell #2, separated from #1 and all of the rest by an array of iron bars. There waiting for me were an agent of State Security and Lieutenant Figueroa, a former military member of Fulgencio Batista regime, having opportunistically joined the next dictatorship in line.

I was searched completely naked. To get me to agree to undress, Lieutenant Tomás argued that we were going to be given new underpants and, indeed, after I gave up the old ones, I was given a new pair. Of course, I knew that our jailers wanted to carry out such a thorough search to make sure we had nothing hidden, especially a radio, as they wanted to control all our information. I still don't know how they failed to discover the package of batteries and documents taped in my crotch in the usual way.

A religious keepsake from my mother, which until that moment had always hung around my neck, was seized by Lieutenant Tomás in a most cowardly manner. He asked me to hand it over just to be checked, with the promise that it would returned. My repeated requests were ignored by Lieutenant Félix Zamora Blanco, appointed by the High Command to oversee the garrison of Boniatico. When a year later, I had an opportunity to address the issue directly with Lieutenant Tomás, he apologized, claiming that he did not remember even having inspected our move to Boniatico, much less the incident of the scapular. But "there is no reason for it not to be returned to you"—he told me cynically— "if it should appear." These last words indicated that I should give it up as lost. Of everything stripped away during my long years of imprisonment, including several books of unpublished poems, my mother's scapular has been for me, without a doubt, the most sensitive loss.

After the search, I was sent to cell #18 on the top floor. Crossing by #11, I noticed Guillermo Escalada Montalvo peering through the tiny loophole in his door. He greeted me with a riotous whoop of joy, as if we hadn't seen each other in 20 years, a quite usual and spontaneous reaction among us political prisoners. It was a measure of our deep affection for each other, and we expressed it almost automatically. No doubt our harmonious coexistence under extremely difficult conditions, the sharing of ideals, the pain and suffering we had all experienced together for years and years, had increased our brotherly feelings toward each other.

At first glance, cell #18 turned out to have features identical to our recently vacated cells in 4B, including the metal plank sealing each door. We already knew about this detail from common prisoners who had worked on the refurbishment of the two Boniatico pavilions, 2A and 2C. The only substantial difference was the steep wall erected around our two floors, designed us to keep us in total isolation. Boniatico thus became a prison locked inside another prison, controlled directly by State Security personnel and kept under the most extreme surveillance imaginable. *Plantado* prisoners were guarded by 36 agents of the political police, including several top officials, comprising an exclusive squad entrusted with our special custody.

A hall ran between two rows of cells in both pavilions. The courtyard was 15 x 35 meters and, outside the west wing and the surrounding high wall, there was a small medical unit, with everything monitored by the electronic eye of closed circuit television. The dining rooms of both 2A and 2C had been reconditioned solely for military use. The guard corps was installed in 2A. The second-floor dining room was a spacious venue used for offices.

Five minutes after having been locked inside cell #18, I felt the door bolt unlatch. I opened the door to see Gutiérrez Menoyo standing there.

"Go on in," Lieutenant Zamora ordered him.

To the surprise of both Eloy and I, we had been placed in the same cell, which certainly pleased us, but simultaneously made us suspicious that an imperceptible listening system could have been installed for spying our conversations. Pablo Prieto Castillo and Eleno Oviedo Álvarez occupied nearby cell #19. A little later, #20 was opened for Carlos Pons Watler and Ernesto Palomeque Bussier. Then Roberto Martín Pérez was assigned to cell #21.

It was already mid-afternoon when the last of the 109 political prisoners considered rebellious had been confined to this new center of experimentation and torture. During the transfer, we had not been given lunch on that memorable November 6 day. The situation was easily remedied for our jailers. We agreed not to eat anything for the rest of the day because we refused to accept being served directly by the military in our cells, which among other things, would prevent or restrict communication among us.

Arriving at an agreement among the prisoners located in Pavilion 2C turned out not to be so easy. A few were of the view that we should abide by the new measure, arguing that in this same prison on previous occasions, the military had served food directly to political prisoners. I think that their biggest concern was that the prison's administration might then stubbornly prevent the head of the floor and the rest of us from staying out in the corridor from after breakfast until 6:00 or 7:00 p.m., which might then lead to a hunger strike. Others, in contrast, posed more radical solutions, like Remberto Zamora Chirino, who proposed that the best answer would be to knock down the doors by hitting them with our beds to face off directly against the guards, which would be courageous but made little sense, especially considering that Remberto Zamora was one of 25 prisoners who only 48 hours before had received the official promise of release. And one of those same 25 prisoners to be released was Armando Yong Martínez, who rushed in to support Zamorita's proposal. Much respect and admiration are due these magnificent men who, up until the very last moment of their long ordeal, managed to remain faithful exponents of national rebellion, showing an exceptional willingness to endure sacrifice and whose gallantry inspired the rest of us to stand fast during the most difficult moments!

Many raised their voices that afternoon to publicize their views. Knowing that a false step at such a pivotal moment could bring about disastrous consequences, the vast majority agreed that under no circumstances would we accept allowing the military to serve us food. That was also my approach, so I resolutely supported that decision.

Having approved the rejection of all food until it could be served to us by our own colleagues, the next issue was to choose someone to represent us in conveying this decision of Pavilion 2C to the authorities. Our former 4D representative, Eusebeio Peñalver Mazorra, had resigned his post on grounds that he had already served his term. His timing was very inopportune, and we all regretted Peñalver's decision. Faced with this embarrassing situation, to fill the vacuum, Remberto Zamora proposed naming Zúñiga and me to the positions of deputy chief and pavilion chief respectively. This forced me to explain that, although I preferred not being named the head of our floor, I would be willing to assume that responsibility if my colleagues insisted. Our official election, which had to be done according to our custom by secret ballot, was scheduled for the next day. However, to everyone's satisfaction, Eusebio

Peñalver agreed to continue representing us meanwhile, a courageous gesture worthy of our most sincere admiration.

The next day, the food situation became normalized. Thanks to the firm attitude with which we confronted the plan to have guards serve us our meals inside Boniatico, the prison's administration was forced to retract the plan. And the chief of each floor and three companions could remain in the hall from breakfast until about 7:00 p.m.

Even better, that same morning, I learned that Reinaldo López Lima had managed to save his transformer radio despite a thorough search. That was stimulating and surprising news. But most exciting and amazing was the fact that he did not suffer the consequences to his freedom that he risked. Remberto Zamora had dared to successfully clandestinely transport the transformer without detection. What a beautiful example of fortitude and courage!

We had been in Boniatico for about two weeks when those who had taken part in the hunger strike were allowed to meet together with us in Pavilion 2C. It was a very joyful reunion among lifelong friends.

For several days, the main topic of conversation in our micro world revolved around the recent hunger strike and the promise by the higher authorities to release all prisoners who had completed their sentences. We still didn't know exactly how or when they would be released. According to the commitment made by the Interior Ministry delegate of Santiago province with the strikers, the group's remaining time in prison would be relatively brief. However, as the time limit set by Colonel Roberto Valdés had come and gone with no favorable changes for those who had served their sentences, many began to experience a growing skepticism, especially when the warden said with his usual distain that for them —the Communists— keeping their word and honor were matters of little interest, much less when dealing with their enemies.

Of course, this casual revelation by Major Israel Cobas Montes was hardly news. Already, Fidel Castro himself had widely demonstrated the practice of reneging on his word, not only vis-à-vis his political adversaries, but, more seriously still, in a 1978 international press conference.

In a press conference, Castro had told journalists that those excluded from the pardons program would be freed when they had completed their sentences. Still, at the end of 1982, 25 political prisoners were still being kept in the dark dungeons of Boniato prison as hostages of the Communist government of Cuba, long after having served their full sentences. Wasn't that proof of contempt for human dignity and justice by those now holding power on that captive island? How could we banish the specter of mistrust and skepticism before the cruel reality assaulting us? It was impossible. If our experience served for anything, it was inevitable that uncertainty caused us to doubt the word of Colonel Roberto Valdés in his agreement with the victorious strikers.

Not until February 21, 1983, did we have a concrete test of the commitment to actually open the prison doors for those who had reached the end of their sentences. That day saw the release of Nelson Eduardo Rodríguez Pérez and Pedro Santana Camejo, to whom we bid goodbye with a round of applause.

The process of releasing completed prisoners was, like everything else, subject to the capricious will of Cuba's rulers, carried out in an excessively arbitrary manner. Each week, only two were released to the street. It happened in the following manner: After Pedro Santana and Nelson Rodríguez were freed, they were followed on February 28 by Roberto Alberto Azcuy Cruz and Manuel Hernández Cruz. Pedro Miguel Montey Hernández and Julio Acosta Lozada were released on March 7. A week later, on March 14, Pedro González Rodríguez and Jesús Sánchez Arango followed, then Augusto Duque Favelo and Julián Domínguez Lima on March 21, and on March 28, Héctor Cabrera Torres and Ismael Hernández Luis. The latter was again on hunger strike, interned in retaliation in a Santiago psychiatric hospital at the time of his release.

Raúl del Valle Vilardel and Ángel Francisco De Fana Serrano were the next two, released on April 6, Ernesto Palomeque Bussier and Remberto Zamora Chirino on April 11, José Manuel del Pino González and Alejandro Miguel Novo Álvarez on April 18, and on the 25th of that same month, Eduardo Capote Rodríguez and Sergio Montes de Oca Gil. And, finally, on May 9, José René Martínez Carratalá and Servando Infante Jiménez walked out of prison.

Of the 25 *plantado* prisoners at Boniato covered by the agreement between the completed strikers and Colonel Roberto Valdés (the official representing the Cuban government), José Oscar Rodríguez Terrero and Armando Yong Martínez were not freed, respectively, until August 18, 1983 and June 27, 1984. Santos Orlando Mirabal Rodríguez, arrested as a child, would remain in the dungeons of Boniato more than 9 years after having served his sentence. What an abysmal difference between the ruthless punishment inflicted on that innocent child and the humanitarian treatment that Fidel Castro had received from his jailers!

The tribulations, the rigor, the extreme cruelty of the punishment inflicted on *plantado* prisoners were evident from the very same day that we had been moved to this new center of experimentation and torture. It would have inflicted physical destruction and mental alienation on any man unprepared to endure with dignity and stoicism the worst possible adversity. To give a precise idea of the magnitude of the repression unleashed against *plantados*, starting on March 10, 1981, we were prohibited from receiving any visits or communication with our loved ones, even to let them know we were still alive. In terms of living conditions, we continued to be cloistered in walled, covered cells 24 hours a day, wearing as our only garment —both in summer and in winter— although the cold could drill into our bones, a single pair of ragged briefs supplied to last for more than year and a half. On the other hand, in all the time we spent in Boniatico, we weren't allowed access to sunlight in the courtyard, since, according to the warden, as he told us in person on September 22, that all depended on our behavior. He said, in other words, that if we relinquished our principles and gave up our rebellious attitude, we would have more privileges. Our medical care was so inadequate that if a disease required a specialist, as had happened to Julio Ruiz Pitaluga, who had spent more than 2 years suffering from a submaxillary tumor according to the diagnosis made by Dr. Stanley, there was simply no solution; we had to resign ourselves to our fate. Perhaps even more significant is the case of Ernesto Palomeque Bussier, who was not treated for his leukemia and who died in a Miami hospital a few months after his release. Or the unfortunate Pitágora Feros, dying in Boniato's clinic from a terrible throat cancer after more than 25 years of incarceration, receiving no medical attention except for a few tablets of analgesic each day, as if he had a simple toothache. But that was not all.

Among the numerous tortures that we had to suffer after being moved, extreme cruelty was shown by the installation of powerful loudspeakers inside 2A and 2C by Deputy Director Captain Alvis Matos Durán. It was one of the "specialties" that he had learned in the Soviet Union during a course on Russian torture techniques. The shrillness of the noise transmitted, starting daily at dawn, caused serious auditory and mental disorders for many comrades.

As part of the same cycle of new repressive escalation, due to our enemies' insatiable hatred of us and their inability to crush our spirits, for many months, in fact since the previous January 19, in a devastating inspection, we were stripped of all footwear, including the flip-flops protecting our feet from the fungus covering latrine floors. Also from that date onward, we were deprived of all jugs and spoons, forcing us to eat with our hands.

Our situation, we assumed, was denounced by Jorge Valls Arango abroad, after being released on June 18, 1984, after having served his 20 years on May 8. Also released were Sturnio Mesa Schutman, Armando Yong Martínez, Basilio Guzmán Marrero, Clemente Rodríguez Isla, Wilfredo Martínez Roque, Arístides Pérez Montañés, Gerardo Martínez Pérez, Justino Ramos González, José López, Juan González, and Rolando García Fuentes, who all of whom suffered in the flesh the infernal repression in Boniatico, having served more than their 20 years each, plus eventually 19 other prisoners, almost all from Combinado del Este prison, also victims of similar abuses. The 26 Boniato prisoners were released on June 28, 1984, and sent on that same day to the United States in a direct flight to Washington, DC. This happened thanks to a list of names and a humanitarian personal appeal made by members of local Amnesty International Group 211 in Washington, DC, directly to the Rev. Jesse Jackson, who raised the issue and delivered the list during talks held in Havana with Fidel Castro. The American president Ronald Reagan, with his goodwill and humanistic orientation, was interested in obtaining the release of many other Cuban political prisoners and presented lists of names to the Cuban government. But Castro, in his usual pettiness, remained intransigent, delivering only the 26 that from many months and years back remained illegally in prison on the captive island after serving their full sentences.

Although no prisoner not included on Jackson's list was freed, it was a very beautiful gesture on his part which deserves public recognition and sincere gratitude, despite the bitter disappointment caused by Jackson's praise of Che Guevara in his speech at the University of Havana and, still more disappointing, was Jackson's urging of parishioners at a service dedicated to Martin Luther King Jr., held in the Methodist Church at 25th and K in Havana, to support the tyrant Fidel Castro and the Communist government of Cuba.

The inhumane prison regime that was imposed on us political prisoners with such rage and cowardice for simply defending with dignity our ideals, makes it necessary to remember each crime, every torture, every vile abuse committed by the torturers under the direction of the tyrant. I cannot help feeling indignation about so much injustice and immorality.

A copy of *The Fertile Prison* fell fortuitously into my hands, a testimonial book telling the story of the survivors of the assault on the Moncada barracks. It recounts the story of the 21 months and 15 days they spent in prison and was published in 1980 by the Cuban government. On page 76, there appears part of a letter written by Fidel Castro in the prison of Isle of Pines dated April 4, 1954, which I consider appropriate to repeat here.

> "I already take the sun several hours every afternoon and on Tuesdays, Thursdays, and Sundays, also in the morning. An isolated large yard, fully enclosed like a gallery, is where I spend very nice, quiet hours.

> "... I arrange my cell on Friday, washing the granite floor with soap and water first, then using marble dust, next detergent, and finally water with Creolyn. I arrange my

things in absolute order. Rooms at the Hotel Nacional are not so clean.

"... I'm going to dinner: spaghetti with calamari, Italian chocolates for dessert, made-to-order brewed coffee, and then an H Upmann 4 cigar. Don't you envy me? They take good care of me; everyone takes care of me a little among them all. They don't listen to me; I'm always fighting so that they won't send me anything. When I take the morning sun in shorts and feel the sea air, it seems to me that I am on a beach, then at a small restaurant here. I will make you believe that I'm on vacation! What would Carlos Marx say of such a revolutionary?"

To the read these fragments of his letter where Fidel Castro has captured his personal experience of humanitarian treatment and the privileges he enjoyed during his brief stay in the model prison of Isla de Pinos after the Moncada attack, one must consider him ungrateful when evoking the appalling cruelties suffered by prisoners of conscience during the long prison night under his despotic and tyrannical rule.

And what astonishment and indignation it has caused to those of us comparing the abysmal contrast between the soft prison life of comrade Fidel Castro Ruz and the regime of misery and barbarism imposed on us, his political adversaries.

It is not easy to predict whether or not this work that I have written here on the sly in the darkness of a torture dungeon of torture will fulfil its important mission, or ever see the light of day.

There is still much more to tell. *Stronger Than Tyranny* is only one subtle link in the rough history of the Cuban political prison.

Ernesto Díaz Rodríguez, Boniato prison, summer of 1984

# CHAPTER 51

# Postscript

When I was released in 1991, having already past the age 50, I was faced with making a new life in the United States, a beloved country, but not originally my own. I reconnected with my three sons by my first marriage, mentioned at times in this book, now all grown up and doing well—fortunately, we were able to make up for lost time after my release. Amazingly, during the years since my release, only slightly exceeding the 22 that I spent in prison, I've been able to create a brand new professional and personal life, but the memories and scars from my prison experience remain. Meanwhile, my nearly lifelong opposition to the Castro dictatorship remains as strong as ever.

We former *plantados* remain true Cuban freedom fighters, dedicated to the rule of law, rights of peaceful association and expression, an independent judiciary, fair trials, humane treatment of all prisoners, and free elections. That is what I have been fighting for my whole life for Cubans and for Cuba, my beloved homeland.

Ernesto Díaz Rodríguez,
Maryland, 2017

## MORE ABOUT ERNESTO DÍAZ RODRÍGUEZ

Ernesto Díaz Rodríguez was born on November 11, 1939 in Cojimar, a fishing village east of the entrance to Havana Bay. He began to study mechanical engineering after graduating high school, at the Escuela de Artes y Oficios (School of Arts and Crafts) in Havana. However, after joining a student group to resist the dictatorship of Fidel Castro, he was closely monitored, threatened, and persecuted.

On March 13, 1961 Díaz Rodríguez and a small group of other activists escaped Cuba in a small boat, reaching Big Pine Key, Florida and receiving political asylum. Upon arrival in Miami, he earned his living as a house painter and later as a painter of skyscraper windows in New York City, but he yearned to return to Cuba to continue fighting for his country freedom. Knowledge of the sea, between 1962 and 1968 he led several armed incursions into Cuba.

On December 4, 1968, during one such operation, Díaz Rodríguez was captured in Cuba and sentenced to 15 years of imprisonment for illegal entry and posing a menace to the "integrity and stability of the nation." On October 9, 1974, after almost six years behind bars, he was accused of conspiring to overthrow Castro's government from *within* his cell and, after a mock trial, was given an additional 25-year sentence.

During his captivity, including seven years in uninterrupted solitary confinement in the most inhumane conditions, Díaz Rodríguez began writing in secrecy, on tiny scrap of paper, documents denouncing the atrocities he and others were suffering. Eventually, at the same time he began writing poems as a vehicle of protest against the brutality of the communist penal system. Soon, his poems which often weave intense images with plays on words and bold tropes, reflected a wider gamut of the human experience, beyond defiance to reflections on courage and love, history and innocence. Surprisingly smuggled his work out to be published abroad.

His first published book was *Un Testimonio Urgente* (Hialeah, FL: Trade Litho, 1977), distributed in Miami and Latin America while Diaz-Rodríguez was still incarcerated in Cuba. As a result of this act of "literary defiance," he suffered further repressions. Díaz Rodríguez's second book *La Campana del Alba* ("The Bell of Dawn," Madrid: Editorial Playor, 1984, 2nd edition Miami: Editorial Sibi, 1986), a book of poems for children, reflects the anguish of his separation from his three sons growing up in American exile.

On February 21, 1989, the P.E.N. Club of France named Díaz Rodríguez an Honorary Member. A vigorous international campaign ensued in which other P.E.N. Club chapters and human rights organizations advocated for his release. Díaz Rodríguez was named Honorary Member of the P.E.N. Club Writer's Club in England and the United States, and the International P.E.N. Club. Also in 1989, and while still imprisoned, Díaz Rodríguez was named Vice-President of the Cuban Committee for Human Rights, a peaceful organization that monitored abuses by the communist government.

On March 23, 1991, after 22 years and 3 months of often brutal captivity in Castro's prisons, Ernesto Diaz-Rodríguez was freed. He returned to the United States where he writes and continues his work as a human rights activist to this day, traveling to many foreign countries to participate in conferences, meet with government officials, and lecture in schools and universities—all to broaden international support for the re-establishment of civil liberties and democracy in Cuba.

Additionally, Díaz Rodríguez's work has been published in the following books and anthologies, listed chronologically:

*Escrito en Cuba: Cinco Poetas Disidentes*, Madrid: Editorial Playor, 1978. Anthology of works by five Cuban dissident poets: Angel Cuadra, Ernesto Díaz Rodríguez, Heberto Padilla, Miguel Sales, and Armando Valladares. Prologue by Ramón J. Sender.

*Mar de Mi Infancia/Sea of My Infancy*, Princeton, NJ: Linden Lane Press, 1991. Poetry, Spanish originals with English-language translations (by Ildara Klee), reflecting on his childhood in Cojímar.

*El Carrusel*, Madrid: Editorial Betania, Colección Literatura Infantil, 1994. Poetry for children.

*Rehenes de Castro*, Miami: Linden Lane Press, 1995. Testimonial of life in the prisons of communist Cuba as a hostage (*rehén*) of the regime.

*Censuré á Cuba: Anthologie de Six Poètes Cubains*, Paris: Gallimard

& FNAC, 2002. Edited by Zoe Valdés, gathers works by censored and imprisoned poets in Cuba.

*Piedra por Piedra/Stone for Stone*, Bloomington, IN: AuthorHouse, 2008. Poetry, Spanish originals with English-language translations (by Ed Winograd & Ildara Klee).

*A Contra Viento*: Trafford publishing, 2011. Poetry, Spanish language.

MAR MID-American Review, 2023 Volume XXXIV, Number 1 Selection of poetry.

Stronger Than Tyranny (testimonio): Amazon-KDP 2018

La Campana del Alba (5th edition). Create Space-Amazon, 2020.

On the Wings of the Wind. Amazon-KDP. 2023

The Fight for Freedom (testimony). Amazon

www.ingramcontent.com/pod-product-compliance
Lightning Source LLC
Chambersburg PA
CBHW031522150726
47990CB00001B/34